'timely and time-centred . . . Mulvey's ability to provoke and stimulate remains undiminished.' – *Popmatters*

'Mulvey has a voice that carries. In the wake of #MeToo, and in an age where being active on social media demands a constant ebb and flow of looking and self-presenting, her coinage has been taken up by a new vanguard . . . A wave of artists and audiences are actively adapting and expanding Mulvey's thinking – and now, so is the critic herself . . . Mulvey's new book is especially pertinent, given the widening rift between her second-wave feminist peers – who are predominantly white academics – and the current "fourth-wave", known for its Twittersphere stomping ground and exacting inclusivity standards . . . Mulvey's voice cuts through generational divides and *Afterimages* strikes a balance between consistency of thought and a willingness to adapt.' – *Financial Times*

'A frank, personal, and critically adroit work, which . . . demonstrates how films – even those that have received the most critical attention – continue to challenge, reveal and provoke . . . a valuable and unique set of responses and arguments by one of the [film studies] discipline's most eminent founding scholars, demonstrating the vivacity of her work.' – *Viewfinder*

'*Afterimages* takes up themes and concepts long central to Mulvey's thinking, particularly feminism and psychoanalysis . . . Her investments persist in altered form as they are rearticulated in relation to the demands of the present.' – Erika Balsom, *Frieze*

'[A] captivating rumination on film theory through a decidedly feminist lens . . . [and a] gorgeously put together book superficially, this release from Reaktion Books is an exciting discovery, a book that challenges classical thoughts around structures in a manner that feels fresh and of this specific moment in time . . . Looking at everything from the use of women as spectacle in fiction cinema to the rise of cinematic language within visual art in the gallery space, *Afterimages* is a wide-reaching collection of essays that all carry with them the same lyrical and compelling Mulvey voice. Toss in a provocative FAQ section surrounding her legendary "Visual Pleasure and Narrative Cinema" essay and you have a release that's essential for anyone interested in the intersection between cinema and gender.' – *Criterion Cast*

'A readable and accessible book by a major author in the field. Highly recommended.' – *Choice*

'Mulvey takes an analytic approach to filmmaking and new technology, focusing on the deterioration of the Hollywood studio system and the emergence of the female voice both in front of and behind the camera ... Future filmmakers as well as art and media students will find this academic take on feminism and cinema a valuable resource.' – *Library Journal*

'*Afterimages* shows a rare quality in academia, the capacity to admit having been wrong at some point, or not sufficiently informed, and re-evaluate past work in light of criticism, and evolution of knowledge. If only for this, Mulvey is an inspirational scholar, and *Afterimages*, an example of accepting that times are changing, but maybe not fast enough or in the right direction.' – *Historical Journal of Film, Radio and Television*

'Over forty years ago, Laura Mulvey's searing polemic "Visual Pleasure and Narrative Cinema" brilliantly articulated why the movies we love also damage us by shoring up patriarchal power. Since that scorched earth moment, Mulvey's analysis of the moving image has broadened and deepened, which makes this book absolutely necessary to today's cultural struggles around gender, race, and class.' – Amy Taubin, critic and contributing editor *Film Comment* and *Artforum*

'As a female film-maker, I owe a debt of gratitude to Laura Mulvey, for her film-making and for her tireless theoretical explorations. She has secured the space in which women are permitted expression and may explore the virtues of silence, stillness and the maternal. It is always exciting when Laura Mulvey publishes new work.' – Joanna Hogg, film-maker

'At once a critical fascination with Hollywood's images of women, a nuanced approach to modern women film-makers, and a consideration of cinema's status in relation to contemporary art: the great skill of Laura Mulvey is to move between these multiple lines of enquiry, taking her reader with her as only a true writer can.' – Raymond Bellour, Director of Research, Emeritus, CNRS, Paris, and author of *The Analysis of Film and Between-the-Images*

AFTERIMAGES

ON CINEMA, WOMEN AND CHANGING TIMES

LAURA MULVEY

REAKTION BOOKS

*For Chad Wollen and for Zoe Wollen with love and
gratitude for their encouragement – especially with the FAQs*

Published by REAKTION BOOKS LTD
Unit 32, Waterside
44–48 Wharf Road
London N1 7UX, UK
www.reaktionbooks.co.uk

First published 2019, reprinted 2022
Copyright © Laura Mulvey 2019

All rights reserved

No part of this publication may be reproduced, stored in a retrieval system, or transmitted,
in any form or by any means, electronic, mechanical, photocopying, recording or otherwise,
without the prior permission of the publishers.

Printed and bound in Great Britain by Bell & Bain, Glasgow

A catalogue record for this book is available from the British Library

ISBN 978 1 78914 122 1

CONTENTS

'We can only grasp silence at the moment when it's breaking' – Sheila Rowbotham.
Great-great-grandmother Nana Peazant stands on the threshold between silence
and its breaking (*Daughters of the Dust*, dir. Julie Dash, 1991).

PREFACE

Afterimages is a selection of lectures and essays that I have given or published since *Death 24x a Second: Stillness and the Moving Image*, which came out in 2006. Although the material has all been rewritten and redesigned to appear in this book, each chapter is still a self-sufficient essay and 'essayistic' in style. The pieces are short and, as they are a close reflection of my personal point of view, the ideas often move quite loosely and subjectively across topics, structures and arguments. The title of the book is a response to various themes that recur across the essays, as I discuss below, but it evokes, in the first instance, an afterword to my early, polemical and feminist concerns with the woman as spectacle and then to my early psychoanalytically influenced interest in the figuration of the mother in patriarchal society. Both these issues are reworked and represented very differently from my earlier essays, and indeed, my films, but the continuum remains in my reading of the works I discuss in Part Two, returning in Part Three with 'Mary Kelly: Speaking Maternal Silence, *Post-Partum Document* and *The Ballad of Kastriot Rexhepi*'.

Some themes from *Death 24x a Second* recur in *Afterimages*. The earlier book analysed modes of spectatorship: not the gendered spectatorship of 'Visual Pleasure and Narrative Cinema', but how the encounter between film and digital technology changed a spectator's perception of cinematic and narrative time, revealing stillness and pose within the hurried flow of traditional film experience. If *Death 24x a Second* took questions of spectatorship out of gender and into film's temporality, here women, film and time are woven together across the different sections of the book. The title *Afterimages* sums up the significance of time as a unifying theme: 'afterimages' conveys 'images of after' or 'from after', bearing on the dislocation of time that runs through so many of the films and works discussed here. There is an echo of 'afterwardsness', the English translation of Freud's term *Nachträglichkeit* that I discuss at the end of Part Two, in 'Clio Barnard, *The Arbor*': how past experience is reconfigured and refracted through the later cinematic process of visualization and narration. In a kind of metaphoric supplement, I use the figure of the ghost and haunting to evoke the complex implication of a past persisting into its future. In *Death 24x a Second* I discussed the ghostliness that has often been associated with the filmic or photographic medium and I return occasionally in *Afterimages* to the way the medium preserves the living presence of human figures, often long dead, through the film machine.

Afterimages, as I suggested above, returns to my longstanding preoccupation with women in film, their histories, their stories and their images. But the important split between Part One and Part Two reflects changes in my perspective on these topics and also changes that have affected cinema itself. The essays in Part One look back to the 1950s, to woman as spectacle and to the decline of the Hollywood studio system (that is, to the source material of 'Visual Pleasure and Narrative Cinema'), but, as I explain in its introduction, more in an elegiac than critical spirit. All the essays in Part Two are about films made by women, signalling that an important and radical shift is beginning to overtake cinema. That I could select these particular films with their special focus, and could have included others, shows how women film-makers have accumulated momentum since I first began to write about cinema more than forty years ago. The films discussed in Part Two demonstrate that when women make films, cinema mutates in their hands and through their eyes. This is not to argue that there is an essential or coherent 'women's cinema' but rather that a 'women-inflected cinema' can take up topics and perspectives hitherto neglected or simply not imaginable by a male-dominated culture. As a woman artist working on women-related topics, the essay on Mary Kelly in Part Three partially belongs to Part Two, and closes the book with a return to these themes. Otherwise, the essays in Part Three reflect my recent interest in the way that avant-garde film of the past has moved into the gallery and reconstructed the relation of spectator to screen using new formal strategies to reflect on long-standing political and aesthetic issues. The chapters in each section are intended, as their introductions point out, to interact and inform each other. I have also added an Appendix, 'Frequently Asked Questions on "Visual Pleasure and Narrative Cinema"', which consists of a selection of questions that have been put to me over the years about my 1975 essay.

Discussed in Part One, the films *Lola Montès* and *Vertigo* are intricately woven across divided temporalities. In my essay on Marilyn Monroe, I construct a temporal discordance between her time as a star of 20th Century-Fox and her later attempts to reinvent her image and her career. The fact that Monroe's trajectory coincides with the decline of the Hollywood studio system carries over into the chapter on Godard's *Le Mépris* and his elegiac reflections on the death of the industry that had given him his love of cinema. All four cases revolve around the gap that separates a past from its later revision, a shift in perspective that stretches across time and alters understanding. A temporal perspective also runs through Part Three. I argue that a sense of the archaic haunts Morgan Fisher's films about film projection as well as Mark Lewis's return to outmoded rear projection technology, and Isaac Julien layers *Ten Thousand Waves* with varying internal references to time alongside the temporal complexity inscribed into the installation itself. The last chapter on Mary Kelly also relates to images of time as *Post-Partum Document* opens up the narrative temporality associated with the Oedipus Complex, delaying the linear pattern to find a maternal time and space. While this chapter relates to the others in Part Three, it also picks up the theme of feminist time discussed throughout Part Two.

The representation of time runs as a theme throughout Part Two, as an essential issue raised by the five films I discuss in that section. The films, of course, vary aesthetically and conceptually and it makes no sense to generalize a filmic coherence across this body of work. However, the films all work to translate the mother's silence into the space and time of cinema, materializing 'muteness' into cultural presence. Sheila Rowbotham has summed up this question of silence:

> The oppressed without hope are mysteriously quiet. When the conception of change is beyond the limits of the possible, there are no words to articulate discontent so it is sometimes held not to exist. This mistaken belief arises because we can only grasp silence in the moment in which it is breaking.[1]

These films bring that moment into being, not within the framework of the story, not achieved by the character or within her story but through the film-maker's use of cinema and mode of narration. Even in *Daughters of the Dust*, in many ways the most positive of all the films' conclusions, Julie Dash's cinematic negotiation between past and future, on poetic and visual levels, transcends the perspective of any character. Overall, Alina Marazzi's comment is applicable to all the films, when she says that she and her editor, in their work on her grandfather's films: 'liberated the feminine spirit . . . as though with Aladdin's lamp'.[2] Here the magic, conjured by the metaphor of the lamp, is the reconfiguration of narrative and character from a feminist viewpoint, through the time and space of film itself. The maternal stories are not just told; as the material is worked through it acquires a sense of 'after' or even 'afterwardsness' that complements the significance of temporality in the films themselves.

In her essay 'Women's Time', Julia Kristeva evokes very vividly the gendered and resonant opposition between two kinds of temporality under patriarchy. Patriarchal time is linear, unfolding in departure, progress and arrival, encapsulated by a teleological concept of history.

Women's time is a matrix of space, unnamable, anterior to God, the aporia of the chora. But Kristeva complicates this opposition through her narrative of two succeeding generations of feminism. She says: 'In their initial struggle for equality, women aspired to escape from their relegation to an a-cultural and pre-temporal space, aspiring to inclusion in the linear, progressive concept of time and the politics that went with it.' Kristeva's second generation however are 'essentially interested in the specificity of female psychology and its symbolic realizations, [and] these women seek to give a language to the intra-subjective and corporeal experiences left mute by culture in the past'.[3]

The films by women discussed in Part Two manifest the characteristics of both Kristeva's generations. In their 'symbolic realizations' the films use cinema to challenge the image of time's linear flow and to visualize in imagery those 'experiences left mute by culture in the past'. Maternal time and the muteness of motherhood become intertwined, no longer in the 'unnamable matrix of space'. Cinema spatializes time and temporalizes space through its own intricate relations with and manipulation of both, as, for instance, in the representation of Nana's island in *Daughters of the Dust*, of Jeanne's flat in *Jeanne Dielman, 23 quai du Commerce, 1080 Bruxelles* and of Tuba's courtyard in *Under the Skin of the City*. There is a way in which the theme of the mother always implies a confusion of time and space, refracted either through the psychoanalytic return to the Oedipus Complex, through a return to myths and knowledge lost under patriarchy, or in the simple sense that a return to the mother is always a return to the past. In Liseli Marazzi and Andrea Dunbar's stories of failed motherhood (*Un'ora sola ti vorrei* and *The Arbor*) both stay close to home and neither manage to create a maternal, enclosing space of their own. Liseli's letters to her own mother from America speak to this longing and seem to suggest that the separation from home had precipitated her breakdown. Andrea always returns home to Brafferton Arbor, in spite of the opportunities for a new life offered by her success in London.

But these films are also a reminder that the 'initial struggle' continues, and broadens out beyond the question of women's equality. Kristeva's division of generations restricts the idea of progressive time to a patriarchal pattern that women aspire to join. As I argue in the end of the introduction to Part Two, these women's films are not detached from history and, while challenging a restricted linear pattern of time, they all address their audiences with the question: what kind of cultural re-imagining of the future can engage with the dream and a politics of 'a better life'? But the progressive concept of time is no longer tied to the linear pattern: temporalities fold back and interweave past, present and future. Out of the films' formal politics, there is a persistent sense that the future cannot be visualized and narrated except through an understanding and analysis of past experience. The compilation 'genre' that I discuss in Part Two is an exemplary form: in a loop backwards, bits of valueless film of forgotten people are brought into historical discourse by their directors and editors. In discussing the compilation film, I cite Jacques Derrida's concept of a 'spectral messianicity': these celluloid ghosts of the past are given a voice in the reconfigured film to address a legacy and a future. The voice carries the idea of a promise, necessarily confusing time and articulating a sense of political obligation that moves backwards and forwards from the 'mysteriously quiet oppressed' to the moment when 'silence is broken'.

These films are also a reminder that not only does women's 'initial struggle' continue, but women's voices and women's understanding of politics can revitalize struggle more broadly. The present historical moment is haunted by those whom history has left behind and abandoned without hope, and the fate of men as well as women are bound together: the desperation left by the scars of slavery (as in *Daughters of the Dust*) and the desperation of post-imperialist migrations (as in *Ten Thousand Waves* and other Isaac Julien works, as well as Abbas's dream of migration in *Under the Skin of the City*). While feminist aesthetic strategies emerge out of women's experience and, I am suggesting, are formed in the very particular experience of motherhood, their messages are relevant to contexts that reach beyond women's oppression and exploitation. On the one hand, there is a specificity to the maternal from which it is difficult to generalize. On the other, just as the muteness of motherhood can be used as a figure for and extended to all groups of the culturally oppressed, so can this confusion of maternal time be used as a figure for and extended to a re-imagination of temporalities. The 'afterimage', evoking the lasting nature of the image left on the eye by the impact of the real, is in *Afterimages* a metaphor for women's use of cinema to offer, not simply to women but to everyone, stories and images thought through this poetic and political film-making.

PART ONE: A LAST CHAPTER

INTRODUCTION: FINAL THOUGHTS ON WOMAN AS SPECTACLE

The essays in this section finally draw a line under my long-standing engagement with Hollywood and its images of women. While they were all written recently, some strands and themes reach back to much earlier phases in my work, which I will trace later in this introduction. But first, the end of the line. I have often described the way that I called upon my familiarity with Hollywood, the 'expertise' of a 1960s film fan, when, influenced by feminism, I wrote about woman as spectacle in the early 1970s. Although I then turned away from spectacle to women and melodrama, 1950s Hollywood was still my main point of reference, above all the films of Douglas Sirk. But as alternative cinemas and avant-garde film came to absorb more of my attention, I lost interest in Hollywood until the mid-1990s, when digital technology enhanced and changed film spectatorship. Then, I went back to rediscover my favourite Hollywood films, perhaps simply nostalgically, perhaps as a tribute to those directors who could so brilliantly conjure up cinema's particular spell.

But a return to Hollywood of the studio system was to see films through a changed political perspective as well as new technologies of spectatorship. In a trenchant critique, bell hooks has pointed out that Hollywood's all-encompassing whiteness had never been addressed by white feminist film theory. On the other hand, she discussed the way that an investigative or 'oppositional gaze' had been habitual for black women, long before white feminism discovered its own mode of distance and critique. 'Whether it was *Birth of a Nation* or Shirley Temple shows, we knew that white womanhood was the racialised sexual difference occupying the place of stardom in mainstream narrative film. We assumed white women knew it too.'[1]

Speaking solely for myself, I only gradually began to realize the way that racial presence and absence dominated the Hollywood screen, with the necessary implication that the excessive investment in the female star as spectacle is symptomatic of racial as well as male sexual anxiety. Thus the female star as fetish, deflecting the male gaze from those aspects of the female body that provoke anxiety, condenses with a white fetishism, deflecting with glamour the anxiety provoked by racial difference. While representations of gender were so obviously on the surface of Hollywood studio-system cinema, James Snead has pointed out that, alongside the stereotyping of black people on the screen, Hollywood's phobic relation to race is manifested through absence: the almost complete erasure of African American presence on the screen.[2] An analysis of this kind of sexual and racial fetishism demands a wider political and historical context, a juxtaposition of screen images with the realities of American life; but just as psychoanalysis needs politics, so psychoanalysis illuminates images of and attitudes to race as well as sex.

The essays in Part One were written separately from each other, out of different circumstances and contexts, but across all four there are considerable overlapping themes, sometimes recurring from essay to essay. And as, inevitably, some ideas lead back to my earlier work, I would like to trace their links. In 2015, the fortieth anniversary of 'Visual Pleasure and Narrative Cinema', I found myself returning yet again (having done so from time to time in the intervening decades) to the 1970s, to the conjuncture of feminism, Hollywood and Freudian psychoanalysis. In this context, I began to think about Hitchcock's 1958 film *Vertigo* and the extraordinary importance it held for the key concepts discussed in 'Visual Pleasure and Narrative Cinema'. I was reluctant at first. *Vertigo* had just been voted the 'greatest film of all time' by the previous *Sight and Sound* poll.[3] Hitchcock had mutated from a renowned maker of cult films into a cinematic cult in his own right, as in *Hitchcock* (2012); the idea of 'the Hitchcock blonde' had also become a cliché of popular culture. However, returning to the film in 2015 and with the help of passing time, *Vertigo* seemed (as I discuss in the second essay of Part One) to be more complex and self-aware than I had previously realized in the early 1970s. Rather than *reflecting* the prevalence of the female star as signifier of sexuality and object of the voyeuristic gaze, *Vertigo* reflects *on* her fabrication, *on* the imbrication between femininity, illusion and film to the point of self-reflexivity.

Crucial to my return to *Vertigo* was the significance of blondeness as a signifier of illusion and artifice that crosses between the luminous figure of the woman and her fusion with the luminosity of the screen itself. 'Marilyn Monroe: Emblem and Allegory of a Changing Hollywood' thus revolves around the iconography of blondeness, and Monroe herself. The essay also returns to the past, to my discussion of Monroe in 'Close-ups and Commodities' (included in *Fetishism and Curiosity*, 1995). To make the move from the Freudian to the Marxist concept of fetishism, I wanted to place Monroe's screen image within the economic and social context of 1950s America, within its consumerist commodity culture. As the early 1950s boom meshed with the politics of the Cold War, America invented itself as the democracy of glamour. Glamour proclaimed the desirability of American capitalism to the outside world and, inside, offered an all-American image to the newly suburbanized, commodity-consuming white population. It was against this background that Marilyn Monroe rose to stardom, supremely personifying the allure of the screen but also suggesting a metaphor for the allure of the commodity. The commodity too depended on a glamorous surface, attracting the eye of the consumer while erasing any trace of the labour power that had produced the product. The intense whiteness of Marilyn's appearance reflected the historical moment, just before the rise of the Civil Rights movement.[4] Out of the artifice of this iconography and the precariousness of its surface masquerade, Monroe's performance comments on and foregrounds its vulnerability, suggesting a kind of self-reflexivity that I argue resounds with her later reinvention of her image and her career. It was when I returned to Hollywood and cinephilia in the late 1990s that I became fascinated by Monroe's performance and her mastery of pose and gesture. Using the 'delayed cinema' of DVD spectatorship, I paused, repeated and slowed her image, moving beyond the film itself to make a video essay, analysing her ability to create stillness within movement.

Although made outside of the Hollywood system, Max Ophüls's *Lola Montès* (the subject of Part One's first essay) shares the self-reflexivity that I argue for in my essays on *Vertigo* and Monroe. During Ophüls's exile in Hollywood in the 1940s, he suffered bitterly under the industry's unrelenting regime. Back in France, his career revived and in 1955 he made *Lola Montès*, his first colour and wide-screen production. Gender (masculinity as well as femininity) had always been central to his films, but, unlike Hitchcock, the highly stylized female star had no place in Ophüls's own highly stylized cinema. There are, however, some parallels between the two directors. Both had long and international careers in cinema when they made *Vertigo* and *Lola Montès*. In spite of differences in style and iconography, their mastery of film form had come to be entwined with their mastery of films about women, as dramatic focus and as cinematic attraction. With the decline of cinema in general as the dominant mode of popular entertainment, it seems unsurprising, but also moving, that Hitchcock and Ophüls should, at that particular moment of their histories and film history, make these self-reflexive movies. Hitchcock focused more on the psychoanalytic and the woman's image as fetish; Ophüls focused more on the economic and the fetishization of the female star as commodity. *Lola Montès* and *Vertigo* were commercial failures, not helped by their thematic darkness and narrative obscurity.[5] These stories of women trapped in the cages of spectacle are told allegorically, although, in retrospect, their meanings are not that hidden. In *Lola Montès*, set in a site of entertainment and quite literally about woman as spectacle, the allegory is not hard to decipher. *Vertigo* focuses on how a woman's image is structured and fabricated precisely according to male desire. While the film references film spectatorship, the allegory revolves particularly around the power of illusion, that of the woman and that of cinema alike.

In all three chapters about the female star image, I return to a key theme of my 2006 book *Death 24x a Second: Stillness in the Moving Image*. Beyond self-reflexive content, that is, how these star images are constructed and displayed as spectacle, their figures have a self-reflexive relation to the film machine itself. The performances and screen presence of Marilyn Monroe, Martine Carol as Ophüls's Lola, and Kim Novak as *Vertigo*'s Madeleine, share a certain mechanization of the body, a draining away of the natural and the human. Their highly stylized bodily movements evoke, in a kind of metonymical reference, the jerky progression of the filmstrip through the projector, as each frame is paused for a 24th of a second in front of the beam of light. In each case, I suggest that these figurations descend from the beautiful automaton, in legend and mechanical experiment, a fascinating fusion of the animate and the inanimate that was finally realized by the cinema. Furthermore, all three figures are under the shadow of death (if, in Marilyn's case, retrospectively) so that film's illusion of movement further conjures up the illusion of the dead repeating their once-upon-a-time gestures in an illusion of life. Although the term has become a cliché, the idea of 'the ghost in the machine' sums up these figures' embodiment of cinema's paradox.

My essay on the three Cinecittà scenes in Jean-Luc Godard's *Le Mépris* forms an afterword to Part One. In the first instance, these scenes allow me to comment on Godard's commentary on the end of Hollywood, returning to my *Cahiers du cinéma* inspired film-going of the 1960s, my own cinephile thoughts and memories both inspired by and superimposed onto his. But the importance of quotation and reference in *Le Mépris* gives the film a further dimension, out of the past and towards a then unforeseen future. Quotation fragments homogeneity, always tending to distract from the diegetic forward flow of a film: when it erupts into a present text, the citation cannot help but bring its past with it. Although Godard inserts his references visually, or in dialogue, into *Le Mépris*, the film's intense reflection on cinema history prefigures a later era in which cinema would be able to quote itself. The pioneering and prime example would be Godard's own *Histoire(s) du cinéma*, made from the late 1980s into the 1990s, in which he reflects back critically on the great days of Hollywood that he mourned in *Le Mépris*.

Jacques Rancière points out that in the very fragmentation of *Histoire(s) du cinéma* Godard portrayed cinema's development into a medium of mass entertainment as a betrayal of its true nature:

> it is presented as having relinquished its vocation as a vision machine relating phenomena to each other to become a glamorous machine in the service of 'stories': the ones in Hollywood scripts or the ones put out by destructive dictatorships bent on reshaping peoples. *Histoire(s)* is thus an enterprise of redemption: Godard's fragmentation is intended to deliver images and their potential from subjection to stories. By inventing original relationships between films, photographs, paintings, newsreels, music and so on, it returns retrospectively to cinema the role of revealer and communicator which it had betrayed by enslaving itself to the story industry. That is why this redemption of the past also announces the end of the history of cinema. The task of a modern cinema, a cinema that has taken the measure of its own historical utopia, would perhaps be to return to the disjunction of the gaze and movement, to re-explore the contradictory powers of the stoppages, delays and disconnections of the gaze.[6]

With these words, Rancière evokes the recent explosion of the audio-visual essay. From a personal perspective, it was precisely out of these 'stoppages, delays and disconnections of the gaze' that I visualized new forms of spectatorship in *Death 24x a Second* that then led me to make the 're-mix' of Marilyn Monroe in thirty seconds of *Gentlemen Prefer Blondes* that I discuss in this part's third essay. And this kind of fragmentation can also, perhaps, redeem moments of cinematic greatness from Hollywood's heyday.

MAX OPHÜLS, *LOLA MONTÈS*

[Ophüls] told me that he included, systematically, in the script of
Lola Montès everything that he had found disturbing and troubling
in the previous three months: Hollywood divorces, Judy Garland's
suicide attempt, the Rita Hayworth incident, the American three-ring
circuses, Cinemascope and Cinerama, competitive bidding over
publicity, the hyperbole of modern life.

François Truffaut, 'Max Ophüls est mort', in *Les Films de ma vie* (1975)

Lola Montès (1955), Max Ophüls's last film, is a complex weave of
allegory and metaphor, a bitter, critical and satirical vision of the
entertainment industry, that is, of his own world. Through the figure
of Lola (played by Martine Carol), he created his most sustained
reflection on the female star as spectacle and commodity and as an
image for circulation and exchange. And the figure of the Ringmaster
(played by Peter Ustinov) personifies the iron and unbending rules that
drive and govern entertainment as a commercial machine.

Ophüls based the film loosely on the real-life Lola Montez. An
Irish-born dancer and courtesan, Montez achieved notoriety in the
mid-nineteenth century through her scandalous love affairs and became
what would now be known as a 'celebrity'.[1] Drawing minimally on her
public performances in later life, Ophüls set the film in a circus in the
u.s. where Lola has been reduced to earning her living by re-enacting,
in a series of highly staged acrobatic acts, the more sensational episodes
of her life. Narrated and orchestrated by the Ringmaster, the tableaux
flamboyantly fill the space of the circus, reaching to its very top with
Lola's rise to power and fame, while a death-defying plunge down into

a small net, precariously placed just above the floor of the ring, represents her fall. The tableaux trigger flashbacks into Lola's memory. In these episodic stories of love, she flaunts her contempt for marriage or any social regulation of female sexuality and her commitment to living only by the rules of her own desire. The flashbacks replace the ultra-stylized scenes in the circus with greater verisimilitude and are dramatized more conventionally in both cinematic and narrative terms. But these fragmentary sequences are also de-naturalized by Ophüls's *mise en scène*: location landscapes are coloured and manipulated almost like film sets. (For instance, in order to achieve an autumnal atmosphere as Lola's affair with Liszt comes to an end, Ophüls had the inn wrapped in 'kilometres of netting' and the road freshly painted reddish brown every morning.[2])

Lola Montès was the first film that Ophüls made in colour (Eastmancolor) and CinemaScope. With it, he made a completely new cinematic departure while simultaneously continuing to develop certain themes that had long been close to his heart. A European consortium, headed by Gamma Films, financed the film on the condition that it should be shot in widescreen and colour. So historically and technologically the film stands firmly within its moment, paralleling those epic spectaculars, those last-gasp attempts to attract an audience to a dying industry, made in 1950s Hollywood. *Lola Montès* is, indeed, spectacular: a lush costume drama with Martine Carol (also imposed by Gamma) in the lead, a star primarily famous for her sex appeal. It was in these demanding conditions that Ophüls made this transcendently self-reflexive film.

There is a remarkable scene at the centre of *Lola Montès* in which the Ringmaster first encounters Lola. It is here that Ophüls clearly articulates, through the Ringmaster, the film's key theme: the marketing of the female star. But it also illustrates Ophüls's ability to integrate ideas and emotions into the fabric of cinema, making maximum use of the aesthetic possibilities afforded by widescreen and colour. Over the course of his long career, Ophüls had mastered a particular cinematic style that could not but be at odds with the constraints of the

CinemaScope format (dismissed by Fritz Lang in Jean-Luc Godard's *Le Mépris* (1963) as appropriate only for snakes and funerals). According to his friend and costume designer Georges Annenkov, it was out of Ophüls's tireless struggle against the widescreen, turning CinemaScope against its own grain, that he came to visualize the film's ingenious and imaginative spatial configurations.[3] In his black-and-white films, the camera, with its forward tracking movements and gravity-defying crane shots, had always been constantly and consistently mobile. In *Lola Montès*, almost magically, he sustains this mobile camera. The widescreen rarely stretches out into a coherent space, but is instead filled by a *mise en scène* in which the frame is organized into multiple planes and layers. Ophüls consistently creates depth and distance, countering the natural tendency of CinemaScope to emphasize width. His characters move through doorways, stand against the glass panes of a window or behind translucent panels that dislocate the screen's coherence, dividing it into distinct spatial spheres.

Ophüls's mastery of CinemaScope and colour comes into its own in the scene between Lola and the Ringmaster. Lola has just reached the height of her notoriety due to a scandalous episode during the summer season in Nice, where 'British bankers and French aristocrats' lined up to court her. The flashback this time comes from the Ringmaster himself, as he intones 'I too went to pay my respects.' And then, in Lola's hotel suite, he begins: 'I am a man of the circus', and proceeds to enumerate the various freaks he has displayed profitably across the u.s. He makes Lola a straightforward proposition: 'You know how to create a scandal and excite an audience. Throughout the world, scandal is money and in America it has no limits. Come with me. I'll pay you top fees. You will re-enact your scandals and if there are not enough, we'll invent a few.' He has drawn up a contract and sits down to sign it. The scene is set in a room layered by glass panels, which enclose the characters in their own distinct but translucent spaces, and points of bright red colour (from candles, small packages, a quill pen) are dotted around the room's decor. The screens and panels separate Lola and the

Ringmaster into different segments of the frame, but a symmetrical balance within the composition implies the sudden mutual attraction between the two. As the Ringmaster moves to screen left, behind another glass partition, to sign the contract, Lola sits for a moment at a mirror in the centre, her reflection filling the screen to the right. Looking at her reflection, Lola seems to see into her future with foreboding, in an intimation of the fate awaiting her in the circus. Announcing that she is not a circus freak, she turns abruptly away from the mirror and returns to her own space by the window. The Ringmaster replies that the contract will wait for her indefinitely; he calls her 'Lola', on the grounds that they are both of the same profession, and he then kisses her. At this moment, the edges of the screen fall into darkness, leaving the central close-up image in something approximating the traditional, pre-widescreen Academy ratio and thus creating the strange sense of a dynamic relation between screen formats. However, the constricted space

also represents the Ringmaster's future hold over Lola; it follows him as he leaves the room and the image only expands back to the CinemaScope format once Lola stands alone in the screen. This scene functions as a premonition of Lola's future fall out of the courtesan's tenuous hold on prosperity. She dismisses the Ringmaster with the prediction that it will not be 'for better but for worse' that she would ever seek out his contract.

Lola's reflection in the mirror as a prefiguration of her future evokes Gilles Deleuze's 'crystal image'. Writing specifically about Ophüls,

Deleuze associates the splitting of actual and virtual in the two-faced crystal image with the splitting of time. Time, he writes, 'has to split the present into two heterogeneous directions, one of which is launched towards the future while the other falls into the past'.[4] While a pre-figured future is launched in this scene, the film's use of flashbacks, so important to Deleuze's concept of the crystal image, falls back into the past. He comments:

Lola looks into the future.

What counts [in *Lola Montès*] is not the link between the actual and miserable present (the circus) and the recollection-image of former magnificence. The evocation is certainly there; but what it reveals at a deeper level is the dividing in two of time, which makes all the presents past and makes them tend towards the circus as if their future, but also preserves all the pasts and puts them into the circus as so many virtual images in pure recollections... The dividing of the two images, actual and virtual, does not go to the limit, because the resulting circuit repeatedly takes us back from one kind to the other. There is only a vertigo, an oscillation.[5]

Although Lola's mirror image is virtual to her actual figure, the mirror image is, at the same time, a shudder, a premonition of the 'actual and miserable', of the circus in the future, of which the Ringmaster himself stands as a foreboding figuration. However, the Ringmaster and the circus have already, from the film's opening moments, been established as a narrative 'present': the actual out of which the flashbacks shift into the virtual, a 'recollection-image'. In this sense, the scene in the Nice hotel offers a miniature of the wider oscillations across the film's splitting of time. This alternation of the actual and the virtual, as Deleuze points out, is literally incarnated in Lola's vertigo as

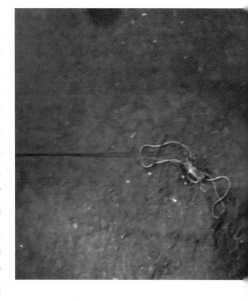

she looks down from the top of the circus tent to the site of her probable death below.

With the Ringmaster's proposal, furthermore, Ophüls makes an explicit gesture towards the film's self-reflexivity. The Ringmaster's words ('scandal is money', 'you will re-enact your scandals') encapsulate the relation between female stardom, spectacle and commercial entertainment that he will stage in the circus. If celebrity depends on the repetition of sex, scandal and gossip, its value as a commodity depends on its repetition within a system of circulation and the production of a paying public. From this perspective, the oscillation between past and future in *Lola Montès* also relates to an economy of female sexuality.

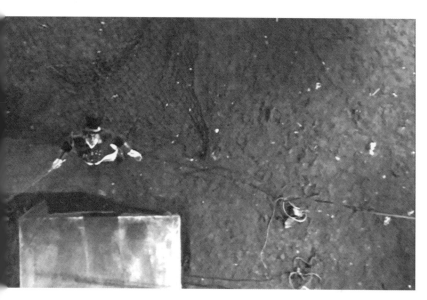

In the future...

Lola looks into the void...

...suspended between life and death.

While the Ringmaster's speculative premise (in Nice) is only realized chronologically later, in Lola's future circus performances, the flashback structure's 'splitting of time' creates a 'circuit' across temporalities and across the different values invested in Lola's body. As she points out: it is only when her sexual value as a courtesan ('the better') is exhausted that she will turn to the Ringmaster to exploit her celebrity value ('the worse'). The circus as an early form of mass entertainment, not yet mechanically reproduced, can only realize a pre-industrial level of circulation and commodification, but the film pre-figures the future of entertainment in two ways. First of all, the circus spectacle is mechanized through the repetitive, synchronized movements of its chorus lines and the plethora of visual tricks. Second, if the circus spectacle in *Lola Montès* stands for a 'primitive' economy of entertainment, then this past presupposes a mirroring into a future industrialized cinema: the film *Lola Montès* itself. In this sense, the Ringmaster's proposal splits the history of the entertainment industry. If Lola's narrative past oscillates into her future as celebrity/spectacle, the circus itself stands as a historical past to the future medium in which the narrative ultimately materializes: the cinema. This fusion of past and future is realized in the visualization of the circus audience, composed, in the first rows, of human-sized papier mâché dolls, properly costumed by Georges Annenkov, replaced in the distance by blown-up photographs.

Annenkov described the idea:

> This was not imposed by budgetary economy. No. It was dictated by Max Ophüls's desire to emphasize the contrast between *the immobility (that is inactivity) of the spectators and the restless agitation of the ring* . . . Ophüls asked to have the figures costumed in black and white . . . In fact, the circus spectators stood, in Max Ophüls's mind, for the public that would come to see his film in those 'darkened rooms' of the cinema.[6]

Lola's compulsive movement from lover to lover, her desire to repeat, mutates into her constantly repeated performance in the circus; she is ultimately a figure for the endless repeatability of the mechanically reproduced spectacle. Out of these themes, Ophüls constructs an image for the film industry's construction of the star, marketed over and over again, an object of repeated exhibition for the desire of an insatiable mass audience.

In Italy in 1934, Ophüls made a film about film, *La signora di tutti* (Everybody's Woman), for the press magnate Angelo Rizzoli's first venture into film production. The film was adapted from the successful 1934 novel of the same name by Salvatore Gotta. Ophüls radically altered the novel and, out of a single-page reference to the heroine's departure for Hollywood at the end of the book, he built the story's present tense around the film industry. Prefiguring the structure of *Lola Montès,* he split the story into a present (the film industry) and a past which tells the story of the heroine's scandalous loves in flashback. *La signora di tutti* also closely rehearses some of the themes of *Lola Montès.* A beautiful young woman, Gaby Doriot (played by Isa Miranda), is being marketed as a new major movie star. But Gaby has a past. In both films, the question of the star's commercial potential is associated with scandal. While the Ringmaster exploits and markets Lola's notoriety, the film studio's publicity machine moves into overdrive to repress any breath of scandal associated with Gaby. Despite the difference in marketing discourse, the stories of both films trace first the scandal of unfettered female sexuality and, then, its exploitation or containment within the entertainment industry. Reconfigured into an erotic spectacle, circulated as an object of mass male desire, neither Gaby nor Lola ultimately threaten the patriarchal order.

Ophüls depicts the cinema's institutional infrastructure highly ironically. He satirizes the all-male studio hierarchy: caricatures of cupidity and hypocrisy, dark-suited, clumsy figures clustering round the glamorous woman on whom their livelihoods depend. Gaby's status as commodity is brilliantly conjured up in the film's opening scene:

in an extreme close-up, a gramophone plays Gaby's theme song 'Io sono la signora di tutti . . .' ('I am every man's woman . . .'). As her agent and the head of the studio bargain over her value, the record is removed and replaced as the bidding see-saws between the two. Here Ophüls uses a modern object of entertainment, the gramophone, to represent Gaby metonymically, as well as to convey the cut-throat nature of the industry in which the star represents profit and profit only. This opening scene is shot with a boldly modernist style: the rhythm of the song and the rhythm of the men's voices as they bargain over Gaby materialize the relation between star and industry. Once the deal is struck, the film cuts from a last close-up on the record to a close-up of Gaby's face on a poster as it comes off a printing press. Once again Gaby's commodity status is clearly signified: as the publicity images appear in quick succession, the name and image 'Gaby Doriot' are repeated over and over again. Mary Ann Doane has succinctly summed up the sequence: 'the woman becomes the exemplary work of art in the age of mechanical reproduction.'[7]

From the mechanical repetition of her name and image as the posters roll off the printing press, the next scene, set in the film studio, immediately takes up the repetition again. Over and over, an assistant director calls for 'Doriot . . . Doriot . . . Doriot . . .'. The camera follows his search, tracking around the chaotic scenes of preparation for the first day's filming, until another underling takes up the same cry, 'Doriot . . . Doriot . . . Doriot . . .', and the camera takes off once again. The rhythm of these tracking shots continues, following Gaby's agent down a hotel corridor and into her suite. Here the camera moves through four interior walls until finally reaching her bathroom: the star herself is then revealed, lying unconscious on the floor after a suicide attempt. These extraordinary and unconventional tracking shots create a cinematic crescendo culminating with the discovery of Gaby's body when, in her first appearance in the film, she lies suspended between life and death. It is during efforts to resuscitate her in hospital that she lives through the memories of her life in a series of flashbacks, prefiguring the relationship between past and future that is so crucial to *Lola Montès*. At the end of the film, Ophüls returns to the printing press. With the news of her death, the production of 'Gaby Doriot' publicity posters slows down and then comes to a halt.

Both *Lola Montès* and *La signora di tutti* deal with the relation between the entertainment industry and the financial structures upon which it depends. Deleuze elegantly relates his concept of the crystal image to films about films, suggesting that their representation of money brings time to the fore because in the cinema 'time is money':

> What the film within the film expresses is this infernal circuit between the image and money, this inflation which time puts into the exchange . . . The film is movement but the film within the film is money, is time. The crystal-image thus receives the principle which is its foundation: endlessly relaunching exchange which is dissymmetrical, unequal and without equivalence, giving image for money, giving time for images, converting time, the transparent side, and money, the opaque side, like a spinning top on its end. And the film will be finished when there is no more money left.[8]

In *Lola Montès* and *La signora di tutti,* Ophüls dramatizes the investment of 'image for money' in the figure of the woman, the essential circuit through which money moves and becomes 'film' (as implied into the future, but equally true in the case of Lola's performance). The actual female body is exchanged into money and materializes in the virtual image on the screen or in the circus ring. But in this version of 'time is money' the flaw, the lack of equivalence and the ultimate collapse of the circuit, is expressed in and through the woman's relation to death and to the actual. This is very clearly the case in *La signora di tutti* as Gaby hovers between life and death on the operating table. And Lola's tenuous hold on life is a dark theme running through *Lola Montès*.

By the time of the circus, the film's present, Lola is ill, her heart is worn out and each performance brings her nearer to death. Although he loves her and has always been in love with her, the Ringmaster steps up the perilous nature of Lola's performances, pushing her to extremes in order to thrill the audience.[9] The question of Lola's health is referred to explicitly throughout the whole of the circus performance, articulated by the doctor with the words 'She has aged before her time. Her heart is worn out.' The question of her illness condenses with the risk of death in the final dive. This is the Ringmaster's gamble: as a showman he delivers the ultimate thrill by removing the safety net, but he also realizes that, sooner or later, with the loss of his star, 'there will be no more money left.'

Ophüls creates an iconography for Lola in which the shadow of death intertwines with the figure of the automaton. At first, Ophüls had doubted whether Martine Carol had the ability to carry the role. But in her performance in the set pieces of Lola's past, Carol has an operatic theatricality, appropriate for her exhibitionist character, also endowed with a certain kind of mechanical quality. In the circus scenes, Lola is drained of human vitality. Ophüls used his star's inherent immobility (of both expression and body) to depict a powerful rhetorical figure, one that juxtaposes her closeness to death, in the narrative, with the kind of lifeless animation associated with a puppet. For her first appearance she is carried into the circus ring rather as life-size, wooden or plaster statues of the Virgin are carried through the streets of Southern European towns on holy days. She is placed in the centre of the ring, silent, immobile and wearing an elaborate gold dress that covers her feet so that her body fuses with the gold platform on which she is sitting. Ophüls cuts from long shots of her figure to sudden close-ups of her face, made-up like the painted features of a doll. These images, the puppet, the plaster Virgin, the doll, find a more mysterious, fascinating realization in the figure of the beautiful automaton, whose exquisite exterior conceals the cogs and wheels that animate her. This structural opposition evokes the cinematic opposition between projector and

Lola as beautiful automaton.

screen, an outside and an inside: the fascinating illusion that holds the gaze but also distracts from the unsightly mechanism that produces it. So too, the shadow of death evokes the cinema's animation of the figures on its filmstrip, traces of once-living gestures, endlessly repeated in the afterlife of their ghostly actors.

There are interesting similarities and differences between Isa Miranda and Martine Carol. Carol was a major French star of the 1950s, with an image built primarily on the pin-up-type attributes of her cleavage. For the character of Gaby, Ophüls and Rizzoli conducted a sweeping search for a new star before casting Miranda. Her screen image exudes the attributes of *photogénie*, that special and indefinable affinity with the movie camera, and plays to her status as star both on the screen and in its fiction. But her acting and performance in general have something of Martine Carol's lifelessness and mechanical gesture, which Ophüls makes use of metonymically in Gaby's association with the machines that embody her and her symbiosis with cinema itself.

Ophüls, at the end of his life, used *Lola Montès* to return to the themes of *La signora di tutti* and to reflect once again on the exploitative, tawdry financial infrastructure of the cinema he loved so much: the subordination of its stars to the mechanisms of the industry and market that produces and manipulates them. The final scene of *Lola Montès* materializes visually, in a single shot, the complex, self-reflexive themes that Ophüls has built up throughout the film. In its combination of conceptual clarity with cinematic brilliance, the shot stands as one of the most extraordinary in the history of film. But it also stands as Ophüls's epitaph. Owing in part to the working conditions Ophüls imposed on himself while making *Lola Montès* and the stressful nature of the production, he died the following year in Hamburg at the age of 55, having just completed an outstanding theatre production of Beaumarchais' *The Marriage of Figaro*.

The final scene of *Lola Montès* is staged outside the circus. Closing the performance in the ring, the Ringmaster announces that Lola will

The commodification of the female body.

receive any and all male patrons and allow each one to kiss her hand for the price of a dollar. The camera begins the shot close on Lola, imprisoned in a wooden cage as though she were a wild animal on display, while the Ringmaster repeatedly exhorts the men to pay just one dollar to kiss her hand. Gradually the camera pulls back with an extensive crane shot that reveals a crowd of undifferentiated male consumers, the film audience *avant la lettre*. In this scene, his last word on the cinema, Ophüls stages the mutation of desire into dollars, an allegorical image that captures cinema's future as a major capitalist industry. Truffaut finished his review of *Lola Montès* in 1955 by citing this as one of Ophüls most Pirandellian moments: 'the spectators advance from *under* the screen in such a way that *we*, the film spectators, merge with them; for the first time, the exit from the cinema is made on the screen.'[10]

In a final moment of self-reflexivity that reverberates into the future, Ophüls reminds his audiences, incorporated as they are into the audience on the screen, of their complicity in the commodification of the female body as spectacle. And all subsequent screenings of *Lola Montès* repeat this message.

The crowd of male consumers.

ALFRED HITCHCOCK, *VERTIGO*

We've forgotten why Joan Fontaine leans over the edge of the cliff and what it was that Joel McCrea was going to do in Holland. We don't remember why Montgomery Clift was maintaining eternal silence or why Janet Leigh stops at the Bates Motel or why Teresa Wright is still in love with Uncle Charlie. We've forgotten why Henry Fonda is not entirely guilty and exactly why the American government employed Ingrid Bergman. But we remember a handbag. But we remember a bus in the desert. But we remember a glass of milk, the sails of a windmill, a hairbrush. But we remember bottles in a line, a pair of glasses, a passage of music, a bunch of keys, because it's thanks to them that Alfred Hitchcock succeeded where Alexander, Julius Caesar and Napoleon failed: to become master of the universe.
Jean-Luc Godard, *Histoire(s) du cinéma*

One could add: 'We've forgotten why Gavin Elster dispatched Madeleine to seduce Scottie, but we remember the perfect blonde.' Godard rightly points out that Hitchcock gave certain objects in his films an emotional and cinematic aura and, even if at a bit of a stretch, Madeleine could belong on the list. But Godard's point extends beyond Hitchcock, to the effect of the passing of time on Hollywood's studio system films more generally. *Cahiers du cinéma*, 'auteur theory' and film studies transformed certain genre films from trash into highly regarded contributions to cinema's history and culture, and, in the process, tended to discard formulaic narrative and character in favour of directorial vision. Nonetheless there are other cases, almost the reverse, clustered around the last days of Hollywood, in which narrative, event and character transcend genre and hold their own dramatically and cinematically. During the 1950s, some directors who had aged alongside the cinema itself, who knew that their own days and that of their industry were numbered, could sometimes make, even as industry pressure intensified in those days of crisis, darker films, emotionally contorted, with haunted characters, challenging narrative convention, overthrowing or ironizing the happy ending. An early example would be Fritz Lang's *Rancho Notorious* (1952), but also Raoul Walsh's *The Revolt of Mamie Stover* (1956), Douglas Sirk's *Written on the Wind* (1956), John Ford's *The Man Who Shot Liberty Valance* (1962) and Alfred Hitchcock's *Vertigo* (1958). These directors, having spent most of their lives negotiating with an iron production system dedicated to standardization, managed to achieve a certain self-awareness, verging, in some cases, on self-reflexivity.

It might seem incongruous, almost perverse, to introduce Edward Said's thoughts on 'late style', developed as they are through Theodor Adorno's thoughts on late Beethoven, to this sphere of popular culture dominated by an industrial production system and market forces. In spite of this clash of cultures, some of Said's reflections relate to the work of these ageing Hollywood masters, not least through the concept of late style itself. The final sentences of Said's essay resonate with not only the personal lateness of these particular films, but a sense of a melancholic liberation as the professional world of the masters faced its own end:

Certain artists and thinkers care enough about their métier to believe that it too ages and must face death with failing senses and memory. As Adorno said about Beethoven, late style does not admit the definitive cadences of death; instead, death appears in a refracted mode, as irony. But with the kind of opulent, fractured, and somehow inconsistent solemnity of a work such as the *Missa Solemnis*, or in Adorno's own essays, the irony is how often lateness as theme and as style keeps reminding us of death.[1]

Hollywood late style reflects back ironically on its own past; but also, echoing Said's final words, the themes and the style 'remind us of death'. Furthermore, in terms of *Vertigo*, what would be a more apt evocation than 'opulent, fractured and somehow inconsistent solemnity'?

These ideas, irony, fracture, the aura of death, are particularly relevant to *Vertigo*; but first of all, there is its lavishly opulent style. The world's most skilled technicians, in its most advanced studios, brought into being the ideas of a director who had honed his command of cinema across a lifetime. Although all Hitchcock's late Hollywood films share his perfectly achieved style, *Vertigo* pushes 'perfection' on to a conceptual level, with a degree of irony that takes it into self-reflexivity. Thus Madeleine's beauty, an illusion that deceives the eye, invokes the illusory fascination of film, recalling, in turn, both Freud's theory of fetishism and its use in film theory. In his meditation on his own world and the phantasmagorias he wove so brilliantly, Hitchcock brutally analyses the symbiosis between the female fetish, the film fetish and the desire of the male spectator for whom both have been conjured up. Reflecting this fractured male psyche, Hitchcock's film is itself fractured into two separate sections. The first part shows the image, Madeleine, embodied in a fascinating illusion; the second part reveals the process of fabrication itself, repeating the process that had, before the beginning, transformed Judy into Madeleine for the first time. Although *Vertigo* is not literally about the cinema, in Scottie's belief in the illusory Madeleine the film reflects on the willingness of the human mind to believe in the illusion that is cinema.

Various themes in *Vertigo* appear in earlier Hitchcock films and then return in some of his later ones. *Vertigo* was immediately preceded by *The Wrong Man* (1956). Shot, appropriately for the plot's darkness, in black and white, the film shares with *Vertigo* something of the Scottie plot: the sense of irrational forces taking over and destroying a human life. More relevant to Madeleine's construction had been Hitchcock's use of colour film to develop the 'Hitchcock blonde' image that has now become a popular culture cliché. But there is a recurrent theme of female duplicity, disguised both by seductiveness and consummate performance: the heroine as undercover agent in *Notorious* (1948) or *North by Northwest* (1959), for instance, or as the compulsive thief in *Marnie* (1964). All these roles highlight Hitchcock's interest in the beautiful but deceitful woman, the focus of *Vertigo*. The iconography of the blonde, essential to Madeleine, dates back, quite obviously, to Hitchcock's films with Grace Kelly. Although she could epitomize sheen, luminosity and surface perfection, there is no deceit in her characters. *Vertigo* makes the connection between blondeness and duplicity that returns with Eve (Eva Marie Saint) in *North by Northwest* and both Tippi Hedren's characters, more marked in *Marnie* but relevant to *The Birds*. All these characters in their visual and narrative construction attract the male gaze, both erotic and investigative, that I analysed in 'Visual Pleasure and Narrative Cinema'. I only now realize, in retrospect, that *Vertigo*'s particular significance for the essay was probably due to a self-awareness that I failed to notice at the time. Then, I was absorbed in critique. Only looking again at the film, seeing it with an altered perspective (that I mentioned at the beginning of this essay), has it become clear that Hitchcock had made a film that was actually about the very Freudian concepts of voyeurism and fetishism that I was attempting to analyse. He visualized my argument and showed that voyeurism, according to Freud a key structure of human sexual pleasure, had been unprecedentedly harnessed by the cinema. And that look, essential to the film medium, has then, in patriarchal commodity culture, been projected onto a particular figuration of femininity.

In *Vertigo*, the figuration is refined around the connotations of artifice. On the one hand, on the side of the plot, Madeleine is an artefact designed by Elster to seduce, but, on the side of the image, it is precisely the artificial nature of her appearance that seduces. *Vertigo* is about the fabrication of a perfect facade, which, in the first instance, is cosmetic:

make-up turns the face into an exquisite mask, and dyed hair gives the look its special sheen. This kind of perfection is demanded of the movie star, and while the camera chooses frame and angle, the lights give her face a further, cinematic, illumination. Madeleine is filmed accordingly. It is, of course, the sight of Madeleine that draws Scottie into the trap. From the moment she stands in profile, in the bar at Ernie's, posing for his gaze, she personifies a cosmetic and insubstantial femininity. *Vertigo*'s brilliant self-reflexivity lies in Scottie's fixation, in Walter Benjamin's words, on 'the sex appeal of the inorganic'.[2]

Madeleine: the sex appeal of the inorganic.

For 'Visual Pleasure and Narrative Cinema' Scottie's gaze represented voyeurism, the active, male sexual instinct, as he secretly watches Madeleine, carrying the spectator's gaze with him. This relationship can be reconfigured, however: rather than acting as a surrogate for the spectator, Scottie has become an ironic, on-screen personification of the entranced spectator absorbed by the hallucinatory quality of its star. Madeleine gives a consummate performance of her story, concocted, as it is, out of a jumble of evocative signifiers and echoes of a nineteenth-century melodrama, haunted by death and apparitions, as insubstantial as Carlotta, Madeleine's great-grandmother. Hitchcock films Madeleine as disembodied, ghostly and filmic. She materializes almost like an apparition, she poses for Scottie's contemplation, strategically and rhetorically enhanced by the resonances of her San Francisco locations, and when she moves she seems to glide across the screen; these ghostly appearances and disappearances culminate when she vanishes from the McKittrick Hotel. After Madeleine has engineered their meeting, she and Scottie begin to roam around together; he seems to have taken that magical step from the theatre audience into the screen, becoming the spectator who crosses over into the film and its story. Her enigmatic dialogue and mysterious character enhance the impression and Scottie tries hard (as in movies of this genre) to adapt to the mysterious ways of the character he has encountered and her preposterous plot.

These scenes all lead towards and culminate in Scottie and Madeleine's first kiss. For obvious and practical reasons, Hitchcock had always conceived of this scene as a rear projection; the plate, the film of the coastal location that would be projected behind Novak and Stewart in the studio, had already been filmed in pre-production along with others which would be used at various points in the film.[3] But the presence of rear projection adds something more to the sequence: the concept of artifice, Madeleine's artificial appearance and her fabrication as artefact, is realized both dramatically and at the level of the cinematic in this special effect. The filming of this crucial scene, however, begins on location at Cypress Point. Although there are cutaways to Scottie, the film concentrates mainly on Madeleine; she looks away from Scottie as she lures him into the last stages of complicity with murder. She recounts her strange dream, her sense of being possessed, her fear of death; her voice sounds strained and forced, in contrast to Scottie's rational, relieved recognition of the San Juan Bautista site. The transition from location to studio is softened by two doubles who run down the edge of the rocks. Then, in the studio, Scottie and Madeleine are in each other's arms, while behind them the pre-filmed Cypress

The artifice of the special effect; the artifice of seduction.

Point plate is projected. As this kiss marks the moment when the trap has finally closed around Scottie, the artifice of Madeleine's seduction resonates with the artifice of the special effect and its spatial and temporal dislocations. However, Hitchcock adds a further twist: during the kiss an immense wave crashes onto the rocks, suggesting a crescendo of sexual desire, soon followed by another just as the scene fades out. On the one hand, the waves draw attention to the artifice, risking audience recognition and amusement; on the other, the wave might signify that Madeleine's duplicitous kiss has been, if only momentarily, replaced by Judy's actual emotion.

The second part of the film revolves around the opposition between Madeleine and Judy. Behind Madeleine's perfect facade lies Judy's tragic reality. Judy, having been the object of such intense passion as Madeleine, is unable to arouse the slightest erotic urge in Scottie. Cinematically, she is filmed as an ordinary girl in an everyday world. When Judy first appears, she is walking down the street with her friends, grounded and physical. But she pauses exactly in front of Scottie and the film finds and frames exactly the same profile as in Madeleine's pose in the bar at Ernie's. Judy's style is markedly cluttered: shoulder-length hair, bulky earrings, patterned blouse with colours

Judy: the ordinary girl.

close to nature, earthy tones such as green and brown, altogether in clear contrast to Madeleine. Kim Novak was dressed by the film's eminent costume designer Edith Head, who has described Madeleine's appearance as stunning but simple: the high heels, grey tailored suit, white overcoat, perfect make-up and blonde hair smoothed back into a bun. Hitchcock insisted on the colour grey for the suit and, apart from the blue-green shawl at Ernie's, Madeleine only wears black or white.[4] The concept of pose was built into the rigid design of Madeleine's look and Kim Novak has described her reaction to the costume:

> I can use that feeling when I play Judy. Judy is trapped into portraying Madeleine and she doesn't want to . . . So I used that feeling of wearing someone else's shoes that made me feel out of place. The same thing with Madeleine's grey suit, which made me stand so straight and erect the way Edith Head built it. I hated that silly suit, to tell you the truth, but it helped me play Madeleine.[5]

Judy's very bodily presence and her characterization as an ordinary girl enhances Madeleine's ghostly, insubstantial glamour. It is only when she submits to being refashioned, from the clothes through to the cosmetic, emerging from the bathroom in the Empire Hotel like a butterfly from its pupa as (apparently) a reincarnation of the already disembodied woman, that Scottie can once again desire her. This opposition between the natural and the artificial woman is also dramatized, almost as an aside, in *The Birds*. In a telling scene, Melanie (Tippi Hedren) goes to see Annie Haywood (Suzanne Pleshette). Melanie is dressed in a mink coat, with white gloves, high heels and perfectly coiffured blonde hair, strongly evoking Madeleine. Annie comes to greet her from the garden, brushing earth off her face, dressed in a red, warm-coloured sweater. *The Birds'* male protagonist, Mitch, is fascinated by Melanie. While he has long since lost interest in Annie's naturalness, his erotic attention is clearly caught by her opposite. A bit later in the film, Melanie rows across Bodega Bay. As in the Cypress Point scene, Hitchcock would have had practical reasons to use rear projection for this sequence, particularly to shoot Melanie's reactions and emotions in close-up. But once again, the rear-projection process brings with it an extra connotation. Framed in the studio, with the sea and coastline projected on the screen behind her, Melanie's personification of the allure of the artificial resonates with the artifice of the mechanical process. Both keep nature at arm's length.

In fashioning a particular figuration of femininity to attract Scottie's obsession, Hitchcock touches, if only implicitly, on male fetishism from a psychoanalytic perspective. There are, however, two strands to the fantasy: both provoke dread, but one is closer to anxiety, while the other is closer to disgust. The first, and most obvious, is castration anxiety. But there is also a residual disgust, a sense of abjection, provoked by the maternal body, that extends more generally to the ageing, decrepit body of the older woman. This iconographical type gradually appeared in Hitchcock's post-war films and coincided with Philip Wylie's pseudo-psychological concept 'momism'.[6] Equivalent dominating and ageing maternal figures, possessively holding on to a son, can be found in Mrs Sebastian in *Notorious*, Mrs Anthony in *Strangers on a Train* (1951) and, in muted form, Lydia Brenner in *The Birds* (1963). Jessie Royce Landis in *To Catch a Thief* (1955) and *North by Northwest*, groomed, permed and with ample make-up to mask indeterminately ageing features, has resonances of 'mom'. Then, with *Psycho* (1960), 'Mother' became a concept rather than a character: the site of the abjection and uncanniness that Freud associated both with the dead and with the maternal body. In a probably unconscious, but satisfying, tribute to Freud, Wylie pronounced: 'I give you mom, I give you the destroying mother ... I give you Medusa.'[7] The complex iconography of Hitchcock's blonde star effectively deflects the gaze from the site of castration anxiety, but also veils that other site of dread, the uncanny body of the mother. The desire to escape from the all-too-physical body invents its eviscerated opposite, the fabricated woman who originated in the myth of Pandora and leads to fantasies of, and experiments with, automata.

Madeleine belongs to the legendary history of beautiful automata, the ancestor of the entrancing mechanical object, the cinema. Film theorists Raymond Bellour and Annette Michelson, quite separately and coincidentally, both wrote essays in the late 1990s about the French symbolist novel *The Eve of the Future* by Auguste Villiers de L'Isle-Adam. In the novel, a fictionalized Thomas Edison creates a perfect replica of a woman for an English lord, who is entranced by his girl-friend's exquisite beauty but irritated by her character and her chatter. Both writers see in the beautiful automaton Hadaly a pre-figuration of the cinema. Michelson sees this embodiment:

Not as the mere object of a cinematic *iconography* of repression and desire – as catalogued by now in the extensive literature on dominant narrative in its major genres of melodrama, *film noir* and so on – but rather as the fantasmatic ground for the cinema itself ... The female body then comes into focus as the very site of the cinema's invention ... we may see the philosophical toy we now know as the cinema as marked in the very moment of its invention by the inscription of desire.[8]

And in a specific reference to fetishism she extends Lord Ewald's fixation on Hadaly to the future film spectator: 'He assents, as the world assents on the eve of its future, to mechanical representation as the simulacrum of the female body. And this world, assenting, murmurs "I know but all the same . . ."'[9]

As Michelson links Lord Ewald's passion for Hadaly to a fascination with the animation of the inanimate, she precisely and significantly points out its gender; the beautiful automaton that seems to come to life is necessarily female. Furthermore, the story directly evokes the fetishist's rejection of the real woman, just as Scottie rejects Judy for the fabricated image, Madeleine. Edison says to Ewald: 'since you prefer an image to reality I shall raise this image to a point of perfection . . . since it is the quality of the image which corresponds to the deepest nature of your desire.' And: 'What you love is this phantom alone. That and that alone is what you recognise as unconditional reality. In short it's this projection of your own mind that you call on . . . and which is nothing but your own mind reduplicated in her.'[10]

Here, the terms 'perfection', 'phantom' and 'projection' suggest the movement between desire for woman as illusion and surrender to the cinematic illusion. Raymond Bellour makes the following point:

> Why, when transposed to the screen, is the construction of the Android found to be so gripping, whether in *Metropolis* or in *The Bride of Frankenstein*? Why do the films dwell on this scene in particular? It pertains, I think, to the nature of the medium. The actual process of substituting a simulacrum for a living being directly replicates the camera's power to reproduce automatically the reality it confronts. Every *mise en scène* of the simulacrum thus refers intrinsically to the fundamental properties of the cinematic apparatus.[11]

Christian Metz emphasizes the significance of belief for the fetishist for whom the fetish must have psychic verisimilitude. So too, for an audience to believe in a film:

> It is understood that the audience is not duped by the diegetic illusion, it 'knows' that the screen presents no more than a fiction. And yet it is of vital importance for the correct unfolding of the spectacle that this make-believe be scrupulously respected ... that everything is set to work to make the deception effective and to give it the air of truth.[12]

Metz argues that the spectator must be maintained in a state of credulousness, and that such a willing surrender of knowledge in favour of belief is an effect of a film's fetishistic disavowal of its mechanics. In Scottie's passion for Madeleine, in the ease with which he is duped by her image, he reincarnates the film spectator's fetishistic credulousness. And, as the story of Hadaly reiterates, both are constructed on disavowal: of the female body and of the mechanical body of the cinema.

Just as the fascination exerted by the beautiful automaton is derived from the mechanical animation of an inanimate object, so the film projector similarly animates the still frames of the filmstrip for the fascination of the film spectator. And, in the same process, the projector resurrects those ghostly figures, whose stilled gestures on the filmstrip come alive with its illusion of natural movement. These material conditions of cinema then mutate into the movement of the storyline, which, in the case of *Vertigo*, reverberates with ghosts and ghostliness. *Vertigo* was adapted from Pierre Boileau and Thomas Narcejac's novel *D'entre les morts* (1954) and Hitchcock used *From Among the Dead* as his film's working title for most of the production, also keeping the name Madeleine for the same character. The first half of the film is under the shadow of tragic Carlotta Valdes and her suicide, whose spirit and whose fate supposedly has possessed Madeleine. In the second half of the film, Scottie is haunted by the 'dead' Madeleine:

in his breakdown, in his search for her and then through Judy. When Judy finally appears transformed into Madeleine, not only has she recreated the original illusion of perfect, artificial woman, but she brings her ghost back to life. There is a poignancy to Scottie's insistence on the precision and polish of the blonde chignon, the last touch that completes the Madeleine look. An eerie special effect illuminates her figure so that she seems to materialize, as it were, out of a mist or fog, somewhere between the living and the dead. However, the special effect goes further: as it fuses the ghost with the beautiful automaton, the cinematic illusion verges on the kind of visibility that threatens its perfect surface and then, implicitly, that of its female star. With Madeleine/Judy and Scottie's last kiss, the instability projected into their first kiss at Cypress Point returns redoubled. Then, the rear projection conjured up the artificial Madeleine and the deceitful nature of her kiss. In the Empire hotel, as the couple are gradually rotated for the camera in their elongated embrace, Scottie looks up and for an instant hallucinates the moment of their kiss in the San Juan Bautista stable. This time, the rear projection seems to emanate from Scottie's unconscious: he knows sexually that the two women are one.

In spite of, even because of, the separation between the two sides of the double Madeleine/Judy, they/she evoke(s) Gilles Deleuze's concept of the crystal image, which he defines first through these oppositions:

> the real and the imaginary, the physical and the mental, the objective and the subjective, description and narration, *the actual and the virtual* . . . the two related terms . . . reflect each other, without it being possible to say which is first, and tend ultimately to become confused, slipping into the same point of indiscernibility.[13]

Although Hitchcock keeps a strong iconographical distinction between Judy and Madeleine, there are hints of indiscernibility, first of all, as the framing of Madeleine's first close-up is reproduced in

Madeleine/Judy: the virtual and the actual.

Scottie's first sight of Judy. But more poignant is the revelatory filming during the scene in which Scottie, having accompanied Judy back to her room after their first date, proposes that he 'take care of her'. Framed almost in silhouette, supposedly but not completely from Scottie's point of view, Judy's profile is first of all clearly demarcated, maximizing her identity as 'Madeleine'. But these shots are interspersed with two of her facing the camera, in which the doubts, the confusion, that beset Judy are marked on her features and also reflected in the more indistinct, dispersed lighting. Deleuze's crystal image is in this doubling; while Judy could incarnate Deleuze's 'actual' and Madeleine his 'virtual', these shots suggest the way that the two slip in and out of each other. Deleuze associates the crystal image with another level of indiscernibility, that is, between past and present: 'Thus the image has to be present and past, at once and at the same time.'[14] In a sense, when *Vertigo* begins, if only retrospectively, Judy is the virtual image. Not yet on the screen, she inhabits an implied but actual past before her fabrication as Madeleine. Whereas Madeleine, insubstantial and artificial, is, of course, closer to the virtual image and lives out both the present time of her persona and the past time of Carlotta. Out of these relations, the film's two parts, divided in narrative, intertwine through the doubled woman's indiscernibility as both one and two. Thus Judy is necessarily embedded in the present tense of Madeleine's story and her consummate performance suggest that a kind of possession has taken place. Just as Carlotta supposedly possesses Madeleine, Judy is under

Judy/Madeleine: the living dead.

the strange spell of the virtual image. Similarly, the dead Madeleine-as-past inhabits Judy's present, until, in their very indiscernibility, the death of one leads to the death of the other. The balance and discordance between the actual and the virtual extracts *Vertigo* from the norm of narrative film. Scottie's inability to control the story adds to its sense of circularity. Scottie is apparently in command of the investigative gaze as he pursues Madeleine through the streets and sights of San Francisco, yet once again the use of rear projection shifts the meaning of image and character. James Stewart is clearly sitting immobile in the studio while footage of the city is projected behind him. As Hitchcock disables his hero, so much more destructively than his earlier figuration of male spectatorship in *Rear Window* (1954), he undercuts the masculinity on which Hollywood's narrative rules depended. In its challenges to convention *Vertigo* stands as a pre-eminent example of Hollywood's late style in its flamboyantly ironic self-reflexivity and its recurring preoccupation with death. As Said puts it: 'the irony is how often lateness as theme and as style keeps reminding us of death.'[15]

As a self-reflexive film, a meditation on film spectatorship, *Vertigo* revolves around the figure of Madeleine as a personification of cinema, standing in a line of descent from Raymond Bellour's androids whose fascination, he argues, duplicates that of the apparatus. Both the android and its medium, cinema, fake the appearance of life and disguise the artifice through a seductive illusion. In *Vertigo*, Hitchcock's success in weaving a preoccupation with death into 'the sex appeal of the inorganic' conjures up Walter Benjamin's thoughts on fashion, the disguise with which Madeleine conceals her deception, with which Judy disguises herself as Madeleine and to which Scottie's fetishism is in thrall:

> Fashion prescribes the ritual according to which the commodity fetish demands to be worshipped . . . Fashion stands in opposition to the organic. It couples the living body to the inorganic world. To the living it defends the rights of the

corpse. The fetishism that succumbs to the sex appeal of the inorganic is its vital nerve.[16]

Hitchcock made *Vertigo* as a personal 'Alfred J. Hitchcock Productions' film, as though aware that with this movie he was stepping out of conventional Hollywood line; but perhaps he also intuited that, in spite of its initial failure, the film would come to be seen as his masterpiece.

MARILYN MONROE: EMBLEM AND ALLEGORY OF A CHANGING HOLLYWOOD

There are only two Hollywood stars, Charlie Chaplin and Marilyn Monroe, whose characteristics can be figured with a few strokes of a pencil in an immediately recognizable caricature. While Charlie is more usually drawn in his full body (with his hat and cane attributes), Marilyn can be evoked simply by her facial features. Both have come to signify 'cinema' as such. Chaplin emerged as a major star at a time when audience numbers rose exponentially, generating vast amounts of money, when Hollywood was still industrially disorganized, not yet the rigid oligarchy it was to become. He (and his less significant United Artists collaborators) understood that industrial independence would be key to artistic and financial success. Thus if Charlie's image has come to be emblematic of the cinema itself, Chaplin's personal rise is emblematic of the rise of Hollywood, its potential in its early days, and his ability to exploit its modernity both on the screen and in its economic infrastructure. If Marilyn's image has equally come to be emblematic of cinema itself, Monroe's superstar persona arises at the time of the Hollywood studio system's decline and is thus further emblematic of the period and its contradictions.

Particularly to the point here, both stars invested deeply in the construction of their images, which were minutely thought through and consciously developed around a surface masquerade. Charlie's mask is descended from the clown's; Marilyn's is an exaggerated mask of cosmetic femininity. As a result, both stars in the everyday could move around publicly or socially without being recognized. King Vidor's *Show People* (1928) plays on this phenomenon: a young actress (Marion Davies) has just had a hit preview, her first step to stardom, and fails to recognize Charlie (then the most famous man in the world) when he asks for her autograph. When Monroe moved to New York in 1955, it was frequently noted that she, then the most famous woman in the world, could move easily and anonymously around the city without the make-up and style that was 'Marilyn'. There are parallels, too, in social and class origins. Both came from the working class of the entertainment industry: Norma Jean's mother and her later foster mother were both cutters of negative film and Charles Chaplin Sr was a one-time music-hall singer. Norma Jean was certainly, and Charlie probably, illegitimate; their mothers suffered from schizophrenia and depression and were confined to mental institutions while their children lived in foster homes. They grew up in extreme poverty and without education, and, although Charlie might have occasionally sighted his around Kennington pubs, neither knew their fathers.[1] Later in life, Marilyn Monroe and Charlie Chaplin had left leanings politically, which they attributed to their childhood deprivation and the tragedy of their mothers' lives as well as a deep consciousness of their lack of education and a consequent hunger for knowledge.

There are other parallels: both were deeply uncertain about their performances and suffered from a disruptive tendency to perfectionism. Whereas Chaplin, with his accumulation of power, his own producer and director, and as a founder of United Artists, could close down a film until he was sure of himself, Monroe acquired a reputation for insecurity: heavily dependent on her various 'coaches'; so often late; always demanding retakes, and never sure of the outcome. In the first instance, there is obviously a gender difference here, but the contrast between the status of the two stars also points to a contrast between the years of the Hollywood industry's rise and its decline. Chaplin made millions at the box office in his early days and could then progress to making his masterpieces (also box-office hits, at least three of which have been cited over the years as among 'the greatest movies of all time') over the long years of his independence. Conditions were very different for Monroe.

CODA 1: Ella Fitzgerald had been a longstanding hero for Monroe and she had learnt to sing from Fitzgerald songs. Fitzgerald had been banned from performing in Los Angeles due to a 'whites-only' policy, and has told this story:

> I owe Marilyn Monroe a real debt . . . she personally called the owner of the Mocambo, and told him she wanted me booked immediately, and if he would do it, she would take a front table every night. She told him – and it was true, due to Marilyn's superstar status – that the press would go wild. The owner said yes, and Marilyn was there, front table, every night. The press went overboard. After that, I never had to play a small jazz club again. She was an unusual woman – a little ahead of her times. And she didn't know it.[2]

To focus now on Monroe: her struggles with 20th Century-Fox parallel historically and allegorically the changes taking place in the industry. As she became the greatest and the last superstar in the 1950s, the Hollywood studio system fell into decline. Undoubtedly, it was her image as the epitome of the 'blonde bombshell' that took her to stardom and made her the most famous woman of her time. As she fought for financial independence, paradoxically it was the meanings and resonances invested in her image that brought her into confrontation with Fox. While this was a battle that she ultimately won against a weakened studio, those paradoxes persisted into her later career.

Marilyn Monroe's difficult relationship with 20th Century-Fox reflects the before and after of the industrial upheavals caused by the Paramount Decree and divestment from vertical integration. During her slow rise to stardom, she had suffered, like so many thousands of others, from the contract system. While a studio could break a contract after six months, the player was at the studio's mercy: for instance, having no say in his or her roles, or being lent out to other studios without consent. Monroe's first contract with Fox lasted only from 1946 to 1947 followed by less than a year at Columbia. It was only through the untiring devotion of her agent, Johnny Hyde, vice president of the William Morris Agency, that she managed to get small parts and press notice. These include her now famous early cameo appearances: the Marx Brothers' *Love Happy* in 1949, John Huston's *The Asphalt Jungle* (for MGM) and, more substantially, Joseph L. Mankiewicz's *All About Eve* (back at Fox), both released in 1950.

Just before his premature death, Johnny Hyde persuaded Fox to give Monroe a new contract. After two more cameos, which introduced her to Howard Hawks, a leading role in *Don't Bother to Knock* (1952) failed to make her into a major star. In spite of some internal support, Fox had never seemed to know what to do with Monroe. As Donald Spoto points out, Darryl Zanuck continued to assert that she was 'not photogenic' and had no future at the box office.[3] By the time he finally gave way and cast her in *Niagara* (1953) she was already a celebrity, receiving regular attention from Hollywood gossip columnists, her still photographs widely circulated and, from early 1952, dating Joe DiMaggio, recently retired from baseball but still America's biggest sporting star. The story of *Niagara* had been conceived by its writer and producer, Charles Brackett, to feature the Falls and once Monroe was cast, Fox built both up into a double spectacular attraction. Although *Niagara* launched Monroe into her future as a superstar, the part of Rose was complex, demanding and very different from her future roles. As a femme fatale in one of Hollywood's last films noirs, her performance is strangely moving (for a character who plots with her lover to murder her husband). Although *Niagara* was her breakthough film, it was her next film, *Gentlemen Prefer Blondes*, that would set the tone for her future, when her acting accomplishments would be routinely overlooked or even decried.

After making a fortune for Fox with *Gentlemen Prefer Blondes* (1953) and *The Seven Year Itch* (1955), for which she never received her promised bonus, Monroe was still tied to her contract. But the breaking point came over her typecasting: once the studio had understood that she was a 'dumb blonde', these were the roles she would play in future. After *River of No Return* and *There's No Business Like Show Business*, both 1954, she rebelled. Later, in the spirit of many other stars before her, such as Bette Davis and Jean Harlow, she succinctly summed up the contract problem:

> I was put into these movies without being consulted at all and much against my wishes. I had no choice in the matter. Is that fair? I work hard, I take pride in my work and I'm a human being like the rest of them. If I keep on with parts like the ones [Fox] has been giving me, the public will soon tire of me.[4]

She wanted, again in the spirit of stars before her, to choose her own scripts and diversify her roles. Monroe's rebellion against Fox in 1954, at the point when the studio oligopoly was cracking, was an emblematic stand against the tyranny of the contract system and the unimaginative, autocratic way in which the studios had imposed it for decades. But it was also symptomatic of the direction in which the film industry was moving.

As the studio system weakened, agents moved into the power vacuum to negotiate a new kind of contract for their star clients, giving them freedom from studio control and financial independence. MCA's Lew Wasserman, very much the architect of the new Hollywood, had negotiated epoch-changing deals for James Stewart and Alfred Hitchcock. Once she was established as a major star, Monroe joined the move towards independent production, setting up Marilyn Monroe Productions in 1956 with her friend the *Life* photographer Milton Greene. Most significantly, the new company was steered into existence by Wasserman, Monroe's agent at MCA. In the final deal, Fox agreed, among other things, that Monroe only had to appear in four films for the studio over the next seven years, with control over subject and director; and, through her own company, she could develop her own projects.

Once she had achieved independence, Monroe was faced with the problem of 'Marilyn' and the future of this carefully crafted image. She would gradually have to resolve a key contradiction between that image and her aspirations as an actress. Monroe knew very well that her rise to superstardom had been due to her fans and had little or nothing to do with 20th Century-Fox. In the industry, her support had come mainly from exhibitors who had quickly realized that Marilyn Monroe was a box-office draw with major financial potential. Even before her beginnings in film, her 'blonde bombshell' image had been the first step in her career and her fragile passport to Hollywood. It was through her success as a pin-up, working for the Blue Book agency from 1946 to 1947, photographed by, among others, Andre de Dienes and Tom Kelly, that she got her 1946 Fox contract. The outbreak of the Korean War in 1950 gave a new lease of life to the pin-up and it was through postcards and magazines that Monroe had built up a very large following. In a sense, her early cameos and small parts are almost animated, dramatized versions of her pin-up image (summed up by Groucho Marx: 'She's Theda Bara, Mae West and Little Bo Peep rolled into one'). At Fox, with her make-up man Allan 'Whitey' Snyder, she evolved and defined the characteristic 'Marilyn' look and there is no doubt that she realized that she had to construct, even exploit, her 'to-be-looked-at-ness' to establish her Hollywood career. By the time *Niagara* was released in early 1953, she was receiving 25,000 fan letters a week. Her pin-up fame was realized dramatically on her trip to Korea (a detour during her honeymoon to Japan with Joe DiMaggio in 1954). As Donald Spoto points out:

> In two days alone, her audience included grateful troops of the 3rd, 7th, 24th and 40th army divisions – 60,000 men. Most

of them had never seen a Monroe film, for they had been in service since her rise to stardom. But they knew her photograph, the calendar, the snapshots, the thousands of pictures in newspapers and magazines.[5]

However, if the 'male gaze' had got her into pictures and made her into a superstar, Monroe had other ideas for her future. At the time of her first Fox contract in the late 1940s, she had already begun to work with the Actors' Laboratory in Los Angeles, where she was introduced to contemporary, socially conscious plays; New York theatre people; and acting. Once she had the power to rebel against Fox, when the now-weakened studio had capitulated to her demands and made a deal with Marilyn Monroe Productions, she began to study her performances and evolve her skills as an actress, most particularly with Lee Strasberg's Actors Studio in New York from 1955. Here again, Monroe's move was in keeping with a new, significant Hollywood trend: the Actors Studio and its method had trained a number of recent stars, such as Marlon Brando and James Dean. Although this reassessment of her performance style at the peak of her career shows that she was aware of changing trends in Hollywood, it also stands as a gesture against industry tradition, and the long-standing contradictions at the heart of a studio's rigid control over the careers and image of their stars and their contract players alike.

Any star system functions as an attraction, bringing an audience into the cinema premised on recognition, return and repetition. To be of value to the studio, to be a marketable commodity, stars had to streamline given characteristics into a reasonably stable personification of self as image. And for a studio, however often characters or costumes might change from film to film, once a star was established, continuity would be of the essence. The trick was to bring a story and its emotions to the screen in an inherently contradictory double act, in which the star's recognition factor always, of course, threatened fictional verisimilitude. As Marilyn Monroe evolved into an ultimate signifier of sexuality, from her pin-ups to her early ultra-sexualized cameos, to her superstardom in the mid-1950s, she was always more image than character. Rather than suggesting character within the continuity of a star persona, she had to personify 'to-be-looked-at-ness' and maintain her highly evolved masquerade, stylized gestures and performance to which a character's interiority would be, by and large, irrelevant. In this sense, the nature of her star image as a commodity for the industry coincided with the structural paradox of the fetishized female body. The perfect surface, epitomized historically by Marilyn and, to return to *Vertigo*, to be epitomized fictionally by Madeleine, holds the fascinated male gaze. But the perfection is in itself fragile; a surface crack might reveal to the vulnerable male psyche the dreaded inside that the fetish denies. While Monroe continued to maintain something of the star's essential duality, she worked to change its meaning.

Monroe's task would be to find a way of moving beyond the fetishized Marilyn. Due to her work with experimental theatre and her interest in social drama over spectacle, she was determined to reconfigure her 'blonde bombshell' image into a completely new register. Needless to say, however, her 'Marilyn' look was essential for the recognition factor that had made her a star and on which her future stardom, her career and the success of Marilyn Monroe Productions depended. The shift, therefore, had to involve a change in the significance of the cosmetic surface and its connotation of vulnerability away from the meaning projected by the industry and male spectatorship. Monroe's achievement (as an actress and as her own producer) would be to evolve a Marilyn with social significance, who could reflect and represent the dilemmas at stake in women's 'to-be-looked-at-ness' and its alienating effects. Furthermore, she could use her constructed image to represent her character's reflections on that image, her interiority, her vulnerability and her uncertainty as the object of male desire. Just as Monroe's innate intelligence, special rapport with the camera and highly developed comic timing all light up

Beyond the 'blonde bombshell' (*The Misfits*, dir. John Huston, 1961).

her 'dumb blonde' roles, her later showgirl films (*Bus Stop*, *Some Like It Hot*, *Let's Make Love* and *The Prince and the Showgirl*) suggest that she was adapting her screen identity to performing the showgirl's dilemma rather than incarnating it.

Monroe aspired, in her experiments with performance, to develop an image that could address ordinary women within the popular culture that she had mastered as a star. She learnt from the high culture of the theatre, but her political commitments were to the socially oppressed and deprived. Ana Salzberg has pointed out that in *The Misfits* of 1961 (written for her by Arthur Miller and on which she pinned so many hopes for her new image and performance style) this aspiration is dramatized in Monroe's first appearance in the film. Her character, Roslyn, is sitting in front of a mirror:

> Captured in the luminosity of the looking glass, her visage wears all its famous beauty: simply, she wears the mask of Marilyn Monroe, movie star. As she turns away from the mirror to face the lens directly, however, the camera reveals a somewhat different figure in medium close-up: a woman with swelling

under her eyes and lines around them, the strain on her face so diffused by the reflection now altogether apparent.[6]

In *The Misfits* Monroe performs an exquisite balancing act, beyond either that of star and character demanded by industry convention or by the naturalism of Arthur Miller's fiction, into a self-reflexive meditation on image that only she could construct out of the ruins of Marilyn. Roslyn is not a showgirl, although the photographs on her cupboard wall hint at a showgirl past, but her character relates to the question of masquerade and vulnerability. If Roslyn is no

The vulnerability...

longer so youthful, she is still glamorous. She represents, as it were, a democratized version of Marilyn, as though Monroe had in mind the multiplicity of women who had fashioned themselves after her image during her superstardom days. She performs Roslyn's outwardly attractive appearance as a defensive surface; vulnerable to the emotional pressures of a woman's life, the image may dissolve, as it were, into tears. Roslyn was the last performance of Monroe's life and, in spite of her disillusion with Arthur Miller, the tensions over the script and the problems with the production as a whole, the character stands as a testimony to her ideas about the social and psychological significance of the cosmeticized blonde.

I began this essay with some reflections on various coincidences between Marilyn Monroe and Charlie Chaplin. I emphasized the way that both produced iconic images that worked as a perfect disguise in their respective superstardoms. In both cases, the will to a reinvention of self might well relate to the difficult childhoods that they both went through. But in Monroe's case, there is a sense that the initial Marilyn masquerade, the successful fetishization of her image, might well have

...of 'to-be-looked-at-ness' (*The Misfits*).

represented the need to escape definitively from Norma Jean. In the characters of her later life, especially, perhaps, with Roslyn, there is a contrary sense that Monroe was bringing something of the inescapable Norma Jean back into her performance and into the characters she chose to embody.

For me personally, my interest in the evolution of Monroe's performance style is in some kind of contradiction with my interest in her performance as superstar, with its connotations of artifice, fabrication

Delayed cinema: between stillness and the moving image (*Gentlemen Prefer Blondes*, dir. Howard Hawks, 1953).

and fetishism. Her extraordinary *photogénie* and her intricate relation to the camera are significant for questions of gender but also lead to the cinematic and to the screen body as a construct that evokes the mechanics of cinema so celebrated by the spirit of modernity.

Although I had written about Monroe's blonde image in *Fetishism and Curiosity*, I began to think more precisely about the cinematic implications of her performance in the context of *Death 24x a Second: Stillness and the Moving Image*. I re-edited the song and dance duet 'Two Little Girls from Little Rock' that Monroe performs with Jane Russell in *Gentlemen Prefer Blondes*. It was one of my earliest experiments with delayed cinema, the shift, that is, in the spectator's attention when a film is slowed down, stilled and sequences repeated, always trying to possess and hold on to the body while reflecting upon and analysing its cinematic nature. I was fascinated by Marilyn's ability to hover between movement and stillness and the way that the pauses, slow motion and repetitions of delayed cinema simply, in her case, materialized something that was already there. I later wrote up my thoughts on the remix in terms of her gestural performance and am partially presenting them here.

Although unnaturalness potentially threatens to break through cinema's naturalistic conventions, further naturalized by narrative, the very mediality of Marilyn's gestures enhances the medium, exhibiting the fusion of the human that the projector animates. Pasi Väliaho argues that cinema takes hold of the animate body: 'The moving image does not simply re-present bodily gestures, poses and movements but, instead, harnesses gestures into its technological positivity by becoming immanent to them in terms of dynamically modulating the body.'[7] Marilyn's gestures are visibly technologically *harnessed* and mechanically *modulated*.

Watching and working on Marilyn's series of gestures in the *Gentlemen Prefer Blondes* sequence, I came to see her as an exemplary figure of *photogénie*.[8] It seemed as though an analysis that simply theorized Marilyn Monroe in terms of the relationship between body and the medium would overlook the intelligence that she brings to film (which goes beyond physical presence and glamour, however essential they may be), that is, her photogenic sensibility. In some enigmatic way cognizant of the tension between stillness and movement in the cinema as well as the tension between film and the photograph, she could take up and hold a pose either within the flow of film or the instant of the photograph. In either case, the pose appears to be fleeting, suggesting continuum of movement in the context of the still image or denaturalized stasis within the moving image. Marilyn's photogenic sensibility inhabits an uncertain space, somewhere between the paradoxical relationship between still and moving images that her *photogénie* touches on.

While her make-up restricted her range of facial expressions, Marilyn's blondeness and her use of cosmetics keep vitally alive the luminosity that produced her special rapport with the photographic medium. Without even slowing down the flow of film or freezing a frame, the graphic nature of Marilyn's 'mask' creates its own slowness, absorbing the camera's attention as though into a slowness of its own, so that her close-ups create a point of comparative repose or stasis. A director would be conscious of this effect and one reason, no doubt, for the particular power invested in the *Gentlemen Prefer Blondes* sequence is that Howard Hawks is, in the very opening number of the movie, highlighting Marilyn as an 'attraction' (in both senses of the word), using the artifice of the dance to give her, and then her close-up, maximum impact.

In the final gesture of the sequence, Marilyn's close-up captures the ineffability of sex and desire. Her pose is elongated and held still for a second, unaccompanied by a phrase of the song. But in the last few frames she turns slightly aside and, as though her luminosity had been crossed by an almost invisible shadow, her features lose something of the distinctive, iconic Marilyn 'look', as though mortality had tinged the celebration of sexuality. Now, with the benefit of hindsight, the spectator who delays and reflects on this image can easily superimpose the close-up 'Marilyns' that Andy Warhol silk-screened as a tribute to her during the four months following her death in August 1962. In these works, he makes the mask of beauty and the death mask uncannily close. The imaginary superimposition of the Warhol images onto the then-living Marilyn has a sense of deferred meaning, as though the pose prefigured the stillness of death. The shock of her untimely death is now so much part of her mystique and her legacy that the artificial and cosmetic nature of her image seems to be already simultaneously defending against and prefiguring it. This kind of additional knowledge, combined with the passing of time, brings the 'shudder at the catastrophe that has already occurred', mentioned by Roland Barthes in relation to Lewis Payne, the young man photographed before his execution. 'I read at the same time: This will be and this has been; I observe with horror an anterior future of which death was the stake.'[9] Here the other cinematic paradox emerges: not only do its machines (camera and projector) animate the inanimate still frames of the filmstrip and give the illusion of movement to the images of its human players, but the illusion also keeps the dead alive, as they perfectly perform and re-perform their once-upon-a-time living gestures.

> CODA 2: Whitey Snyder tells this story about Marilyn Monroe. While *Gentlemen Prefer Blondes* was shooting, she had to go into hospital. When she was preparing to leave, she called Whitey to do her make-up 'so when she met the public or the press or anybody, she'd look alright'. She asked: 'Will you promise me that if something happens to me in this world, when I die, promise me you'll do my make-up so I look good when I leave.' He answered 'If I get you while you're warm, Marilyn.' She gave him a money-clip that said: Whitey Dear, While I'm still warm, Marilyn. When she died, Joe DiMaggio called him and said 'Whitey, you promised.' So he went to the mortuary and did her make-up for the last time.[10]

This anecdote, to my mind, gives a poignant verisimilitude to Marilyn's 'photogenic sensibility', almost as though she grasped the relationship between the cosmetic mask, the photographic image and the mask of death. But the anecdote leads back to the allegorical relation between Hollywood and Marilyn Monroe's career. As a globally recognized emblem of Hollywood glamour, her iconic image might have helped to conceal the decline of the studio system that was taking place precipitously during the 1950s. But her own death on 5 August 1962 certainly seemed to sound the death knell for the Hollywood that had flourished as an industry since its rise, alongside Charlie Chaplin, in the years after the First World War.

THE DECLINE AND FALL OF HOLLYWOOD ACCORDING TO JEAN-LUC GODARD'S *LE MÉPRIS*

Although the whole of *Le Mépris* (Contempt, 1963) is a film about making a film, the first section is a more complex meditation on the cinema, most particularly the crisis of the Hollywood studio system and its aftermath. The film's initial premise brings the central characters together around a film of *The Odyssey*, produced by the fictional Jeremy Prokosch (Jack Palance) and fictionally directed by the great Fritz Lang, as himself. The other story is told in signs, images and allusions that reference the world of *cinéphilia*, Godard's formative years as a critic for the *Cahiers du cinéma* and the Hollywood films and directors he had written about and loved during the 1950s. That world had, by 1963, moved into a past tense: the Hollywood studio system that had been revalued by the *politique des auteurs* had aged, overtaken by industrial changes. Godard was no longer a *cinéphile* critic but a successful New Wave director. Elegiacally, Godard uses quotation, an aesthetic device that always comes out of the past, to evoke the lost great days of Hollywood (Lang) in contrast to its degraded present (Prokosch).

Godard's 'taste for quotation' is well known, and he himself used the phrase in a long interview in the special *Nouvelle vague* issue of *Cahiers du cinéma* in December 1962. He said, in relation to *À bout de souffle* (Breathless, 1960):

Our earliest films were simply films made by *cinéphiles*. We could make use of whatever we had already seen in the cinema to deliberately create references. This was particularly the case for me . . . I constructed certain shots along the lines of ones that I already knew, Preminger's, Cukor's etc. Furthermore, Jean Seberg's character follows on from *Bonjour Tristesse* [Hello Sadness]. I could have taken the last shot of that film and added an inter-title Three Years Later . . . It comes from my taste for quotation that has always stayed with me. In life, people quote things that appeal to them . . . So I show people quoting: except I arrange their quotations in a way that will also appeal to me.[1]

Quotation, Godard seems to be saying, offered a point of cinematic transition in his trajectory from *cinéphile*/critic to *cinéphile*/director, from the days of the *Cahiers* to those of the *Nouvelle vague*, from loving a particular shot to using it in his own films. About thirty years later, this lifelong partiality for quotation culminated in *Histoire(s) du cinéma*. *Le Mépris*, released in 1963 as a comparatively large-budget fiction film with corresponding production values, adapted from a quite conventional novel, benefits from the retrospective shadow cast by *Histoire(s)*. Not only are both made up of a tissue of film quotation and reference, but both were made during transitional periods in film history. Looking back at *Le Mépris* from this perspective, the fiction dominates less, the characters give way to their emblematic casting and the network-like structure of the *Histoire(s)* aesthetic comes to the fore. Furthermore, *Histoire(s)* draws attention to the place *Le Mépris* itself occupies in film history, how close it lies, in 1963, to 1950s Hollywood, a time of industrial decline, but also the decade in which some of the greatest films of the studio system were made. It was these films that Godard and the other *Cahiers* critics had seen on their release in Paris. But the presence of history draws attention to an aesthetic shift. Quotation in *Le Mépris* is no longer simply 'a taste'. It enables an elegiac commentary on the decline of one kind of cinema while celebrating another: the style, that is, that Godard had himself developed within the context of the French New Wave. Summing up the cultural shift, Michel Marie says: 'The aesthetic project of *Le Mépris* is entirely determined by the context of the end of classical cinema and the emergence of new "revolutionary" forms of narrative.'[2]

It was Alberto Moravia's novel *Il disprezzo* (1954), from which *Le Mépris* was adapted, that gave Godard, in the first instance, the necessary film-within-a-film framework from which to develop his own themes and reflections. The novel was based on Moravia's own real-life encounter with the Italian film industry, when, as a journalist, he visited the location of Mario Camerini's 1954 spectacular *Ulisse* (a Lux Film production with Kirk Douglas as Ulysses, also starring Silvana Mangano and Anthony Quinn). *Il disprezzo* uses a film production of *The Odyssey* as the setting for a tight group of characters (producer, director, screenwriter and screenwriter's wife) that bring together the story of a film in production, a marriage in decay and intellectual debate about Homer's epic poem. The novel shows no interest in either the mechanics of film-making or the history of cinema. Unlike a novel, a film about a film in production is necessarily self-referential and modernist and Godard took the opportunity to insert into it his story of the cinema.

In the first instance, the 'end of classical cinema' was set in motion by the Paramount Decree of 1948. The Federal Government wanted to break the restrictive practices inherent in Hollywood's vertically integrated system of production, distribution and exhibition. After the Decree, the studios had to sell their cinemas. The old financial mode of self-investment, through which production was supported by box-office returns, was gradually replaced by individual package deals put together by independent producers, stars and increasingly powerful agents and agencies, boosted by financial backing from banks and other outside investors. Furthermore, during the 1950s the industry struggled for survival when box-office receipts declined, from $90 million circa 1946 to less than $40 million by 1960, due to the rise of television.[3]

Fazed by new industrial conditions and a declining box office, the old studios turned to mega-productions, the spectacular historical blockbusters of which *Le Mépris' Odyssey* is a caricature. While Fritz Lang metonymically represents old Hollywood, Jack Palance's Jeremy Prokosch stands for new Hollywood, and the investment in one spectacular blockbuster production, *The Odyssey*, that might, with luck, pull off a major box-office hit. This new combination was very different from the returns made from 'a feature a week' that had sustained the Hollywood genre system and its auteur directors. Several of Godard's favourite directors were caught up in the blockbuster trend. The impact can be seen, for instance, in the case of Anthony Mann. In one of his last *Cahiers* reviews of a Hollywood film (issue 92, February 1959), Godard argued that just as Griffith had invented the cinema in each frame of *Birth of a Nation* (1915), so Mann had reinvented it in each frame of *The Man of the West* (1958). Ultimately, he claims, Mann had created a work of modern cinema. But in 1961 Mann directed the spectacular *El Cid* in keeping with changing conditions in Hollywood and continued to make, for most of the 1960s, films with overblown casts and budgets in which opportunities for cinematic and aesthetic innovation would be limited. He was more fortunate than others. Some favourites of the *Cahiers du cinéma* who had regularly produced movies year after year during the post-war years, such as Sam Fuller, could no longer find work in the new Hollywood film industry, only occasionally managing to make a few independent productions over the coming decades. Nicholas Ray made no more movies after *King of Kings* in 1961 and *55 Days at Peking* in 1963. Joseph Mankiewicz, for whom Godard had a particular admiration and had described, as early as 1950, as 'one of the most brilliant of the American directors', was in 1963 directing *Cleopatra* (ironically for a director with a particular talent for spare, witty dialogue and sophisticated direction of actors).[4] This long decline is vividly reflected in the *Cahiers du cinéma's* annual list of the 'Ten Best Films of the Year'. Dominated throughout the 1950s by their favourite Hollywood directors, by 1958 only three

Hollywood films appear: Mankiewicz's *The Quiet American* stands at number one, Preminger's *Bonjour Tristesse* at number three and *The Man of the West* at number five. The following year, no Hollywood films are included in the Ten Best list.

Leaving aside its subsequently inserted 'prologue', *Le Mépris* opens with three sequences set in Cinecittà, the film studios outside Rome, which were as evocative of the Italian film industry as

The end of cinema: Jack Palance as the new Hollywood producer.

Hollywood for the u.s. or Pinewood for the uk. Together, the three sequences form a triptych in which the 'old' cinema that Godard loved, especially Hollywood, is enunciated through a 'new' modernist cinema, his own film style. In his book on Fritz Lang, Tom Gunning uses the screening-room sequence in *Le Mépris* to discuss the complex question of film authorship. He says: 'The film-maker functions less as a scriptor than as a fashioner of palimpsests, texts written over other texts creating new meanings from the superimposition of old ones.'[5] For all three of the triptych sequences, the concept of palimpsest has special relevance, evoking the way that quotation and reference create layers of time, bringing something from the past into the present, which then inscribes the present onto the past in a similar but different manner, ghostly rather than textual. The actors too bring the resonance of the earlier films layered into their present fictional roles.

As Jacques Aumont puts it:

Jack Palance, Georgia [*sic*] Moll and Fritz Lang are vehicles, in the flesh, of part of the past, of history. They are living quotations and, already, survivors of a vanished world . . . through them, Godard quite consciously evokes not only his own immediate past as *cinéphile* – *The Barefoot Contessa*, *The Quiet American* – but a more distant, already heroized and mythic past.[6]

Just as these actors come from the past, Brigitte Bardot and Michel Piccoli stand for the new French cinema.

In the first sequence of the triptych, the studio lot stands idle and deserted. Francesca (Giorgia Moll as Francesca Vanini, the producer's assistant) explains to Paul (Michel Piccoli, the screenwriter): 'Jerry has sent everyone home. Things are hard in the Italian film industry at the moment.' Jerry, the American producer, then appears on the edge of the sound stage and proclaims, in long shot and as though addressing a vast audience, that he has sold the studios for real-estate development. Francesca's final remark, 'C'est le fin du cinema', carries the sense of crisis beyond Cinecittà to the general decline of industrial cinema by the late 1950s and even to the question of cinema itself. The studio lot is itself, in Aumont's terms, 'a vehicle, a part of the past, a history', and, as such, might be understood as *mise en scène* as quotation. Poignantly, the scene is, in fact, set in the lot belonging to Titanus (the studio that had produced Roberto Rossellini's *Viaggio in Italia* in 1953) and which was, in actual fact, just about to be demolished. The fate of Cinecittà corresponds to that of the Hollywood studios at the time, more valuable as real estate than for film production.

The second sequence of the Cinecittà triptych brings together the central group of *Le Mépris'* characters, who all, fictionally, belong to the cinema through their various roles in the production of *The Odyssey*. It is here that Godard introduces most intensely the aesthetic of quotation. Set in the studio screening room, the confined space is criss-crossed by quotation and reference of all kinds: spoken, enacted, written, personified, discussed. Francesca and Paul join Prokosch and Lang to watch *The Odyssey* rushes. The conversation between the characters enables Godard to juxtapose references to the contemporary state of cinema and classical European culture; these two themes are reiterated, on the one hand, by literal quotations from European literature, and on the other by the presence of figures with an emblematic association with Hollywood. Louis Lumière's grim prediction, written in large letters under the screen, 'Le cinéma est une invention sans avenir' (the cinema is an invention without a future), creates a link to the elegiac spirit of the first and third sequences.

While the literary quotations are, by and large, overt and attributed, the conjuring up of Hollywood is more complex, taking place through the signifying properties of the actors as living quotation. Fritz Lang, as the fictional director, obviously brings his own cinematic history with him, but so do Jack Palance and Giorgia Moll. Michel Piccoli (as Paul Javal) brings to the group a particular resonance of Paris: as an actor, he evokes the French New Wave; as a character, he evokes Parisian *cinéphilia*.

As well as having appeared in Italian peplum productions, Giorgia Moll had played the French-speaking Vietnamese heroine in Joseph Mankiewicz's *The Quiet American*, thus creating a direct link to one of Godard's favourite directors. He had reviewed the film on its release with his usual admiration but was disappointed that Mankiewicz's intelligent, elegant script was imperfectly realized as film.[7] In *Le Mépris* Godard has invented the character Francesca Vanini (she is not in the Moravia novel) whose name refers directly to Roberto Rossellini's then-recent film *Vanina Vanini* (which will represent him on the line of posters in the third sequence). As Prokosch's interpreter, she comes to stand for living quotation in a different sense, repeating the words of others, translating, often very freely, between the mono-linguistic Paul and Camille (Bardot) on the one hand, and Prokosch on the other. As well as her own native language, Italian, with Lang she can speak English, French or German and gains his approval for her recognition and translation into French of his quotation from the German poet Friedrich Hölderlin's 'The Poet's Vocation', written at the turn of the nineteenth century.

Jack Palance brings Hollywood into *Le Mépris* in several ways. As a star in his own right, he represents the Hollywood star system as such. He also represents a link, both as a star and through his fictional character Jeremy Prokosch, to a cluster of Hollywood films-about-film that had been made in the 1950s, all of which include an unscrupulous and exploitative producer or studio boss. In the first instance, Palance would, for Godard, evoke Robert Aldrich's 1955 film *The Big Knife*, an adaptation of a Clifford Odets play about the conflict between a star (Palance) struggling to maintain his ethical principles in the face of the power and persistent bullying of the studio boss, played by Rod Steiger. Palance thus brings with him a complex double quotation: he is the star who had played the role of a star, while in *Le Mépris*, in the persona of Jeremy Prokosch, he references the character personified by Steiger. Furthermore, as Michel Marie points out, Prokosch is a direct descendent of Kirk Edwards, the megalomaniac, casually brutal and sexually predatory Hollywood producer in Joseph Mankiewicz's *The Barefoot Contessa* (1954), a film that had been highly prized by *Cahiers du cinéma*. Palance's chiselled, mask-like features (due to plastic surgery after being wounded in the Second World War) and his slow, zombie-like movements recall Warren Stevens's stony, almost motionless performance as Kirk Edwards. To these two Hollywood-on-Hollywood films should be added Vincente Minnelli's *The Bad and the Beautiful* (1952), in which Kirk Douglas plays the prototypically unscrupulous, if more engaging, producer Jonathan Shields.

Although Prokosch has been said to evoke Godard's real-life producers Carlo Ponti and Joe Levine, the iconographical legacy of these Hollywood movies is probably stronger, due to Godard's preference for quotation over immediate reference. However, as well as inscribing these iconographical traits and characteristics, Godard uses Prokosch specifically to signal the decline in Hollywood production values in the face of cynicism, philistinism and a taste for kitsch. A throwaway remark by Fritz Lang indicates that Prokosch is not, for him, within the true tradition of Hollywood independent production. Refusing his invitation for a drink, Lang quotes a famous Goldwynism (Samuel Goldwyn tended to mix up language): '"Include me out", as Sam Goldwyn, a real producer of Hollywood once said'. Prokosch's first appearance in Cinecittà underlines the new commercialism. While Godard's citation of the Hollywood-on-Hollywood films puts *Le Mépris* within this 'subgenre', evoking a tradition of films of self-reference (that does, of course, pre-date the 1950s), he is also clearly gesturing towards the industry's uncertain future, underlined by the Lumière quotation.

Fritz Lang is first introduced to the film by the most well-known anecdote of his career. Goebbels offered Lang a privileged position in the German film studio the UFA in 1927, to which he had replied by leaving the following day for Paris and then the United States.[8] Godard follows this up with an enacted confrontation between Lang and

Prokosch in the screening room. In a moment that seems anomalous and strange, Prokosch violently interrupts the screening, claiming that the images on the screen were not in the script. Lang brings the argument to an end by saying calmly: 'Naturally, because in the script it's written and on the screen it's pictures, motion pictures it's called.' According to Tom Gunning, this is a re-enactment of a confrontation between Lang and Eddie Mannix, his first U.S. producer.[9] Both these anecdotes show Lang confronting authority; but one is given its place in Lang's biography, while the other floats, functioning dramatically as a fragment but without explanation. Together, these two anecdotes represent two very different kinds of quotation with very different aesthetic implications.

If Prokosch, in his *Le Mépris* role, is emblematic of a changing Hollywood, Lang stands, in stark contrast, for a long history of the cinema, some of its most outstanding films and its more generally changing fortunes. Born in 1890, shortly, that is, before the cinema, and making his first film in 1919, Lang and cinema matured, as it were, side by side. Due to the *Mabuse* films, *Metropolis* and his prolific output during the Weimar period, as a 'living quotation' Lang brings to *Le Mépris* the memory of aesthetic achievements of German silent cinema, then, with *M* in 1931, early experiment with synch sound. (It might be worth remembering, in the context of the late 1950s blockbuster, that Lang had almost bankrupted UFA in 1927 with his spectacularly expensive spectacular *Metropolis*.) In 1933 he joined the stream of exiles from Nazism who then contributed so much to Hollywood during the years of the studio system. From *Fury* in 1936 to *Beyond a Reasonable Doubt* in 1956, he made a film, sometimes two or three, almost every year. Although by and large successful (unlike some of his compatriots), he too had found it increasingly hard to direct by the mid-1950s. Leaving Hollywood for Germany in the late 1950s, he directed his own versions of 'spectaculars': *The Tiger of Eschnapur* and *The Indian Tomb* as well as an attempt to return to the *Mabuse* cycle. By the time he appeared in *Le Mépris*, he had made no films for three years; on the other hand, as an early pantheon director of the *politique des auteurs*, his critical status had risen in France and Luc Moullet's book *Fritz Lang*, which Camille reads and quotes from in the apartment sequence, had just been published when the film was made. Godard treats Lang reverentially, himself acting the role of the fictional director's assistant. He frames and films Lang so that his literal presence takes on the mythical quality due to an old man, no longer employable but, more than any other director still living at the time, stretched across and emblematic of this complex cinematic history. Lang, still wearing the monocle that signifies the old days of Weimar as a badge of belonging and distinction, is quotation as embodiment, summoning up the past and inserting it into a present to which he no longer belongs.

In the third sequence of the triptych, Godard realizes and confirms his themes through a very different mode of quotation. Outside the screening room, the characters act out the scene in front of a wall of posters: Howard Hawks's *Hatari!* and Godard's own *Vivre sa vie* (both 1962), Roberto Rossellini's *Vanina Vanini* (1961) and Hitchcock's *Psycho* (1960). Apart from Godard, the three were great directors celebrated and defended during Godard's time as a *Cahiers du cinéma* critic, but all were, by this point in time, nearing the end of their careers; and Fritz Lang is filmed with them in such a way as to join the old masters. The presence of the *Vivre sa vie* poster creates its own distinctive chain of female beauty reaching back across the history of cinema. Later in the film, Camille wears a black wig, bobbed in the style worn by Anna Karina in *Vivre sa vie*, which in turn reaches back to Louise Brooks's incomparable flapper look. Much admired by the director of the Cinémathèque française Henri Langlois for an insouciante seductiveness in films such as Hawks's *A Girl in Every Port* (1928) or Pabst's *Pandora's Box* (1929), Louise Brooks might be seen as a pre-figuration of Godard's fascination with a feminine beauty synonymous with the beauty of the cinema.

The history of cinema: Fritz Lang as the great Hollywood director.

The bracketing of Hawks and Hitchcock represent the French critical tendency known as Hitchcocko-Hawksianism. Both directors had started their supremely successful careers in the 1920s and had flourished under the studio system, with comparative independence (Hitchcock, of course, arriving from Britain in the late 1930s). By the early 1960s both were now ageing, but both would make films occasionally until the 1970s. Although he was to make one more film (*Anima Nera* in the same year), Rossellini's career in cinema was also just about over. From 1961 to the end of his life in 1977, apart from a few documentaries, he would work exclusively for television. *Vanina Vanini* was adapted from a novella by Stendhal. As if to emphasize its significance, 'Francesca Vanini' had been summoned by name over an intercom a few seconds before the film's poster appears on the screen.

Godard inserts the figure of Fritz Lang into this series of *hommages*. Framed alone, in front of the posters, Lang walks quite slowly towards the camera as he lights a cigarette and, emphasizing the mythic nature of this portrait shot, music briefly appears on the soundtrack. In the next couple of shots, Paul, as a *cinéphile*, brings cinema directly into his conversation with Lang. Lang brushes aside Paul and Camille's admiration for *Rancho Notorious* ('the western with Marlene Dietrich') with 'I prefer *M*.'

The posters: a backdrop for cinephilia.

The posters: a backdrop for a new star.

A *cinéphile* moment: *Rancho Notorious* (dir. Fritz Lang, 1953).

But Paul persists and mentions the scene in which Frenchy Fairmont (Mel Ferrer) allows Altar Keane (Dietrich) to win at chuck-a-luck, a favourite moment of Godard's (to which he refers in his general discussion of the Western in his *Man of the West* review).

The sequence outside the screening room is the turning point of the film. It begins with the first appearance of the real star of *Le Mépris*,

Brigitte Bardot, as Paul's wife Camille. As she stands against the backdrop of posters, she personifies new cinema, a new kind of stardom, as well as a new kind of glamour. European as opposed to Hollywood, her blondeness resonates with the sunlit Riviera as opposed to the Elizabeth Arden beauty salon (in *Vertigo*, for instance), and she dresses like an ordinary girl of the time, gingham skirts and sailor shirts as opposed to Hollywood's haute couture. Bardot might have been the most famous movie star of her day, but she signified a weariness with the old movies and the rise of something new. However, when Bardot agreed to appear in *Le Mépris*, the producer, Carlo Ponti, managed to raise more money for the film from the American producer Joe Levine. Levine had understood that Bardot would bring to the screen her natural sexuality, including nudity (still impossible in the United States); he was enraged by the film's first cut and the 'absence of Bardot's naked body for which he had paid so much'.[10] It was at Levine's insistence that the film's opening prologue was shot, in which Godard duly shows Bardot nude but with a kind of Brechtian distanciation somewhat at odds with his producer's expectations. It is, in a sense, appropriate that the Hollywood producer should so conform to type as to demand the woman's image as sexual spectacle in return for his investment.

Roberto Rossellini's presence in *Le Mépris* persists after the opening triptych through various references to *Viaggio in Italia*. For instance, Godard's filming of the statues of gods, as well as his use of music, directly evokes the style of the Museo Archeologico scene in *Viaggio*. While the film is a story of a marriage in crisis, it is also, more significantly, a film of modernism and quotation. From this perspective, the presence of *Viaggio in Italia* in *Le Mépris* does considerably more than cite a director of the greatest importance to Godard. The links bear witness to quotation as a modernist strategy and the way that a citation from the past defies tradition and convention to produce the modern. Quotation is also fragmentary, heterogeneous and incoherent, fracturing the smoothness and self-sufficiency of a text. The film posters outside the screening room superimpose, as in a palimpsest, another layer of time and of meaning over the fiction, with a detour into the quite different discourse of cinema history. It is the interaction of these different layers, simultaneously detached and dependent on each other, that is contradictory, modernist and, ultimately, moving in Godard's meditation on the decline of Hollywood and the rise of his own New Wave.

PART TWO: THE NEXT CHAPTER

INTRODUCTION: TIME REBORN – WOMEN'S STORIES, WOMEN'S FILM

In general, as one second-century AD guru put it, 'a woman should as modestly guard against exposing her voice to outsiders as she would guard against stripping off her clothes' . . . This 'muteness' is not just a reflection of women's general disempowerment throughout the classical world: no voting rights, limited legal and economic independence and so on . . . But we're dealing with a much more active and loaded exclusion of women from public speech than that – and, importantly, it's one with a much greater impact than we usually acknowledge on our own traditions, conventions and assumptions about the voice of women. What I mean is that public speaking and oratory were not merely things that ancient women didn't do: they were exclusive practices and skills that defined masculinity as a gender . . . Public speech was a – if not *the* – defining attribute of maleness. A woman speaking in public was, in most circumstances, by definition not a woman.[1]

Part Two of this book is designed around five films, all directed by women, all produced within very divergent social and cultural contexts, but all revolving around the figure of the mother. In thinking or writing about the films over the past few years I have found certain ideas and cinematic strategies recurring across them and interconnecting with each other. These films have given me new perspectives on a topic that has always been close to me, dating back to my early interest in the iconography of the maternal in Hollywood melodrama and to *Riddles of the Sphinx* (dir. Laura Mulvey and Peter Wollen, 1977). With the figure of the mother central to all five films, their directors have found words and images, figures and stories with which to approach issues associated with motherhood that had, by and large, been relegated to silence under patriarchy. The films I discuss, rather than simply sites of storytelling or accounts of women's lives (however effective they may be as such), break away from a neutral lens and narrative transparency. Experimenting with time and space, the directors' aesthetic strategies move towards a defamiliarization of film language, reconfiguring the idea of the maternal conceptually and from a feminist perspective. Ultimately, the films address the 'ineffable' and the 'unspeakable' through the material of film itself, exploiting its potential as a visual and conceptual medium that can challenge patriarchal representations. And these formal challenges are indissolubly linked to issues of women's cultural silence.

Part Two opens with an essay on Chantal Akerman's *Jeanne Dielman, 23 quai du Commerce, 1080 Bruxelles* (1975) and the extraordinary impact it had on feminist thinking about film, and, of course, film in general, at the time of its release. This was a formative period for me. Ideas relating both to feminist theory and film practice that date back to the mid-1970s are still important for my thoughts here and now. It was then that I first moved from a critique of images of women in film, particularly Hollywood (reflected in Part One of this book), to an attempt to envisage a radically different, future, film language. In the early films I made with Peter Wollen, the question of women's silence and women's relation to language were central themes that inevitably brought questions of form with them. *Riddles of the Sphinx*, made in 1977, revolved around the mother and grew out of the influence of psychoanalytic theory as well as the new possibility of making 'theoretical' films. We took as a starting point Freud's concept of the Oedipus Complex and the place the maternal occupied within it. Also influential was Lacan's reworking of the Freudian Oedipus Complex that specifically located women's silence at the foundation of patriarchal society.

To summarize, although I sometimes found Lacan difficult, his three orders of psychoanalysis, the Symbolic, the Imaginary and the Real, had a revelatory impact on my ideas and have been essential for my project of feminist political, cultural and psychoanalytic analysis of patriarchal culture. In the Lacanian formulation, the origins of the Imaginary are found in the pre-Oedipal sphere of the maternal, the pre-linguistic, and marked by the bodily closeness of mother and child, their mutual dependence and their love. This is the bond that must, ultimately, be broken by Law of the Father. Out of the loss of maternal plenitude and in the emptiness that follows, the child turns towards language under the aegis of the father's closure of the Oedipal trajectory. If learning to speak and to signify is initially an individual and maternally orientated experience, ultimately the child gains entry to the pre-established Symbolic Order that guides and dominates *his* conceptual understanding, and leaves *her* understanding distanced from patriarchal culture and society. This is because, in the last instance, woman signifies the difference on which the Symbolic, a linguistic system, depends. This rigorous, psychoanalytic and cultural account of the mother's secondary status, locked into the Imaginary, marginal to the Symbolic, offered feminists a convincing 'explanation' for the exclusion of women from the patriarchal public sphere and relegation to cultural silence of all kinds. Furthermore, the concept of the Symbolic Order also points specifically to the question of language and its place in the Lacanian Oedipus Complex. To continue with the Lacanian terms: feminism could work to reveal ways in which the Imaginary co-exists with, and penetrates, patriarchal culture while also exploring and experimenting with language and culture in the interests of a counter Symbolic. As an aside: the movement from the maternal to the paternal is marked in psychoanalytic theory by a complex initiation into gender in which the image of the mother as castrated plays an essential role, underpinning the fetishized iconographies of the feminine discussed in Part One.

Thus *Riddles of the Sphinx*, as well as other feminist work influenced by psychoanalytic theory, confronted a double dilemma in terms of the silencing of women. On one side, women were marginal to the Symbolic Order through which a society constructs and imagines itself; on the other was the difficulty of finding adequate words to express emotions and experiences outside and irrelevant to male and mainstream culture. Thus a politics of language had to address language, as such, and as an issue in its own right, in its less abstract and more imaginary poetics. For instance, while the very words I have used spatialize women (that is, their exclusion, their marginalization, their position outside the mainstream and so on), they also illustrate the way that language turns to metaphor to visualize meaning and the way its imagery often has recourse to material shapes and forms, playing on, in Julia Kristeva's term, an 'indefinite *fuzziness*' of language.² For instance, the Oedipus Complex has been understood in terms of a journey, reconfiguring time into space. The sequence from maternal silence to the language of the Symbolic opens out, as it were, into a threshold, on which a range of communicative systems can spread out; gestures, images or other forms of mute signification mutate into figures of speech and permeate the materiality of language itself. Owing to its expressive malleability, film flourishes in the time/space of the threshold. Feminist film-makers can find ways of representing silences and new ways of expressing ideas and emotions at a knight's move away from established and traditional ways of making meaning.

In 'Rakhshan Bani-Etemad, *Under the Skin of the City*', I use the concept of the 'mute text' taken from Peter Brooks's discussion of nineteenth-century theatrical melodrama. He sums up the dramatic significance of muteness and, in spite of the different frame of cultural reference, his points are acutely relevant to my context:

> Mute gesture is an expressionistic means – precisely the means of melodrama – to render meanings which are ineffable, but nonetheless operative in the sphere of human ethical relationships. Gesture could perhaps then be typed as in the

nature of catachresis, the figure used when there is no 'proper' name for something . . . Yet of course it is the fullness, the pregnancy, of the blank that is significant: meaning-full though unspeakable.[3]

At dramatic moments when formal language is inadequate or irrelevant, other means of expressive modes come into play. It was this kind of muteness that drew feminist film-makers and critics in the 1970s to the Hollywood melodrama as a genre that addressed a female audience and that had evolved an expressive mode of *mise en scène* to evoke the 'unspeakable' of women's lives. These are stories of strained emotional relationships that are unable to find expression in the transparency of day-to-day language or to find escape through dramatic action. In climactic moments and in extreme situations, the melodrama has recourse to non-verbal means of expressing its meanings, and the melodramatic message is configured through other registers of the sign. In response to unspoken emotion, cinematic language has to carry meaning through specifically filmic values: camera movement, sound, framing, lighting, colour, objects and so forth. This kind of non-linguistic speech and its close associate, music, had a certain influence on the 1970s feminist avant-garde. There is a direct reference to early melodrama in Sally Potter's *The Gold Diggers* (1983), and the traces of its influence can be found across the films I made with Peter Wollen. Yvonne Rainer subtitled *Lives of Performers* (1972) 'a melodrama' and here she draws attention to her search for a new language:

> Having survived my various physical and psychic traumas and emboldened by the women's movement, I felt entitled to struggle with an entirely new lexicon. The language of specific emotional experience . . . promised all the ambivalent pleasures and terrors of the experiences themselves: seduction, passion, rage, betrayal, grief, and joy.[4]

To sum up: the cinema, changed by the challenge of finding new ways of representing women and their lives, would, in the process, be liberated into new forms, images and modes of expression.

Needless to say, the decades that have stretched between those early 1970s speculations and the present of 2019 have seen women's writing of all kinds, art, film and so on, expand exponentially. It might almost seem as though the long-standing questions of silences and marginalization have been, if not completely at least considerably, filled and shifted. However, as these five films continue to explore legacies of silence in a variety of different ways, the mute text becomes a site, in itself, of richness and poetic invention. Out of the sphere of the mother and women's marginalization, out of apparent cultural deprivation and lack, new ways of depicting affect and the ineffable in human communication begin to take shape.

Jeanne Dielman, 23 quai du Commerce, 1080 Bruxelles substitutes gesture for language in key aspects of the narrative: the film's initial, careful and poetic record of women's domestic routine, as both labour and culture, is later overtaken by the symptomatic gestures of the unconscious as Jeanne's life falls into crisis. *Under the Skin of the City* (2001) similarly traces the family's ordinary routines in the first part of the film until everyday life is disrupted by crisis; both the film's style and the characters' actions respond gesturally to the impossibility of expression or escape. Class is a crucial factor of constraint in both films, in spite of the radical difference between the petty bourgeois Brussels housewife and the working-class family in Tehran. Across these, and other examples, the problem of expression cannot but be intertwined with the presence and pressure of forces beyond individual control. For instance, Tuba, the mother in *Under the Skin of the City*, has a persistent hacking cough, a symptom of the conditions in the cotton-combing factory where she works; but at times of emotional stress, her cough takes over, wracking her whole body, doubly signifying the speech that evades her.

Cinema is essentially temporal. It records time as it passes and reproduces it on film as well as using it as a storytelling medium. Film has so often been associated with the linear, that is, with a narrative unfolding along a road taken by heroic journeys, and subject to the sequence of cause and effect. But the films discussed here disrupt and confuse temporal logic and make visible and material a complicated temporality. In her essay 'Women's Time', Julia Kristeva cites the tradition: '"Father's time, mother's species," as Joyce put it; and, indeed, when evoking the name and destiny of women, one thinks more of the space generating and forming the human species than of time, becoming, or history.' And then: 'time as project, teleology, linear and prospective unfolding; time as departure, progression, and arrival – in other words, the time of history.'[5]

Just as public speech and language is associated with the authority of patriarchy, so is this linear concept of time. From a feminist perspective, however, and as represented in aspects of these films, the figure of the mother can conjure up time within space, on a threshold, as it were, and also find meaning that fuses words, objects and gestures through the text of muteness that is the film itself. In *Jeanne Dielman* the passing of time becomes palpable as the film dwells on Jeanne's domestic rituals; but for most of the film the temporal frame of reference remains in the present. *Daughters of the Dust* (1991), *Un'ora sola ti vorrei* (2002) and *The Arbor* (2010), however, present time as layered, with differing timeframes overlapping one another. In *Daughters of the Dust*, the focus of Part Two's second essay, Nana, the great-grandmother, succeeds in carrying her archaic time forward by means of a restorative ritual that closely links 'in between' time and the language of gesture and object. She takes things of symbolic significance from her past, treasured in a tin box across her lifetime, and weaves them into a magical 'hand' according to the traditions of her African ancestors, juxtaposed with her granddaughter's Bible. She then creates a ritual of departure for her family as each one kisses the sacred objects, inscribing their past heritage onto their future. She reconfigures rather than represses the traumatic experience of slavery, dispatching her African American descendants out of their individuality, preserving the fragility of a maternal 'Symbolic' into a collective, self-conscious history.

In very different cinematic registers, moving away from fiction into biography, *Un'ora sola ti vorrei* and *The Arbor* bear witness to the fact that neither of the two articulate and intelligent women at the centre of these films could find a way to survive their failure as mothers. As retold by their daughters, directly by Alina Marazzi and through Clio Barnard in Lorraine Dunbar's case, their stories reach beyond the individual, and through their complex use of different temporalities, towards the future. The cinematic fusion of differing dimensions of time restores some kind of efficacy to the mother's story. Both Liseli and Andrea succumbed to pressures of class, in spite of their class difference. I have drawn on psychoanalytic theory in Part Two's concluding discussions of both these films, to locate them beyond their own timeframe and in relation to their future audiences.

There is a strange but telling resonance across the endings of all five films that seems to touch on something beyond the reassuring, however experimentally reworked, time and space of narrative film. *Jeanne Dielman*'s seven-minute shot of Jeanne, after she has murdered her client, stands as an image outside the rationale of the narrative. The shot floats in its own temporal dimension, defying structure and pattern. The last shot of *Daughters of the Dust* stays with the figures of the remaining characters as they walk along the beach, emblematic of the film's fusion of temporalities, from Nana's links back to the older world of the African ancestors to the unborn child of the not-yet-realized future. In the last shot of *Under the Skin of the City*, Tuba looks directly through the camera to the film's future audiences to demand, 'Who sees these films anyway?', and the question carries her desperation into and across cinematic time and space. *Un'ora sola ti vorrei* ends with a newspaper report of Liseli's suicide, difficult to decipher and untranslated in its foreign versions, that seems to refuse the finality of death and the film's narrative closure. *The Arbor* ends with archive footage of Andrea with the baby Lorraine, resonating with the film's complex interweaving of cinematic time, returning in the last shot to the later children, in 2010, of Brafferton Arbor and the doubtful future that still continues to hang over them.

These final images all evoke the metaphor of haunting. In the end, the films refuse to 'give up the ghost', that is, refuse to give up the voice of protest around and about the ideas and events that have been evoked in their stories and through the language of the film. And the metaphor of the ghost insists that the words and images embedded in these stories of mothers should haunt the future until addressed by the future. All five films embody a promise to the silent image of the ghosts that moves from the past to the future: their stories, translated into cinema, have been told and will be heard by generations as yet unborn.

CHANTAL AKERMAN, *JEANNE DIELMAN, 23 QUAI DU COMMERCE, 1080 BRUXELLES*

I first saw *Jeanne Dielman, 23 quai du Commerce, 1080 Bruxelles* at the Edinburgh Film Festival in 1975. There were two striking aspects to its screening. First, the festival that year vividly reflected the energy and fertility of its contemporary cinema: it showed, from the United States, *Film About a Woman Who . . .* and *Lives of Performers* (both directed by Yvonne Rainer), *What Maisie Knew* (dir. Babette Mangolte, the cinematographer for Chantal Akerman, Yvonne Rainer and later Sally Potter), *Rameau's Nephew by Diderot* (dir. Michael Snow) and *Speaking Directly* (Jon Jost); from the UK, the festival screened *The Amazing Equal Pay Show* (The London Women's Film Group) and *The Nightcleaners* (Berwick Street Collective); and from Europe, *Moses und Aron* (Jean-Marie Straub and Danièle Huillet) and *In Gefahr und größter Not bringt der Mittelweg den Tod* (The Middle of the Road is a Very Dead End, dir. Alexander Kluge and Edgar Reitz). Furthermore, 1975 was the year of the Brecht Event, a collaboration between *Screen* and the Edinburgh Film Festival, that included Godard's *Deux ou Trois choses que je sais d'elle* (Two or Three Things I Know About Her, 1967) and more Straub–Huillet, as well as relevant German films from Brecht's time.[1] The Brecht symposium was emblematic of the spirit of the 1970s: the conscious return on the part of the contemporary cinematic avant-garde to that earlier moment of dialogue between radical politics and radical aesthetics.

Second, within the festival context and alongside the other films, all remarkable in their different ways, *Jeanne Dielman* stood out as something completely new and unexpected. It was the film's courage that was immediately most striking. On the one hand, Akerman's unwavering and completely luminous adherence to a female perspective (not so much via the character Jeanne Dielman, but embedded in the film itself); on the other, her uncompromising and completely coherent cinema, her use of film language, produced a film that was both feminist and cinematically radical. I clearly remember that *Jeanne Dielman* was screened twice in the medium-sized theatre in Edinburgh's Filmhouse, to the attentive audiences for which it was intended, and that it was the wonder and the puzzle of that year's festival.[2] It felt as though there was a before and an after *Jeanne Dielman*, just as there had once been a before and an after *Citizen Kane*.

Chantal Akerman has described the more difficult atmosphere when *Jeanne Dielman* was first screened at the Directors' Fortnight in Cannes as she and Delphine Seyrig sat at the back of the cinema listening to the seats banging as the audience walked out. However, she eventually added:

> The next day fifty people invited the film to festivals. And I travelled with it all over the world. The next day, I was on the map as a filmmaker but not just any filmmaker. At the age of twenty-five, I was given to understand that I was a great filmmaker. It was pleasing, of course, but also troubling because I wondered how I could do better. And I don't know if I have.[3]

Akerman went on to make many excellent films but it seems that the extraordinary power that radiates from *Jeanne Dielman* was not to be repeated. I would like to suggest that this phenomenon, this 'unrepeatability', might be due to the way the film captured the spirit of women's film-making at the time. While Akerman's extraordinary qualities as a film-maker made the film what it was and is, the consciousness and the possibilities associated with experimental film and feminism of the 1970s were an essential part of its grounding. *Jeanne Dielman* was, to my mind, the outstanding film of that particular conjuncture of radical politics and radical aesthetics. However, there is a difficult-to-articulate conundrum: how the energy and creative demands of a political movement interact with the energy and creativity of an individual; when, that is, someone touches and then draws on a nerve of urgency beyond the sum of his or her parts, the product is more exemplary than personal, more transcendent than individual. At the same time, in a similar but almost contrary phenomenon, out of that sense of collectivity, the enabling power of a political movement, valuable films are made that would not, in other contexts, ever have seen the light of day.

It was also the foundational moment for thinking about 'women' and 'cinema', as the two terms were clearly articulated for the first time as a problem and as a possibility. Moreover, for the first time, women began to make films within the collective consciousness of a women's movement. Before then, there had, of course, been great films made by women, and women had contributed in different capacities and at different epochs to the cinema as an art and as an industry. From the early 1970s women and film events and women's film festivals not only brought this hidden history into visibility but created sites of solidarity, of excitement and enthusiasm, in which new films could be shown and discussed. It is hard to overestimate the significance invested in the cinema at the time, as it seemed to mutate from a cult object of women's oppression to a utopian instrument of women's liberation. To sum up: the Women's Liberation Movement gave women the confidence to speak and to speak about issues that needed to be voiced, but also the sense of urgency that turned these issues into material 'things' that mixed art, politics and ideas together; ultimately, too, the movement provided the energy to organize events of all kinds in which the 'things' could be recognized and taken further.

The processes of thinking about and with cinema had a direct effect on the aesthetic and narrative strategies of the films made at the time. Due to its conceptual malleability, new ways of visualizing ideas could be found with film and, at the same time, cinema itself could be freed from subordination to narrative and become an instrument for thought. A body of feature films emerged, each film roughly ninety minutes long (although *Jeanne Dielman* is longer), that broke with the tradition of the avant-garde short while still working with radical aesthetics and broke with the classic form of the art film, due to a refusal to compromise or capitulate to audience expectations. Finally, these films were all shot on 16mm sync-sound cameras, very often by newly emerging women cinematographers. This light, more informal technology had a comparatively short life within the history of cinema. If the spirit of radical aesthetics, feminist aspirations and utopian confidence marked 1970s experimental cinema, so did its technology. It would be difficult, perhaps impossible, for this 'movement' cinema to survive in the context of 1980s austerity and political disenchantment. Great films would, of course, continue to be made by some of the women film-makers with their roots in this period, but, as the movement lost cohesion, inevitably they came to be more scattered and individual.

One particular perspective, or theme, out of the many taken up by feminist cinema during the 1970s is especially salient for *Jeanne Dielman*: how to find a voice for women's interiority, for the inside of the mind itself, as well as for its silences. Yvonne Rainer's *Lives of Performers* and *Film About a Woman Who . . .*, Valie Export's *Invisible Adversaries* (1976), as well as Akerman's earlier *Je tu il elle* (1974), all reflect on women's relation to language, storytelling and the unconscious. The inside of the mind, as in the case of *Jeanne Dielman*, also intertwines with the inside of domestic space, the home and, most of all, the mother. *Riddles of the Sphinx*, the film I made with Peter Wollen in 1977, and Sally Potter's *The Gold Diggers* (1983) take motherhood as a key political and psychoanalytic issue for feminism. However random this list may seem, however disconnected the individual films, as a group they make some important points that connect to *Jeanne Dielman* and attest to a certain unity in 1970s experimental film.

Jeanne Dielman consistently depicts language as difficult. In the first instance, Jeanne lives in a constrained environment in which communication with others is not easy; her daily life is one of almost unbroken silence. The painful silences that separate mother, Jeanne, and her teenage son, Sylvain, at the dinner table are interrupted by occasional and embarrassed attempts at communication. Then there are sudden eruptions of excessive speech, for instance, Sylvain's bedtime Freudian streams of consciousness that his mother listens to, unhappy and embarrassed. Although a lack of speech pervades *Jeanne Dielman*, the screen itself is filled by the figure of Jeanne and an intricate tapestry is made up of her daily rituals, gestures and habits, inexorably accumulating significance with repetition. Delphine Seyrig's extraordinary performance is at the heart of this process.

During the first half of the film, which establishes Jeanne's everyday domestic routine, Seyrig performs Jeanne's domestic tasks with an exact precision. In the first instance, she is creating a character, Jeanne Dielman, who personifies the meticulous domestic culture that characterized Belgian middle-class housewives, among whom Akerman had herself grown up. She has pointed out, and this is one reason why the film has been so important to feminists: 'I made this film to give all these actions typically undervalued a life on film.'[4] Akerman creates a kind of lexicon of domestic gesture that takes this underground culture, as it were, and puts it at the centre of an avant-garde film, of art. But there is more to Jeanne's action than a simple record of the everyday: Seyrig invests her meticulousness with tension.

Across the film, cinematic space and cinematic time are intricately woven into the fictional 'space' of the small flat, where Jeanne lives with Sylvain, and the fictional 'time' of her daily routine, divided between her role as housewife and prostitute. She shops, prepares supper (*cuisine française*) and each afternoon receives a different client. Her life pivots on the essential separation of these roles. Order and cleanliness fill her daily existence, also representing the need for surface propriety that her double life demands. Jeanne's own outward appearance is similarly constructed around an unassuming elegance that belies any connotation of prostitution; but the absolute perfection of her clothes, make-up and hair paradoxically might suggest something to be concealed. Jeanne's daily life is separated into spheres: the clients follow a strict line from front door to bedroom, her domestic tasks take place by and large in the kitchen and she and Sylvain eat their supper at a dining table in their sitting-room.

Although Jeanne leaves the flat for daily chores, the heart of the story, its actions and events, are mapped across its interior space. For the first half of the film, Jeanne's temporal and spatial relations seem to be in harmony; she moves through her surroundings with calm composure, never deviating from the exactitude of her schedule. The film, however (in keeping with Akerman's lexicon), allows some of Jeanne's actions to develop in their own time, throwing the spectator's understanding of cinematic convention into disarray. Filmed always from the same frontal position, at Akerman's own eye level, the camera records, for instance, Jeanne as she does the washing up and then, with a kind of anthropological exactitude, follows the intricate details involved in French traditional cooking. Jeanne is shown preparing two meals: first, *pain de viande* (meatloaf), with her patient kneading of the mince and careful addition of other ingredients, then *escalope de veau*, with the tricky process of dipping the meat in milk and coating it with flour. These actions, and peeling the potatoes, are shown in real time and include every part of the process, the precise positioning of milk and flour, and clearing and tidying afterwards. Other activities, for instance her sandwich lunch and preparation of her coffee, are also shown in full duration. Time envelops the screen and the space of Jeanne's kitchen is filled by the temporal rhythm of her life.

But onto this devoted tribute to women's work, Akerman has superimposed an aesthetic and theoretical dimension, involving awareness of time and its place in the complexities of cinema. Only film can record the image of a chunk of time as it passes. Usually convention demands a shift in point of view, camera movement and so on before the spectator is confronted by the strangeness of seeing time itself pass. But when a shot is held beyond normal expectation, the flow of time belonging to the fiction begins to fade and the time of its recording comes to the fore. In this sense, to continue with the metaphor, on the tapestry that fills in for silence in *Jeanne Dielman* the texture of cinematic time interweaves with the texture of Jeanne's movements, gestures and rituals. Thus the content of the screen image (Jeanne) becomes inseparable from cinematic form as a temporal medium. In a still further dimension, a third level, as it were, emerges out of Seyrig's performance, creating a relation between Jeanne's body and the body of film. In the actual precision of her movements and actions and the exactitude of their timing, Jeanne's humanity drains away and is replaced by a sense of the automatic. In a fascinating discussion (which, in the first instance, is about Robert Bresson but leads to *Jeanne Dielman*), Ivone Margulies argues that a perception of cinema's mechanical reality can free it from representational enactment, through

> the automatism proper to the cinema (which transfers mechanical reproduction to bodies and gestures) . . . In this new form, the filmic body as well as the performances are suffused by a sense of the mechanical, by an automaton quality, resulting from massive stylisation and from processes of textual inscription . . . this quality is transferred onto characters and performers.[5]

Thus the (possibly) dialectical relation between the texture of Seyrig's performance and the material presence of time merge into the figure of the automaton, in which the materiality of performer and film are embodied.

However, halfway through the film the initial harmony between Jeanne's time and space is shattered. There have been intimations of this instability from the very beginning, through the tension in Seyrig's performance and the suggestion that, in her obsessive attention to cleanliness and order, Jeanne is hiding some secret. From early on in the film, Jeanne's interior autonomy is complicated by a presence from outside: a neon light flashes continually into the sitting-room, its penetrating beam hitting a glass-fronted case that stands directly behind the dining table. Almost invisibly, the flashing light unsettles the interior space, like a sign from the unconscious pointing to a site of repression. Then an innocuous domestic object becomes a metonymic representation of Jeanne's prostitution. After each client leaves, she immediately puts her money into a decorative soup tureen that stands

An innocuous domestic object: the soup tureen.

on the dining table. As she does so, she walks past the flashing light reflected in the glass behind her and the semi-darkness of the room accentuates the reflection. As Akerman characteristically holds her shots for a few seconds after Jeanne has left the frame, the flashing light has time to become more acutely significant. Each evening, mother and son sit at the dining table. When the camera faces Jeanne, the soup tureen is half visible to her left at the edge of the frame, while the light flashes beside her, creating, as it were, a triangle of guilt. Furthermore, as Sylvain sleeps on the sofa-bed in the sitting-room, during his nightly monologues about sex the tureen can be clearly seen in the background, speaking the mother's secret sexuality that her son so embarrassingly attempts to articulate.

The narrative is shifted when Jeanne's sexuality and, consequently, her unconscious begin to disrupt the balance between time and space on which her precarious control had depended. The shift in narrative has a crucial effect on the film's depiction of time and the significance of Akerman's extended shots. *Jeanne Dielman* takes place over three days, marked by the afternoon visits of Jeanne's three clients; and the moment of change revolves around the second client's visit. The film's opening sequence featuring the first client has already established Jeanne's normal routine. Jeanne is finishing her advance preparation for dinner, putting the potatoes on to cook, just before the first client (played by the Belgian documentary film-maker Henri Storck) rings the bell. The camera stays outside the bedroom and only a darkening of the light in the corridor indicates the passing of time; when Jeanne and her client come out of the bedroom, she immediately turns on the light. Then, in quick succession, she is paid, she sees her client out and she puts the money in the soup tureen. She then drains the potatoes and has a bath. A careful and thorough cleaning of her body is followed by an equally careful and thorough cleaning of the bath and its surroundings. She continues to prepare supper and for Sylvain's return from school. On the second day, she puts on the potatoes, precisely and according to routine, just before the second client (played by Jacques Doniol-Valcroze, a critic for *Cahiers du cinéma*) arrives. This time, however, Jeanne emerges disorientated from the bedroom. At first, she forgets to turn on the light in the corridor as she sees out her client. Then, as she puts the money in the soup tureen as usual, she forgets to replace the lid. Following this, she tidies the bedroom and has her bath, forgetting that the potatoes are still cooking on the stove.

This symptomatic action is the crisis point for Jeanne and the narrative; the overcooked potatoes signal a loss of control over her balanced routine; in an immediate knock-on crisis, her planned supper is ruined.

The film responds with a sequence that functions like a pivot, shot with quick cuts and a very different rhythm from the rest of the film. Jeanne is suddenly spatially disorientated; she wanders from room to room with the saucepan. Ultimately, the spatial disorientation becomes temporal. As Jeanne then has to buy, peel and cook another lot of potatoes, time is thrown out of joint and her hitherto perfect synchronization between time and space falls apart. (Later she mutters to herself and an indifferent Sylvain that potatoes could have been mashed but 'pureé' was scheduled for the next day.) Thus mother and son wait in silence at the table while the potatoes are cooking. The camera faces Jeanne, framed between the flashing light and the soup tureen, both signalling the intrusion of the sexual into the domestic space. For the first time, the extended shot is of Jeanne inactive and the accumulated hints at enigma congeal into a puzzle, directly addressing the spectator. There is now a hieroglyphic thread in the texture of the screen: the heavy significance of the client's visit, the possibility of Jeanne's capitulation to her sexuality and the loss of bodily control inherent in orgasm.

On the third day, Akerman ratchets up the time-space dislocation as Jeanne wakes unusually early and embarks on her daily routine an hour before the correct time. She has to wait for the post office and the greengrocer to open; her domestic routine is disrupted by slight parapraxes; and she wanders aimlessly between activities and different rooms. She suddenly sits, staring into space as though the automatic links from action to action and gesture to gesture have broken down. Akerman holds this moment of emptiness and inactivity in an extended shot so that the presence of Jeanne's unconscious seems to materialize into the screen. In Freud's highly figurative description, consciousness struggles to censor its unconscious, and the instincts and experiences that it manages to repress are gathered into the mind's lower depths. In this imagery, traces of time, moments of trauma for instance, that have been imprinted in the unconscious over the course of the subject's history, are visualized within a spatial pattern: surface (consciousness) overlays its underneath (unconsciousness). The complex play of time

The forgotten lid.
The dinner table: waiting for the potatoes.

and space in *Jeanne Dielman* reflects something of this pattern: in the first part of the film, Jeanne's too-perfect gestures suggest a covering over of something that should be firmly repressed; when the 'non-time' of the unconscious breaks through the defences of her conscious mind, it intrudes into the surface of Jeanne's life. While, in the first instance, the image of doubled space might suggest the incompatible worlds of housewife and prostitute, as the portrait of Jeanne unfolds, the site of repression seems rather to be her own sexuality, the abject nature of the female body and its ultimate and uncontrolled subordination to pleasure.

On the afternoon of the third day, after her routine is thrown further out of kilter by a combination of external misfortunes and her internal disorientation, Jeanne comes home to find a parcel from Canada, an anticipated present from her sister Fernande. Distracted, she fails to put the potatoes on to cook at all. Just before the third client (played by Yves Bical) rings the doorbell, she fetches a pair of scissors and unpacks a pink nightdress with a white satin collar that she holds

Seven minutes to think about the film.

up against herself, looking in the mirror. This and the next scene form the film's ultimate conundrum. For the first time, the camera comes into Jeanne's bedroom as she undresses and has sex with her client; and, also for the first time, Jeanne's mask of composure, that had only slightly begun to fade in the second part of the film, disintegrates into a series of grimaces as she lies under the client, seeming to signal an oscillation between disgust and pleasure. Her composure returns as she gets dressed, carefully buttoning her blouse: she is reflected in her mirror that also shows the man lying on the bed in the background. Suddenly Jeanne grabs the scissors and stabs him.

The significance of the murder has been discussed by many commentators with many varying perspectives over the many years since the film came out. As Margulies has pointed out, there is a definite resonance between the ending of *Jeanne Dielman* and that of Akerman's first, thirteen-minute film *Saute ma ville* (1968), in which Akerman shuts herself in her flat and, having made anarchic chaos of her domestic environment, blows herself up. Akerman has cited the influence of Jean-Luc Godard's *Pierrot le fou* (1965), in which the hero blows himself up on the top of a cliff, having run out of any remaining options in life. From the perspective of narrative, Akerman has closed in on Jeanne, narrowing her parameters, just as Michael Snow's zoom in *Wavelength* (1967, also cited by Akerman as a key influence) reaches the end of its focal length. There is also a death in *Wavelength*, but the film continues to zoom over the body with increasing abstraction until it closes on a still photograph. When asked 'Why end with a murder?', Akerman replies: 'It didn't end with a murder. There are seven very strong minutes after that.'[6]

In these seven minutes, Jeanne sits in shadow at the dining-room table, her white blouse slightly stained with blood. The blue neon light seems to be heightened in intensity in its reflection behind her, further accentuated as its beam hits a white china dog on the top shelf of the cabinet; Jeanne and the soup tureen next to her are both reflected vividly in the shiny surface of the table. The image and its composition directly recall the elongated shot of Jeanne at her first moment of crisis, sitting similarly framed while waiting at her dining-room table for the potatoes to cook, the first moment, that is, when the sexual intrudes into the domestic sphere. The last shot, from this perspective, summarizes the film and the spectator can use the seven minutes to think back over the course of events that brought Jeanne into this final image. Nevertheless, there is a more polemical resonance to the shot. There is something of a Brechtian gesture in the murder, an explosive event that leaves the spectator uncertain and wondering; beyond problems of narrative logic and verisimilitude, the murder punctuates the film with a question: what does this mean? Over the following seven minutes, the spectator is taken into the emblematic silence of Jeanne's existence and the gradual eruption of her unconscious into the symptomatic actions, slips and parapraxes that he or she has just witnessed. These moments bring a series of dark, brooding signs into that threshold space between silence and language; this trajectory brings women's social and cultural oppression into dialogue with the sexuality that constitutes the unconscious. Akerman has made use of the language of film to inscribe mute meanings onto the screen and bring these questions into the public sphere of cinema.

JULIE DASH, *DAUGHTERS OF THE DUST*

I wanted to use the power of the motion pictures. For there are many
stories to be told and many battles to begin.[1]

With *Illusions* (1982) Julie Dash dramatized, in 34 minutes, the
historic exclusion of African Americans from the Hollywood screen
and the consequent contented, approving, apartheid cinematic image
of the United States as white (with a few menial exceptions). As
the character Mignon Dupree puts it: 'Your scissors and paste have
eliminated my participation in the history of the country.' Dash
emphasizes throughout *Illusions* that 'the influence of that screen
cannot be overestimated.' Furthermore, the loss to the history of
cinema embodied in that heavy silence cannot be overestimated.
Only occasionally would black directors be able to make films for the
'race market', away from the mainstream industry, and there were no
women equivalent to the aberrant presence of Dorothy Arzner or Ida
Lupino, the only women directors in post-silent Hollywood. Julie
Dash's *Daughters of the Dust* (1991) was the first feature film made by
an African American woman to be released, and, although African
Americans have recently gained significant presence behind and before
the camera, she has yet to make a second feature. In *Daughters of the
Dust*, Dash directly addressed not only the 'stories to be told' but the
ways and means of their telling: women are at the centre of the film
and the story unfolds with and through their perspective, narratively
and cinematically.

The film's historical moment and geographical place configure
the dilemmas at the heart of *Daughters of the Dust*, structurally and

cinematically, through ideas and images of time and space that disperse a conventional narrative line into multiple layers and interwoven strands. The story takes place on one of the Georgia and Carolina Sea Islands over a single day. The Peazant family has come together, joined by family members who had already moved away, for a picnic before a number of them make the journey to the North. Dash has set the film in 1902 (a little before the main migration north that began in 1910), when the first generation born after slavery had become adults. The island and the single day form a poetic pivot, circling around the story of the picnic and bringing into intense focus the Peazant family's debates and dramatization of the traumatic legacy of slavery and how the new generation might transcend it. Dash has described the process of structuring the film: she reconfigured her careful research, documentation of the place, its people and their history, into something built out of, but quite beyond, the factual, that would show 'black families, particularly black women, as we have never seen them before'. She continues:

> I came up with the idea of structuring the story in much the same way that an African griot would recount a family's history. The story would just kind of unravel. This very important day would unravel through a series of vignettes, if you want to call them that. The story would come out and come in and go out and come in, very much the way that in Toni Cade Bambara's work one character would be speaking to another and then it goes off on a tangent for several pages and then she brings it back and goes out and back again.

In Dash's discussion with bell hooks, it is pointed out that this mode of narration 'defamiliarizes' (in Viktor Sklovsky's term) a given, pre-existing concept of reality with a new way of seeing.[2]

In terms of film, the editing process weaves scenes and dialogue in and out of each other across different spaces, creating unexpected montage juxtapositions between people and ideas. Conventional cinematic perspective shifts as the mobile, wandering camera moves from place to place, inscribing the island's topography into the film and narrative image through its varied, visually rich locations. The island includes the wide sandy beaches and dunes of the ocean where African captives had been landed, as well as the waterways of the marshy backwoods (along which family members arrive at the beginning of the film and leave for the North at the end) and the huge oak trees that shelter the Peazant shacks and graveyard.

The narrative process of coming out and coming in, as Dash described it, is spatial and drifting, unlike the more usual and conventional linearity and homogeneity of narration. In *Daughters of the Dust* the cinematic organization of space resonates with the significance of geography for the film's ideas and overarching structure; the spatial drift then leads, in turn, to the film's layering of time and its use of flashback and flashforward. The micro-dimension, the island and the day, opens up into the macro: place reverberates into time, reaching back to Africa as an original home and a remnant of memory. The Sea Islands, cut off from the American mainland, a site where slave ships had unloaded their captives, preserve something of Africa in the local legends, customs and memories that are inscribed into the film through the Gullah language and everyday rituals of cooking and communication, for instance. Through its location in Ibo Landing, the film cites a moment in the history of slavery that had become legendary. While the different versions are all founded on the Ibo's immediate refusal of slavery, in the legend they had walked back to Africa across the water; in the history, recounted in the film by Bilal Muhammed, they had chosen to drown, and had walked into the sea weighed down by their chains.

Nana Peazant (Cora Lee Day), the family's mother, grandmother and great-grandmother, embodies the island as place of memory and as a trace of Africa, her voice introduces the story and its tensions between past and future. At the heart of the film is Nana's spiritual attachment to the family's ancestors, rooted in the relics of African religion and rituals, and her belief in their healing and protective powers. Deeply marked by the experience of slavery, in which collective memory and the memorizing of family genealogy had been an essential defence against a systematic destruction of family ties, Nana understands her heritage as both a source of spiritual transcendence of the past and of its destructive legacy, and as a means of holding her family together. But in another, opposite, gesture towards a transcendence of the trauma of slavery, still persisting in the Jim Crow South, the younger members of the Peazant family have decided to leave the island for the industrialized North, investing their hopes in the future as represented by city life and modernity.

The conflict between the belief in the past and the hope of the future is dramatized through the daughter-in-law, Haagar (Kaycee Moore), who rejects Nana Peazant and the memories she holds on to. Two journeys meet in the island, as though at a crossroads: on the one hand, the Middle Passage, with its complete destruction of humanity and community, leaving only a few partial memories; on the other, the Great Migration, its utopian dream of forgetting the past and founding a new African American culture and way of life. Daddy Mac, the eldest male Peazant and Nana's surviving son, rationalizes the journey: 'The only thing left for us will be scrap iron stills and tenant farming . . . Listen to what I tell you . . . if Roosevelt does anything at all, it's going to be for Northern industry and not for us.'

Haagar's investment in the journey north is rooted in a deep desire to escape from the past, from Nana's archaic superstitions, in order to give her children something new:

> Those old people, they pray to the sun, they pray to the moon . . . sometimes just to a big star! They ain't got no religion in them. No! This is a new world we're moving into and I want my daughters to grow up to be decent 'somebodies'. I don't even want my girls to *hear* about all that mess. I'll lock horns against anybody, anything that tries to hold me back. Now

Nana Peazant: preserving the past and the old magic.

> I say if Nana Peazant wants to live and die in Ibo Landing,
> then God bless her old soul.

The opposition between Haagar and Nana is, on one level, between an attachment to the past and a hope for the future that is clearly articulated by the characters in the film. Two other family members who returned to the island for the picnic represent divergences from the isolated life of the island. One of Nana's great-nieces, Viola (Cheryl Lynn Bruce), has become a devout Christian; another, Yellow Mary (Barbara O), has gained financial and personal freedom through prostitution and is able to live as a 'new woman'.

Throughout the film, there is an underlying tension derived from the traumatic experience of motherhood under slavery and its continuing legacy, one strand of which is dramatized through the relationship between Eli (Adisa Anderson), Eula (Alva Rogers) and their unborn child. In one of the film's opening sequences Nana is with Eli, her great-grandson, in the family graveyard. He is deeply distressed by his wife Eula's recent rape by a white man, which he sees as a violation of his

The unborn child: the old magic conjures the future.

own possession of her, and he is obsessed by doubts over her pregnancy. Nana's reasoning, her argument that no person can belong to another, falls on deaf ears and in response to her pleas to call for help from the ancestors, he destroys her sacred tree, decorated with bottles representing and memorializing the dead. But Nana persists, and calls upon the ancestors to save Eli and Eula. In a beautiful image, arising slowly out of a blank screen, the spirit of their unborn child is summoned into the story by the ancestors with a mission to reconcile her father with her mother. Her voice already joined Nana's in the voice-over narration at the very beginning of the film, but here she materializes into the possibility of reconciliation and a new dialogue between the spirits of the past and their future urbanized descendants. The unborn child's spiritual force convinces Eli that she, Eula's baby, is his. The reconciliation gives Eula the strength to make the film's ultimate statement on women's sexual oppression and the tragic uncertainty that haunted pregnancies during slavery.

Although Nana and some of the younger island women have welcomed Yellow Mary, Eula's speech is triggered by most of the women's collective hostility to her. Eula directly addresses these women, who are deeply embarrassed as she speaks the unspoken: 'If you so ashamed of Yellow Mary, 'cause she got ruined . . . Well what do you say about me? Am I ruined too?' She continues: 'As far as this place is concerned, we never enjoyed our womanhood . . . deep inside we believed they ruined our mothers, and their mothers before them . . . Deep inside we believe that God cannot protect us from the world that put shackles on our feet.' She warns that without reconciliation with the past, the journey north will be simply an attempt to escape from it.

> We are the daughters of those old dusty things that Nana carries in her tin can. We carry too many scars from the past. Our past owns us. We wear our scars like armour . . . for protection. Our mother's scars, our sister's scars, our daughter's scars. Thick, hard, ugly scars that no one can pass through to ever hurt us again. Let's live our lives without living in the folds of old wounds.

Alongside the persistence of sexual violence against women as a key feature of the culture of slavery that Eula articulates so clearly, is the traumatic loss suffered by mothers whose children were taken from them as either mother or child were sold into further slavery. Dash had planned a scene of separation that was not included in the final film, showing the mother's tradition of cutting off a lock of her hair as the only token she could pass on to her lost child. She says: 'I really hated not being able to include that in the film because for me, no matter how much I read about it or heard about it, I really could not fully understand what it meant to have a child or an infant taken from you.'[3] She does, however, include the memory of this loss. At the end of the film, Nana constructs a 'hand', a spiritual bond, through which she will preserve links to her family into the future and across the distance between them:

When I was a child, my mother cut this from her hair before she was sold away from us. Now I'm adding my own hair. There must be a bond, a connection, between those that go up north and those who across the sea . . . A connection! We are as two people in one body. The last of the old and the first of the new. We will always live this double life, you know, because we are from the sea. We came here in chains but we must survive. We must survive. There's salt water in our blood.

Nana meets the departing members of the Peazant family as they gather at Ibo Landing. All her family kiss the 'hand' that she has laid on top of Viola's Bible and tied with Yellow Mary's St Christopher medal; while Viola makes the gesture finally and with difficulty, Haagar is unable to join the ceremony. In her final words, Nana pronounces: 'Morning would bring a new life for my children and me. They would carry my spirit. I would remain here with the old souls.'

While Julie Dash dwells most particularly on those aspects of African American life and its ancient traditions that she had to reconstruct out of their near invisibility, she makes an elegant, thoughtful parallel between Nana's spiritual magic and the magical aspects of cinema. Mr Snead (Tommy Hicks), the photographer commissioned by Viola to record the last family picnic, functions as a kind of 'medium'. In addition to his camera and equipment, he brings optical toys with him to the island. During the morning boat journey to Ibo Landing, he shows off his kaleidoscope to Yellow Mary and her friend Trula. Later, the unborn child brings the two strands together: as she looks through a stereoscope, the street scene of a northern city comes to life, as though the still photograph had mutated into a movie fragment under her vision of the future. More strikingly, she intrudes, for a fraction of a second, magically into the icon and epitome of modernity, the camera. As a group of Peazant men pose for a collective portrait, the unborn child comes to stand by her father, Eli. Looking through the camera, Mr Snead is shocked to see her and jumps out to

'Morning would bring a new life for my children and me.'

look, but she has disappeared. The series of shots of the group of men and Mr Snead finding a site for the photograph take on a cinematic magic of their own, slowly dissolving the black-coated figures across the reflections on the wet sands. Furthermore, *Daughters of the Dust* makes a particular use of slow motion, mutating from 24 frames a second to take particular moments out of the everyday and its reality. During Nana's confrontation with Eli in the graveyard, the film cuts away to the Peazant girls in their Sunday-best white dresses, playing dancing games on the beach and thus juxtaposing but also fusing the past and the future. Nana insists: 'The ancestors and the womb, they're one, they're the same. Those in this grave like those that are across the sea, they're with us. They're all the same.'

As their dialogue continues, images of the girls, of Haagar's elder daughter Myown, later continued with the girls' dancing feet, mutate into a slow motion that defies the cinema's normal subordination to the illusion of real time. In this sense, Julie Dash uses cinema for its dual potential. While the camera, as a recording instrument of unprecedented power, captures, for instance, the carefully recreated scenes that celebrate the Gullah culture and its traces of Africa, this same camera also recognizes and expands its inherent ability both to transcend human vision and to visualize time and space as imaginative rather than literal concepts. Julie Dash has described the importance of her collaboration with Arthur Jafa on the look of the film and has described the slow-motion effect in terms of its magical qualities:

Photography: towards the future and the modern magic.
The old and the new magics.

We had a camera that was a prototype. Sometimes someone would be walking, then she'd wait, then it goes into slow-motion (in the middle of a shot). The speed-aperture control thing used to keep freezing on us. We had a hair-dryer we had to keep putting on it because of the humidity down there because of the ocean. So it would shut down. But that variable-speed motor – it was called speed aperture computer at the time – now they have it together but it was a prototype at the time. That was part of the – I don't want to say 'magic' – but of the voodoo of it, the science fiction. It's almost imperceptible: someone's moving and then the motion changes. It does have a visceral effect. It's like visual dubstep.[4]

Nana's relation to the spirit world lies alongside a life of hard reality, stretching back to the brutal indigo-dyeing process under slavery, freed with her husband, Shad, into the cultivation of the infertile land of the Sea Islands. In a recurring image of both histories, shot in slow motion and close-up, the dusty earth falls through Nana's indigo-dyed hands. Julie Dash brings to this intractable history the imaginative powers of not only the camera but narrative. She calls her film 'speculative fiction', to which she adds the 'what ifs?':

Like *what if* we could have an unborn child come and visit her family-to-be and help solve the family problems.

What if we had a great-grandmother who could not physically make the journey north but could send her spirit with them.

What if we had a family that had such a fellowship with the ancestors that they helped guide them, and so on.[5]

There is an essential optimism to this magical mode of storytelling. Forces are conjured up from collective consciousness as a means of alleviating the heavy weight of history. *Daughters of the Dust* ultimately overcomes the binary opposition between Haagar and Nana: as Nana becomes spiritually part of the migration north, a kind of dialectical relation between the past and the future comes into play. The optimistic spirit of the 'what ifs?' prefigures the complex transformation of dream and imagination into political struggle, into an optimism of another conceptual level that dreams for but also fights for a better world. At the end of the film, the unborn child finishes the story: Yellow Mary stayed on the island to spend time with her great-grandmother; Eli and Eula stayed behind and Eli became involved with the anti-lynching

Looking into the future.

movement. Also, in a beautiful gesture to the ancient history of the locality, Haagar's daughter Iona stays behind to be with her lover, St Julian Last Child (M. Cochise Anderson), the last Cherokee to survive on the Islands.

Julie Dash has used the cinema and its special attributes to visualize a time and a space of African American women, outside the linearity associated with the traditional conventions of film narrative and teleological history. This is time imagined by the matriarch, with her perspective on history then taken up by the film's narration to extend out, spatially, as it were, from the single teleology, to discover and include the nearly lost and almost forgotten. Returning to the island and to August 1902, *Daughters of the Dust* constructs a threshold on which time is momentarily paused and on which the Peazant family also pause for a collective ritual. Nana's 'hand' is a mute object but one layered with symbolic significances drawn from African slavery and the early days of freedom. But the 'hand' and Nana's maternal power also lead into the future: she holds open the door to African American past culture that then leads into the future of its cultural descendants. Eula uses the image of the scar, once again mute but symbolic of the specific, silent suffering of women, and of women as mothers, under slavery. But her words themselves open up the legacies of silence grasped (to cite Sheila Rowbotham) at this moment of their breaking, that is, in the process of their cinematic transformation into African American women's history.

RAKHSHAN BANI-ETEMAD, *UNDER THE SKIN OF THE CITY*

Rakhshan Bani-Etemad's films, whether documentary or fiction, are about those on the margins, at the lower echelons, of contemporary Iranian society. Throughout her career she has worked tirelessly to expose the injustices that society tolerates, giving, at the same time, a public voice and presence to those who suffer from them. *The May Lady* (1998) was the film in which Bani-Etemad first focused specifically on the figure of the mother, so central to her later films and to her next feature, *Under the Skin of the City* (2001). As silence is central to women's oppression under patriarchy, what form of language might adequately 'fill in' for those silenced for so long? What mode of expression might bring private silences into the public forum of culture? Furthermore, poverty, hunger, lack of sanitation and day-to-day conditions suffered by women urgently need to be recorded and brought to the attention of society in general and the authorities in particular. In keeping with this desire to reflect the problems of contemporary Iran, and sharing the well-known influence of the Italian neorealists on Iranian cinema (as evidenced in a few pre- but mostly post-Revolutionary films), Bani-Etemad's work is, by and large, within the tradition of social realism, associated with a transparent cinematic style. But, to my mind at least, *The May Lady* and *Under the Skin of the City* address the cultural oppression of women's silence alongside urgent social issues. Both films acknowledge the film-making process; as a film about film, with a protagonist who is a documentary film-maker, *The May Lady* cannot help but lead to reflection on cinema as such.

Ultimately *The May Lady* leaves silences unbroken, and film as a language fails its subjects. The failure, however, is embedded into the film's message. As *The May Lady* actually depicts, and is about, the silencing of women, it stands, to adapt Peter Brooks's term, as 'a text of muteness'.[1] That is, even if the film fails to give women a voice, it powerfully represents their mute condition. *Under the Skin of the City* is bookended by two short but important self-reflexive scenes in which a TV reporting team interviews women workers about the forthcoming election, held in 2000. The final scene restages film's failure to capture working-class women's words and emotions. Apart from these brief moments of self-reflexivity, *Under the Skin of the City* addresses the depiction of silences with a formal stylistic step that reaches beyond *The May Lady* to another cinematic level. Although the characters in *Under the Skin of the City* are constrained by the muteness of class and gender, Bani-Etemad turns to the language of film itself to express the experience of injustice, helplessness and shock. As the story goes into crisis, social realism gives way to a more melodramatic style: sounds and images, detached from the transparency of events, capture emotions when words fail.

The protagonist of *The May Lady* is Forough Kia (Minoo Farshchi), a middle-class, prize-winning documentary film-maker.[2] Her role as a film-maker with a deep commitment to observing her world is figured in a striking image at the beginning of the film. Shot through the window of a car standing at a traffic light, Forough takes off her dark glasses and looks intently out into the city. The previous establishing shots of a wide Tehran motorway have shown cars swirling around small figures, seemingly risking their lives as they dodge among the traffic. Forough's look links the two shots together: the small children run up to the car offering flowers and cigarettes for sale. Forough then questions them about their origins with warnings about their safety. The lights change and the car drives on. But the film has established Forough as a woman with a strong, inquiring gaze directed with curiosity and concern at the marginal and the vulnerable.

The next scene establishes her as a film director. She is first shown, in close-up, looking through the camera, setting up the image for the cameraman; she looks intently at the scene, arranging the group of children for the shot, and then, stepping forward, she asks them about their ambitions. In an interview, Bani-Etemad commented on the scene:

> The sequence in *The May Lady* was actually based on a documentary that I filmed earlier where I asked a group of poor children what they wanted to become, and they came up with all of these jobs, including acting and film, and they had no idea what it takes to become a doctor, lawyer, engineer, or an actor. They didn't realize that they wouldn't be able to receive the education and that they would never go to college . . . It was very moving for me, behind the camera, to see these children talking about their hopes and dreams.[3]

Forough receives an important commission from the national television station to find and to film the 'exemplary Iranian mother'. Through this project, Bani-Etemad introduces the lives of, and the problems of representing, working-class women as a major theme in the film, counterbalancing the class status of her protagonist. As Forough interviews countless women in her search for an exemplary mother, two themes predominate in the stories she hears. There are mothers whose sons have either been 'martyred' or wounded during the recent Iran–Iraq war, devoting their lives to mourning or to nursing a dependent son. There are the desperate working-class mothers, abandoned by their husbands, bringing up their children alone and in poverty. Forough watches the fragmentary raw material she has collected, trying to select one story from among so many. She stares at the accumulated portraits of the tired, distraught women on her editing-room monitors, she watches and re-watches the interviews. The women's voices are shrill with pain and their feelings of despair are conveyed through gestures and facial expressions. Some try to tell their stories but often their words fail in the face of the camera and the expectations it places on them, only recording their inability to speak. Others turn away wordlessly, rejecting the camera's intrusion and challenging Forough's right to film them.

Forough decides to give up the project. She takes photographs of the women to a meeting with the committee responsible for the commission, spreads them out, in a mass, all over the table and says: 'All these mothers are exemplary. I am unable to choose one from all of these. Another director might be able to, but I cannot.' In the first instance, her gesture is political. These lives, represented by the photographs, are not simply of individuals but bear witness to endemic injustice and oppression; society itself bears down with extra weight on these women struggling to keep their families together emotionally and materially. But her gesture more implicitly rejects the cliché image behind the committee's concept of 'an exemplary mother'. The film, moving beyond Forough's fictional world, challenges an image so central to a society in which mothers suffer silently, highly idealized but heavily oppressed.

The decision is aesthetic as well as political. The images document the suffering of the women, but also the intractable process of translating their voices into a conventional cultural object. The raw reality, captured in the fragments that Forough has filmed, cannot be contained in an exemplary story, narrated through proper editing and traditional modes of documentary presentation. Once she refuses to take the project to its next stage, Forough steps onto a significant threshold. Here she confronts two kinds of silence, one affecting the film-maker and the other affecting the women she films. As a woman film director, Forough sees, feels and understands the material she has gathered together; but, as a woman film director, her form, film itself, fails her. As the women's suffering is caused by class (poverty), patriarchy (male oppression and violence) and nationalism (war and its aftermath), their voices cannot make themselves heard. Relegated to the margins of society, they are living symptoms of society's true nature. Bani-Etemad, staying herself within a social-realist aesthetic, reflects on and visualizes the limits of the form while also visualizing the problems at stake. It is in this sense that *The May Lady* functions as a mute text: although the film fails to find a voice for the women filmed, it bears witness to their unheard voices and the social silence that envelops them. Furthermore, in the film's main narrative strand, *The May Lady* develops the theme of silence through Forough's personal life and her own intractable problems as a mother.

Forough is divorced from her husband and lives with her teenage son, Mani, who deeply resents his mother's relationship with another man. While her film project takes her to working-class women whose immediate, desperate struggles contrast with her privileged and financially secure existence, Forough's relationship with Mani demonstrates that women's secondary status runs across class boundaries. She is faced every day with the problems of her own motherhood. Caught between the demands of her son and her lover, she questions the tradition that a mother should give up her own affectionate life for her son's exclusive, possessive, love through which he asserts his masculine right of ownership and control over her. As a sign of Mani's control over his mother, Forough's lover is never seen and their personal communication is limited to telephone and letter. Forough's attempts, as an intellectual and articulate woman, to reason with Mani are met with a blank wall of jealousy. In the last shot of the film, Mani and Forough, mother and son, sit side-by-side watching television with the framing and direct camera angle suggesting a long-married couple. When the telephone rings, the son turns up the sound on the television, preventing his mother from answering. Although the film ends with Forough's voice as she telephones her lover, there is no sense that she has resolved her dilemma. As a mother, this mature, successful, professional woman is at the mercy of her teenage son's rejection of reason and his refusal to accept her right to an emotional existence outside of her relationship with him. *The May Lady* traces the story of language's double failure: in Forough's story, her failure to reason with her son, and in the story of her project, the failure of film to provide a voice for working-class women. The impasse in which the fictional film director finds herself in *The May Lady* has a bearing on the more formal expressive codes that characterize the later sections of *Under the Skin of the City*.

Under the Skin of the City was Bani-Etemad's next feature after *The May Lady* and the most ambitious film of her career. Her previous films had concentrated, by and large, on a main woman protagonist and one specific issue. Here she extends the scope of the film to the fortunes of a whole family and a wide range of social problems. Tuba (Golab Adineh) is the mother of five children, whose husband is an invalid and unable to work. She and her beloved eldest son, Abbas (Mohammed Reza Faroutan), support the family and their close relationship lies at the heart of the film. Abbas works as a messenger or 'gofer' for the boss of a small business; Ali, the second son, is at university and is involved in politics; the eldest daughter, Hamideh, is married to a man who ill-treats her; Mahboubeh (Baran Kosari), the youngest daughter, is at school. The closeness between Mahboubeh and her neighbour and best friend, Masoumeh, is the other heart of the film.

Tuba and Abbas embody contrasting narrative spaces, representing, on the one hand, the male dynamic of narrative drive and, on the other, the stasis of the domestic sphere. Early on, the space of the family home is established: the small house with its courtyard surrounded by high walls, typical of the working-class districts in the south of Tehran. For Tuba, the house stands for her and her family's happiness and resilience, her love for her children and their love for her and for each other. It is, that is, the space of the mother. (The house next door, identical in layout, is tyrannized by a brutal and conservative eldest son so that the high walls are more resonant of a prison than of maternal comfort.) The characters, the central family, look forward to a future that, although precarious and fragile, should conform to their aspirations. For the first third of the film, that forward direction persists. Tuba's family house is a place of embrace and enclosure, while Abbas moves around the city on his motor scooter, across wide shots of cityscape, motorways and surrounding urban development. For him, this should be a success story, an escape from the constraints imposed by class, his lack of education and the destiny that seems to hold the family in poverty and impotence. He saves money for his ticket to Japan, seeing migration as the almost magical means to establish control over his own story, to rescue his mother from her debilitating job in a textile factory, to ensure a better life for Ali and a university education for Mahboubeh. He dreams that, on his successful return, he will marry the young woman he longs for from afar, now way beyond his social reach. This is the pattern of the folk tale: the linear direction of the story encapsulated in the linearity of the hero's journey along a road to success. Freud used this pattern, transferring it to a nineteenth-century milieu in his essay 'On Creative Writers and Daydreaming'; the 'princess' of the fairy tale becomes the daughter of the hero's employer, just as, in the transposition here, Abbas loves the beautiful secretary in Mr Marandi's office. In order to pay for his ticket to Japan, and although he knows how devastating the loss of her home and all it symbolizes will be for Tuba, Abbas persuades his father to sell the family house to a builder/speculator.

Three events disrupt the precarious hold that Tuba's family has on day-to-day well-being and the collective affection that shelters them from the hardness of their existence. Two events stem directly from women's oppression and lack of legal rights. Masoumeh, beaten by her brother for going to a pop concert with Mahboubeh, runs away from home to join the child fugitives who haunt the parks and public spaces of Tehran, all victims of domestic violence. The second event involves Tuba's lack of ownership rights over her own home, which is dramatically realized as her husband and son sell the house without her knowledge or permission. Third, to include the vulnerability of the working-class in general, Abbas discovers that the travel agent has absconded with his money, the proceeds of the sale of the family home.

These events effect the film's language. The conventions of transparent style are thrown out of kilter; the shock and alienation the characters experience, and to which they cannot begin to formulate a coherent response, estrange sounds and images from the cinematic norm. These shifts are reminiscent of the melodrama's recourse to non-verbal means that 'fill in' the lacuna of silence. Here, shock and the breakdown of the everyday reinforce the structural muteness of class and gender oppression. The family story in *Under the Skin of the City* demonstrates that

Tuba in her courtyard with Mahboubeh and Masoumeh, the two friends.

conditions of working-class daily life lack buffer zones or safety valves. Misfortune or error can quickly mutate into disaster, leaving its victims struggling to comprehend, unable to articulate the fate that has overtaken them.

Realism records the state of things, without extra-diegetic intrusion into a representation of the norms of everyday life and its fragile survival strategies. *Under the Skin of the City* breaks with stylistic transparency, opening up another level of cinematic signification. In one of the film's most moving scenes, Mahboubeh secretly meets Masoumeh in a park and the film responds to the girls' intense emotion and the acute injustice of Masoumeh's fate. Strange diegetic music and non-diegetic sounds slow the scene when the two girls first see each other and extend their long, tearful embrace. The sense of shock intensifies. The police arrive to harry and arrest the fugitive children. The scene ends with the camera holding the image of the empty path down which the children had fled, with Maboubeh's abandoned bag in the foreground and a colourful bunch of balloons floating ironically in

The two friends' meeting: cinema as expressive code.

mid-distance. When Abbas goes to the travel agent to reclaim his money, he finds the building deserted. He bangs helplessly on the metal gate as a voice shouts out: 'They took the money and ran.' Back on his scooter, Abbas is pursued by these disembodied sounds; the moment of shock continues to reverberate as the clang of the gate pursues him along the motorway. Once again, as in the scene in the park, an estrangement or dislocation of sound and image breaks with the norms of social realism. The director creates an emotional space in which moments become elongated in time, conveying the intensity of the experience and allowing the spectator to take in the instant and its implications. No longer a detached observer, the spectator registers and understands the meaning inscribed by the language of film. In subsequent scenes, *Under the Skin of the City* continues to convey its characters' helplessness with camera angles and framings tinged with strangeness. Conventional narrative continuity fragments into emotionally charged tableaux in which the characters, hitherto naturally centre screen, are displaced by a foregrounded image into semi-distance,

Abbas pursued by disembodied sound (or cinema as expressive code).

underlining their helplessness. This shift is quite slight rather than heavily marked, so that the film's use of a more melodramatic style demands attention and interpretation.

The intense affection between Tuba and Abbas resonates with the tropes of melodrama: the discordant aspirations of mother and son, one centred on maintaining the family home, the other sacrificing it in the hope of escaping from a class-bound world, lie at the heart of the crisis; one represented visually by the stasis of domestic space, the warmth of affection and family, the other by the space of the city, invested in narrative drive and desire. External forces brutally block the kind of narrative linearity in which the hero brings the story to a satisfactory end, after a certain number of trials and tribulations. But as crisis puts an end to his hopes, Abbas has to search desperately for another road or narrative line that will allow him to assert control over his and his family's life. Tuba, with the developer about to claim her family home, retreats into her domestic space.

Abbas turns to the drug dealer who, on several occasions, had offered him the chance to better himself by smuggling heroin across the Turkish border. As Abbas drives along the winding road through the snow-covered mountains, Ali, hidden in the back of the truck, throws the white wedding dresses, in which the dealer smuggles the white heroin, out into the snowy road. Both objects gesture, ironically in their whiteness, to the social pain, the dulled hopes, that the film has depicted. For Abbas, at this moment, the whiteness of the snowy, desolate landscape stands in only for the blank of his despair.

Tuba's despair and desolation at the disintegration of her family and the loss of her home finds expression in this short scene. A single static shot is preceded by a blank, black screen crossed by intermittent flashes of diagonal light. The flat, unreadable space of the screen seems to summon up, in the first instance, cinema itself and the essential elements of light and dark out of which, potentially, recognizable forms and meanings may emerge. This (very short) initial moment creates a visual disorientation in the spectator that evokes, but is not, of course, adequate to, the black hole of hopelessness that has overwhelmed Tuba. In the main shot, the flat blackness mutates into the darkness of night, showing the inside of the (by now familiar) courtyard shot from a high angle on the outside wall. The flashes of diagonal light also mutate, out of abstraction, into streaks of pouring rain. In the courtyard, in long shot, Tuba is sitting on the ground in front of a small basin in which she is washing clothes with obsessive intensity. Her automatic actions are precisely in keeping with her lifetime of caring for her family, in which hard labour is inextricably involved with deep affection. This confusion is, of course, central to the mythologies of motherhood and, in these extreme circumstances, Tuba resorts to a performance that poignantly reflects those underlying contradictions. Washing clothes literally gives her an occupation in a moment of crisis, but in the pouring rain and darkness, her habitual actions are obviously absurd. The rain, metaphorically and metonymically, stands for her tears; but more brutally, as a natural, uncontrollable force, it soaks the pathetically domestic water in the small basin, rendering Tuba's gestures grotesque. It is on these various levels that the aesthetic of melodrama works: the literalness of visual images becomes figurative under emotional pressure, accumulating implicit meaning without recourse to external symbolism.

Overwhelmingly conscious of her inability to 'do anything', Tuba does 'something' that is symptomatic of the maternal unconscious. As the camera maintains a distance from the scene of Tuba washing clothes, it draws into the shot all the constituent elements of the *mise en scène*: the space of the courtyard, the darkness and the rain. It also shows, without any sentimentality, Tuba's crippled husband, who briefly remonstrates with her ('this is no time for doing the laundry') and wraps his jacket around her shoulders before slowly and painfully retreating back into the house. His gesture is not empty but personal, affectionate and in character; nevertheless, it marks, at this point, the inability of any individual to penetrate the mother's despair, which this scene renders with a fusion of melodrama and restraint.

Tuba's action displaces the typical and homely into an empty gesture that caricatures the domestic, and its very irrationality becomes the sign of a core resistance to a dominant 'rationality'. From a dramatic perspective, there are two aspects to the scene. In the first instance, it vividly shows that, in this relentless situation, Tuba is able to transform an action belonging to the everyday into a symptomatic action that evokes both her unconscious and a wider, collective unconscious of women unable to express, speak or articulate the pain and injustice they suffer daily. Second, Tuba's intense feelings are woven into the *mise en scène* and cinematic style, so that the spectator is forced to read the screen and move beyond any straightforward identification with character. Although the film has often shown the mother's face (lined by hard physical labour and unrelenting anxiety but enlivened by humour, affection and intelligence), there is no cut to close-up to break up the integrity of the shot. The whole space evokes Tuba's emotions but also presents a topography that demands a further reading from the spectator.

On one level, her irrational action expresses the way that Tuba's situation is beyond words. On another level, the film responds to that wordlessness and compensates for it cinematically. Here again *Under the Skin of the City* suggests that *mise en scène* and the language of cinema must, and should, acknowledge silences rooted in oppression and repression and find some way to fill in visually for the inadequacy of language. From this perspective, the cinema's ability to move beyond language, into the cinematic, lends itself to this political form of expression and draws attention to particular conjunctures in which the political and the cinematic come together. Ultimately, the single shot of the courtyard, its melodramatic *mise en scène* that fuses the gesture of washing with the pouring rain and the mother's tears, leads beyond the drama of *Under the Skin of the City* to the difficulty of representing the problems of motherhood. By and large, the mother is easily transformed into a visible cliché or disappears into a miasma of ideological or psychic confusion, as witnessed by Forough's commission in *The May Lady*. Bani-Etemad, as a woman director, has confronted these contradictions: in *Under the Skin of the City* she has woven the ideological and political contradictions inscribed into the concept of motherhood into the essentially gestural form of cinema itself.

Bani-Etemad ends *Under the Skin of the City* with a concluding or summation scene. The television crew is once again recording the women's view on the coming election in Tuba's factory. Tuba makes an impassioned statement to camera, citing the patience that the people have shown over the years as the government failed to improve their lot. The cameraman abruptly asks her to repeat her words, due to a technical fault. Looking at the (diegetic) camera, she says: 'I have lost my house. My eldest son is on the run.' Striking her chest, she adds: 'Why can't you film what's in my heart?' She then looks straight past the camera to address the cinema audience, saying: 'Who do you show these films to, anyway?' Tuba succinctly challenges film's ability to either hear the words of impoverished women or to register their emotions. Although her statement reiterates the mute text of *The May*

'Who do you show these films to, anyway?'

Lady, the film *Under the Skin of the City* has pushed beyond the limits of simple recording, as exemplified by the TV crew, using the language of film to materialize women's silences, estranged but expressed in cinematic sound and image.

Tuba's question leads both back to the beginning of Bani-Etemad's career and forward to *Tales*, her latest film released in 2015. In 1993, she made a three-part documentary, *Rapport 72*, in which an elderly woman had challenged her with the same question; the second part of the trilogy is titled *To Whom Do You Show These Films?* Although she stopped making feature films during the repressive presidency of Mahmoud Ahmedinejad (2005–13), Bani-Etemad was able to put together *Tales*, composed of a series of short films she had made as fragments to avoid censorship, then released as a feature after the election of the Rouhani government. In *Tales* she imagined the futures of several characters who had appeared in her previous films. Once again, she returns to the closing question of *Under the Skin of the City*. Tuba and her fellow workers have been swindled of many months' wages and are trying to enlist government help. Once again, a documentary cameraman (although in this case sympathetic to the workers' cause) is filming them as they prepare to demonstrate. As Tuba rehearses her speech, she looks into the camera and says: 'Honourable authorities, whoever you are, wherever you are, whatever you're doing, please come and see for yourselves our miserable life.' And then she directly addresses the cameraman, 'Who do you show these films to, anyway? And even if someone watches them, so what?'

ALINA MARAZZI,
UN'ORA SOLA TI VORREI

Autobiography, diary, gossip, love stories – women have more often
inhabited the margins and peripheries of language, its interstices,
minor or oblique discourses. Outside the signs and the time of the
Father, before Oedipus, the nurse's tongue appears, rather than a
system, a subterranean archipelago of signals and symptom which
point to a 'black continent' of femininity, women's dark world, history
of phantasms behind the frail history of facts and certifications, built
on its own repression, fed of its own censure.[1]

Film has a privileged relation to the representation of time. So often it is
associated with the linear, that is, with a narrative that unfolds along the
road taken by heroic journeys, subject to cause and effect. As alternative
film-making demonstrated across its history, cinema can potently
disrupt and confuse temporal logic and make visible its complicated
temporality. Not only do sequence (the time of the shot) and instant
(the time of the frame) paradoxically coexist, but film easily reverses
time and movement, juxtaposing repetition with extended duration.
Cinema embodies time as contingent and subject to the imagination.
But, more to the point in this context, the compilation film integrates
pre-existing footage into a newly configured text, layering time, bringing
a past into an ever-receding present. Double temporality has long been
considered an essential attribute of the form, as witnessed, for instance,
by the title of Jay Leyda's early book on the topic, *Films Beget Films*
(1964), and by Christa Blümlinger's term 'second-hand film'.[2] Although

existing footage has been reassembled since the beginnings of cinema, there are landmark moments in its history. The Soviet film-maker Esfir Shub pioneered the use of found footage as critique in her film *The Fall of the Romanov Dynasty* (1927), Joseph Cornell pioneered its use as art in *Rose Hobart* (1936), and the form has continued along these paths as well as deviating into others.

The compilation film has no inherent relation to women, but its formal properties fit well with stories that emerge out of silence and cultural marginalization, tentatively making the shift from an individual and private world into circulation in the public sphere. The process of collecting and rearranging primary material has a certain similarity to 'history from below'. Parallels between this kind of historical process and the compilation film are accentuated by the specific nature of film. As its images are inscribed onto photosensitive material, found footage preserves the presence of its past, carrying into the future the imprint of the moment of time when the image was recorded. Even once reorganized into something new, even in the final version of the edited film, a sense of temporal heterogeneity persists. This refusal to be neatly integrated into a new and homogeneous text seems to preserve a ghostly voice of a kind, insistently searching for a social space in which it might be, perhaps, addressed in the future.

Although there are many kinds of compilation, appropriation or found-footage film, the form has relevance for feminist history in both its questioning of historical narrative and its means, as cinema, for reconfiguring patterns of time. Feminist methodologies privilege informal materials (often the only traces left of women's difficult everyday lives), constructing the past out of personal relics such as memorabilia, letters and diaries. These scraps of sources are necessary for a picture of the past to emerge in which women's lives are central rather than marginal; and, in the absence of public events usually associated with politics, women's everyday struggles challenge given boundaries of formal, political history. Problems associated with the female body, with sexuality, emotion or motherhood, for instance, can be extracted from the taboo of the feminine, from the silences of embarrassment and shame, to find a historical discourse in the public sphere. Beyond the question of content and untold stories, this kind of gathering together of disparate material affects the formal structure of the text and its process of narration. On the one hand, these texts tend to be made up of heterogeneous fragments; on the other, feminist history, once having given space to unheard voices, has a commitment to their integrity; a balance must be made between creating a political discourse and fidelity to the material from which it is drawn. Aesthetics and politics intertwine to form textual heterogeneity, an unfinished and unpolished final product.

However conventional the compilation film may be in its straight-forward documentary form, it carries within it an essential temporal complexity. In a feminist context, layered time can be exploited aesthetically and politically for narrative and narration that deviate from a traditional linear pattern. Recently, as seen in radical challenges to historical narrative and avant-garde challenges to narrative film, for instance, there has been widespread reaction against temporal linearity. But the search for another, non-linear concept of time, and attempts to give it an appropriate pattern or configuration, come up against the actual difficulty of pinning down time and how, in keeping with the demands of human imagination and social organization, it shifts, twists and turns. Time is hard to articulate or to conceptualize but culture and society are 'possessed' by patterns of temporality, habitual and intangible, which form an essential part of the fabric of everyday life and its ideological structure.

The characteristic gaps between the found footage and the completed compilation film can be arranged into these four tropes:

PALIMPSEST: evokes the gap in time between the original footage and the final film. A palimpsest refers to a double inscription: one text is laid over another; the original might be partly erased but still haunts the later text. Similarly, as found footage is overlaid by its later reconfiguration, two time levels exist simultaneously. This persistence of the past generates its own metaphor of haunting.

DÉTOURNEMENT: refers to the frequent, but not essential, ideological gap between the original footage and the final film. The term cites the Situationist practice in which a pre-existing cultural text (usually of high standing) would be distorted for political critique, producing an antagonistic or antithetical meaning.

GLEANING: relates to the gap in value between the found material and the final film. The term, suggested in Agnès Varda's film *Les glaneurs et la glaneuse* (The Gleaners and I, 2000), gives a cultural lineage to the process of collecting, accumulating, sifting through and recycling discarded materials. Gleaning not only refers to what was, once upon a time, a specifically female task (collecting the unwanted residue of an agricultural harvest), but evokes the kind of apparently trivial things, personal or emotional, collected and saved, in which women invest value. By extension, the term also evokes the often apparently valueless nature of found-footage material that, almost by definition, has no place in film culture; only when re-evaluated and recycled does it acquire significance and, consequently, value.

HAUNTING: In the dislocations between found footage and its reconfigured form, ghostly figures, preserved as they are on film, refuse to be laid to rest. Film's preservation of images of the living dead, figures from long ago that still move, gesture, perform exactly as they did when registered on film, gives substance to a message from the silenced and oppressed of the past brought back to light by new political perspectives. In the meantime, they have, if only metaphorically, refused to 'give up the ghost' or to be laid to rest.

In *Un'ora sola ti vorrei* (For One More Hour with You) Alina Marazzi reconstructs the story of her mother, Luisa Hoepli/Marazzi (known as

Liseli). Alina was seven years old when her mother died. Although she was never subsequently mentioned by her family Marazzi discovered, years later, that even the slightest document relating to her mother's life, her illness and her death, and every trace of her presence, had been carefully preserved by her husband Antonio, kept in a trunk in his mother's attic. She also discovered a cupboard full of home movies, shot by Liseli's father, Alina's grandfather. As a young film-maker, Marazzi began to analyse and catalogue the endless reels, in different formats and varying states of preservation, and gradually began to formulate the film that became *Un'ora sola ti vorrei*. The film is constructed out of the traces of Liseli's life, that is, out of intrinsically informal materials: extracts from letters and diaries make up the soundtrack, read by Marazzi herself and augmented by music that she had either found or commissioned; the home movies, augmented by photographs and medical documents, make up most of the image track.

Un'ora sola ti vorrei is constructed out of the residual traces of Liseli's life: diaries, letters and memorabilia. The film thus exemplifies the gap of gleaning: things without value are revalued into a historical record with social relevance. However, central to the film is the gap of *détournement*. When she began work on the raw film material, Marazzi was searching, on a personal level, for her lost mother, but she gradually came to the realization that Liseli's story has a significance and importance beyond the individual. Her grandfather's overarching intention, as his granddaughter perceived it, was to record a particular bourgeois way of life, through that of his own well-to-do and cultured family. In the context of Marazzi's feminist consciousness, the footage finds a changed, or charged, significance; that is, the film moves the story from the realm of women's silence and suffering to recognition within a feminist discourse of history. Liseli, although an articulate and intelligent young woman, had been unable to break through the silence surrounding intractable social pressures involved in motherhood, succumbing to depression and ultimately to suicide. The lack of social discourse around the experience of motherhood, its silences, affects the films' aesthetic strategies and the way that political, feminist significance is woven out of this difficult material.

The aesthetic of compilation, its fragmentary and unfinished nature, reflects the difficulty of telling Liseli's story; but, while using the course of Liseli's life as a 'vertical' form, the film breaks up linear chronology with 'horizontal' insertions. The non-chronological editing enhances both the temporal layering inherent to the found-footage film and the gap between Liseli's father's home movies and the final film. Furthermore, as the footage is slowed down and stilled and repeated, the photograph's instant of registration emerges into visibility, accentuating the presence of the past. Due to the editing, to the association between the photographic image and death, as well as stilled and repeated images, the film casts the shadow of her future death over even the young Liseli. But, to reiterate, ultimately, and beyond the 'double' temporality characteristic of the compilation film, *Un'ora sola ti vorrei* moves from the individual instance into the realm of history, sharing the aesthetic of compilation film as critique initiated by Esfir Shub. This ideological gap comes from the shift in consciousness between the grandfather's filming and the two women compiling his footage into a new text, the gap between the bourgeois and patriarchal vision behind the Hoepli home movies and the vision of their young female editors, working after the Women's Liberation Movement and educated within feminism. Marazzi and her editor, Ilaria Fraioli, found themselves questioning, not in the first instance but ultimately, the nature and authority of the original material. In commenting on the precision of her grandfather's style, his command of *mise en scène*, as well as the technology of filming, Marazzi refers to this as 'highly controlled self-portraiture' noting that 'no image was casually made'. She continues:

> there was something we could not avoid and that did, in fact, generate a useful dialectic: the 'look' of the camera operator. It was impossible to forget that these images were all made by a man filming his women, his muses: his wife, his daughter . . .

The looks at the camera reveal a game of complicity between the film-maker and those filmed. These women are beautiful and charming, captured by the equal charm of the camera work. But in my mother's case, these images of happiness are shown to be false: it was as though the camera was not able to capture an essence beyond an appearance … For his whole life, this man had filmed his wife and then his daughter without succeeding in actually seeing them, without capturing the looks that these women gave him in return. The letters and diaries put this appearance of happiness continuously in question.[3]

Un'ora sola ti vorrei raises questions about the status and significance of an archive, the relation between the film and the material from which it was drawn, and its future address to its audience. When Marazzi, as an adult, questioned her father about her mother, he told her that she should look in his mother's attic where everything relating to Liseli had been stored. There, she found a trunk containing letters, photographs, medical records and Liseli's teenage diaries. Marazzi describes the experience of being the first person since Liseli's death to look through it as both magical and macabre. Marazzi then found her grandfather's home movies in a cupboard; boxes and boxes of films (16mm and 8mm) covered the Hoepli family's life since 1926, but had been left unopened and unwatched since Liseli's death. In his discussion of 'archive fever', Jacques Derrida characterizes the archive initially in terms of a topology (a site) and a nomology (an authority). In the Hoepli case, there is a definite sense of a topology: the attic, the trunk and the abandoned cupboard are all spaces of the relegated but preserved materials of a family's memory, but especially the secret and the unspoken. Derrida's topology resonates, in this case, with Gaston Bachelard's 'poetics of space': the spaces in which these memories are housed have a particular significance within the topography of the family home. However, the informality of the material, its domesticity, even its femininity,

Luisa's mother (home movie).
Luisa's wedding (home movie).

Luisa and Alina.

Young Luisa (polyphoto).

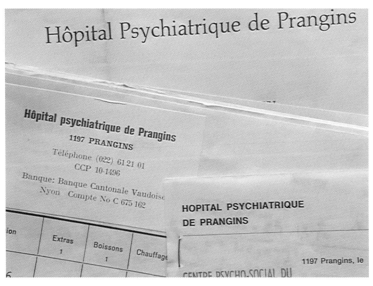

Letter from Luisa to Antonio.

Medical reports from the clinic.

The end of the home movies.

indicates that the material resists the patriarchal authority that Derrida considers to be fundamental to the archive. The grandfather had indeed recognized this himself, saying to his granddaughter: 'Why bother to look at all this? These are *sciocchezze* [mere stupidities] that I made as a young man for fun; they are without any historical interest.'[4] And Ilaria Fraioli, commenting on the intrinsic value of Signor Hoepli's material, points out the contradiction between his assessment and its actual historical relevance: 'he considered the films only to be a pastime without any value. This is confirmed by the fact that he hardly ever filmed his prestigious Hoepli bookshop, perhaps to avoid mixing the serious with the frivolous.'[5] However, the material could find its authority, its nomology, through Marazzi and Fraioli's shared vision. In describing the process of producing the film, Marazzi says:

In the dialogue between the images and the words, beyond the letters and diaries, there is another level of writing: Ilaria's and mine. We edited and re-edited, subverting the original intention of the images, appropriating and retelling the story as it seemed to us, taking up the point of view of the filmed. In a certain sense we liberated the feminine spirit imprisoned in those boxes, as though with Aladdin's lamp.[6]

Marazzi also comments on the private nature of the material, not only as home movies but as depictions of both the everyday and the relation between mother and daughter: gestures repeated by women across time and generation. It is possible to understand Derrida's concept of the fever that disturbs the archive in the incomprehensibility of Liseli's life and death (and indeed he relates the fever specifically to the death drive). However, a more relevant disturbance might be found in the women's feminist reworking of the material to create 'women's history'.

While the confusion of time that exists between found footage and its reconfiguration lies at the heart of the compilation film, the politics of compilation as critique ultimately depend on an exchange that will only happen in the future: that is, how the retold story will deliver its message. Jaime Barron uses the term 'archival effect' to underline the specificity of the relation between the form and its double temporality:

Hence I suggest that we regard archival documents as – in part – the product of what I call 'temporal disparity', the perception by the viewer of a 'then' and 'now' generated within a single text. Indeed, the experience of temporal disparity is one of the things that gives rise to the recognition of the archival document as such, or, in other words to the 'archive effect'.[7]

In Barron's terms, the archival effect is produced by the spectator's response to the temporal complexity of the material, emphasizing the crucial place of the future in the work of the compilation film. In his reflection on the temporality of the archive, Derrida emphasizes this future dimension. He says:

> In an enigmatic sense, which will clarify itself *perhaps* (perhaps because nothing should be sure here, for essential reasons), the question of the archive is not, we repeat, a question of the past. It is not a question of a concept dealing with the past that might be already at our disposal, *an archivable concept of the archive.* It is a question of the future, the question of the future itself, the question of a response, a promise and of a responsibility towards tomorrow. The archive: if we want to know what that will have meant, we will only know in times to come. Perhaps. Not tomorrow but in times to come, later on or perhaps never. A spectral messianicity is at work in the concept of the archive and ties it, like religion, like history, like science itself, to a very singular experience of the promise. And we are never very far from Freud in saying this.[8]

In *Un'ora sola ti vorrei* the implication of the promise moves personally, from Alina to her mother and her story, and then politically, to the film's future. Liseli's image moves from her ghostly presence on film (celluloid's characteristic illusion of the living dead is further enhanced by her actual untimely death) to the ghostly spirit that refuses to be put to rest, perhaps until a feminist future can make at least a gesture towards the silenced past. This is the point at which, after decades of invisibility, the emotional significance of the film's actual instances and split seconds become political. In the last resort, this material carries in its celluloid footprint something that can be returned to the historical consciousness of Liseli's future. Just as celluloid confuses temporality, so does the concept of promise: speaking towards a time in which unrecognized experiences might find recognition or even redemption.

Alina Marazzi showed *Un'ora sola ti vorrei* widely. It won prizes at Locarno and Torino Film Festivals in 2002. She has described the emotional responses that the film elicited, particularly from women of Liseli's generation who had suffered from and survived similar psychological problems. And sometimes from younger women whose mothers had succumbed to depression and had also committed suicide. These responses confirm the importance of the way the film negotiates two shifts in time and space. First of all, through the screenings, the private nature of women's suffering and the muteness of the maternal voice could enter into a 'social space' and into public discourse. Second, Liseli's story could find recognition, so that the previously lost and silenced voice could be found within feminist historical consciousness and in a 'social time' of the future.

CLIO BARNARD, *THE ARBOR*

I think I'm a bit suspicious of naturalism and realism. Life is complicated and doesn't really have neat storylines. There are always several different versions of a story you could tell at any one time, so it's more fractured and complicated than that. I think that's why I want to put the two together somehow: the artifice and the real.[1]

The Arbor is in an acute reminder of the fragility of women's cultural production, and thus their social and aesthetic public voice. This fragility is personified by Andrea Dunbar and her plays, and the tenuous but significant link between her brief moment of public recognition in the 1980s and her subsequent return through Clio Barnard's 2010 film. Both the plays and the film depended on progressive arts funding to come into being.

The chances, in the first instance, of Andrea Dunbar's voice finding a public hearing was slight, with all the odds of class, gender and post-industrial social deprivation stacked against her. But the English teacher at her local comprehensive school encouraged the working-class fifteen-year-old, living on a run-down post-industrial council estate outside Bradford, to submit a play to the Royal Court Theatre's annual Young Writers' Festival. Max Stafford-Clark, the director of the Royal Court, picked up and staged *The Arbor* in 1980, commissioning a follow-up, *Rita, Sue and Bob Too*, which was performed in 1982 and then made into a film, directed by Alan Clarke, in 1987. Dunbar's words came from her own immediate experience on the Buttershaw estate, drawing directly on her very difficult experiences as a young woman, but she also bore witness to the conditions of life in a post-industrial working-class community, with neither hope nor any means of expression. By the mid-1980s Dunbar had three children by different men, had spent over a year in a Women's Aid refuge and had begun to drink heavily. She died of a brain haemorrhage in 1990 at the age of 29.

In 2000 Clio Barnard saw the Royal Court's staging of Robin Soans's verbatim play *A State Affair*, constructed from interviews with Andrea Dunbar's surviving relatives. Interested in what had happened to Andrea's children, Barnard went to the Buttershaw estate and found members of the family still living on Brafferton Arbor, the street that gave its name to Dunbar's first play and to Barnard's film. Barnard recorded interviews about Andrea from her family and friends, gradually building up a portrait of her from their memories. Then she traced Andrea's daughter Lorraine to a drug rehabilitation clinic outside London and interviewed her extensively. It was at this point that her plans for a documentary changed direction. Lorraine agreed that her interviews could be used but refused to appear on film. Barnard decided to use a device with which she had experimented in an earlier work: to use actors to lip-sync the words of the people she had interviewed. The second part of Barnard's film, which is the third iteration of Andrea's story, focuses on Lorraine, in a tragic sequel to Andrea's tragic life. Barnard's film emerges out of her hybrid work between art and the moving image and *The Arbor* was financed by Artangel, a charitable foundation that funds art destined for exhibition outside of the gallery. It won multiple international awards and was given a general release in London cinemas.

The Arbor can only be understood through its history and geography. First of all, England is scarred by the unbridgeable gulf between its south and its north, exaggerated by the magnified status of London as the site of government, the finance industry and culture. But the division is also economic. In 1845 Benjamin Disraeli wrote his novel *Sybil*, subtitled *The Two Nations*, to draw attention to the conditions of extreme poverty and deprivation in the early industrialized north, which has returned today with post-industrialization.

Bradford was a world centre for textile production that exploded in the mid-nineteenth century, attracting mass immigration from Ireland and then, in the 1950s, from Pakistan. The post-Second World War Labour government, elected in 1945, pursued a policy of widespread urban renewal through council housing, of which the Buttershaw estate is an early example. Built in the late 1940s, before the domination of the high-rise model, the estate is made up of self-contained, semi-detached houses, designed around a kind of village green. Bradford's textile industry, which had dominated the world since the nineteenth century, went into a decline that was aggravated by Thatcherism in the 1980s. The mills closed down, bringing massive unemployment. Paul Harrison introduces his book *Inside the Inner City* in the following terms:

> As recession deepened and the monetarist policies initiated in 1976 were pursued after 1979 with increasing vengeance and disregard for the consequences . . . Swathes of industry were mown down, increasing numbers of human beings and communities were marginalised, inequalities deepened and disadvantages accentuated . . . declining industry, decaying housing and abandoned people spread like a cancer affecting areas where it had been unknown before and growing more and more malignant where it was established.[2]

Andrea Dunbar's parents had both worked in the textile mills; by the mid-1980s unemployment brought with it the descent into alcoholism, racism and domestic violence that Dunbar's plays capture so vividly. And then, in an even further deterioration, drug addiction swept through the next generation, exemplified by Andrea's daughter Lorraine.

The break-up of industrial capitalism eroded the concept of progress that had been built into working-class militancy, which was necessarily directed towards a better future. Unemployment, and the loss of hope that went with it, blocked any sense of a way forward. The Buttershaw estate that might, once upon a time after the Second World War, have stood for a utopian aspiration of a kind, collapsed into itself in an image of temporal stasis and spatial desolation. The opening shots of Barnard's *The Arbor* show feral dogs inhabiting the overgrown 'village green' and throughout there are shots of boarded-up and abandoned houses. In the catastrophic decline into which Thatcherism consciously precipitated the British working class, material deprivation was accompanied by, in the Italian theorist Franco Berardi's phrase, 'the slow cancellation of the future'. Max Stafford-Clark gives his impressions of the estate in these terms:

> Some houses were boarded up, some gardens were a tangled mess of grass and weeds, often featuring rusty bits of car engine mounted on breeze blocks. Like the occasional battered caravan that blossomed in some garden, they were dreams of escape – hopeless male fantasies doomed to remain for ever in a state of incompletion.[3]

The strong contrast between the sense of time embodied in Andrea Dunbar's plays and Clio Barnard's *The Arbor* is partly due to the backward look, across two decades, that gives the film a sense of the past. The intense impact of a cancelled future is fundamental to Dunbar's depiction of her environment. Writing for the stage, she found a voice that exists intractably in the present tense, without any exterior perspective. Her characters are trapped in their immediate surroundings and the violent emotions swirling around and between them have no temporal dimension beyond the immediate present. Sex for Rita and Sue is a way of filling this vacuum that Dunbar's witty dialogue fills further as she details the intricacies of the two girls' negotiation of intercourse with Bob in the confines of his car. Sex fills up time and extends the moment of now; and the resulting emotions, anger and recrimination, become the stuff of everyday life and a means of interpersonal communication.

It is particularly this unrelenting emphasis on the immediacy of the word as spoken, as inevitably enacted in the 'now', that gives Dunbar's plays the effect of a verbal photograph. Her characters and their situation embody a material deprivation that brings with it the deprivation of any sense of either past history or future possibility. Dunbar produces this effect not only through her skill at writing and her gift for words, but through carefully structured events, overshadowed by essentially doomed emotional relationships. Furthermore, the desperate, angry 'speech' of those subordinated to fate in the guise of capitalism stands in direct opposition to the transcendent 'language' of power (and the Symbolic Order). In a sense, Dunbar's characters' words have only the inarticulate significances of gesture.

The portrait that *The Arbor* builds of Andrea shows her, herself, trapped in a present, without a sense of a future, although she was able to capture that loss of temporality so clearly in her writing. Her relations with her children lack the usual maternal investment in their futures and her decline into alcoholism seems symptomatic of a refusal to 'escape' her fate, even when her plays offered her a way out. On one level, the complex depiction of time that lies at the heart of *The Arbor*, its form and its filmic structure, responds to Andrea's situation; it finds a future for her in which her difficult relationships can be retold. But on a more theoretical level, Barnard has used cinema's temporal complexity to fragment the time of narrative into multiple strands that bring past and present into a dialogue that will reverberate into the future. Although not strictly a compilation film, *The Arbor* reworks footage of the past into its reconfigured form. Film of Andrea, taken from television documentaries made at the height of her celebrity in the 1980s, inserts her in her own time and space, showing her as she gets the train to London with Lorraine or walks around the Estate with Lorraine in a pushchair.

The lip-syncing adds a particular temporal complexity to the film. Although the lip-sync is by and large accurate, there is a slightly uncanny dislocation between the performers and the voices of the original interviewees, materialized in a kind of bodily palimpsest: the actor's performing, filmed body overlays the real person whose voice remains a present trace of the past recording. A disembodied voice emanates from the photographed body, redoubling the inherent ghostliness of the photographic image. The ghostliness of the recorded voice, usually naturalized in film by its perfect alignment with the body, can be easily overlooked. Simon Reynolds points out: 'Recording has always had a spectral undercurrent.' He goes on to cite Barthes description of the photograph as 'ectoplasm of the "what has been"', to add: 'Like a spectre a recorded musician is at once present and absent.'[4] Creating two incompatible emanations of an inscribed reality, *The Arbor* harnesses the denaturalization of the body/voice relationship, pushing the uncanny towards the spectral.

On yet another level, extracts of Dunbar's *The Arbor* are staged at the edge of the 'green' for Barnard's *The Arbor*. Local residents gather round to witness a re-enactment of the Dunbars' tempestuous family life, bringing back scenes from several decades ago into the now of their everyday lives. This fragmentation of time then allows the layers to be interwoven into a different pattern, also interweaving performance and reality, as characters are also fragmented across media. For instance, Cecília Mello, in her fascinating essay on Barnard's film, points out that Andrea's brother David is personified in three forms during the performance of the play: first, his actual and previously recorded comments that are then lip-synced by the actor playing 'David' in the film, who watches another actor perform the young 'David' in the play. Her argument adds the film's use of different media to its layering of time, as

> it gently interweaves the different inter-medial strands as though in a mosaic. Hence the impossibility of solving this film's paradox by either saying that it introduces fictional elements into a documentary or that it brings the 'document' (such as interviews, letters and television/film footage) into

Manjinder Virk and Christine Bottomley lip-sync the voices of Lorraine and Lisa Dunbar.

fiction. The vague impression one has when confronted with its heterogeneous structure is that *The Arbor* cannot be defined in or against these terms. Documentary is no longer the opposite of fiction, and fiction no longer the opposite of documentary, just as cinema is neither the same nor the opposite of other media.[5]

The Arbor, in a sense, has no categorizable body and this formal insubstantiality underpins its aesthetic refusal to clearly identify a stable relationship between the past and how it is narrated. In the first instance, the ghostliness of the lip-sync device is augmented by the ghostly presence of Andrea herself, in the footage of her with the infant Lorraine. The apparent closeness between the two is rendered almost unbearably poignant in light of both of their future lives. As Andrea carries Lorraine onto the train to London, the scene enacts a 'before', a pre-conscious moment haunted by hindsight of what is to come. The sense of haunting is then carried into Lorraine's unforgiving relationship with her mother, who is kept alive, as it were, by

Andrea Dunbar's *The Arbor* (1980) performed for Clio Barnard's *The Arbor* (2010).

her daughter's anger, further accentuated by certain parallels between the two. Lorraine too had become pregnant as a teenager, suffered from violent partners, lived in a Women's Refuge, and rather than alcoholism she had descended into the more destructive heroin addiction and the prostitution that maintained it. But many women in that community suffered this kind of fate. Lorraine also, and more to the point, inherited her mother's ability to articulate and analyse the most difficult aspects of her life. As Clio Barnard puts it: 'Both Andrea and Lorraine have a gift with words in that they are both very direct, straightforward communicators.'[6] But their relationship is overshadowed by Andrea's implicit racism, epitomized by her remark,

overheard by Lorraine, that she would rather have had an abortion than a multiracial child. This is the bitterness that Lorraine is unable to lay to rest; in the film's first words, she says: 'Can I forgive her? No.' This Andrea, embodied in Lorraine's emotion, haunts the film. Furthermore, Andrea's second daughter, Lisa, is more understanding and her memories of and reflections on her mother's life create a direct contrast to those of Lorraine.

When Barnard first met Lorraine, she was in prison serving a sentence for manslaughter after her two-year-old son, Harris, had swallowed her methadone and died. Barnard has described her hope that the film, although painful for the family, would work therapeutically in the retelling of these stories. She said of her final interview with Lorraine: 'she began to accept that Andrea did love her, was able to stop blaming her and she was able to find it in herself to empathise with her mother.' She continues:

> I hope that the film allows people to grieve for the loss of Andrea at such a tragically young age, for the loss of Lorraine to heroin addiction, and to grieve for the loss of Andrea's grandson, Harris, and to empathise with the Dunbar family. Why make private grief public? Because I think we all have a collective responsibility for Harris and all children in his circumstances.[7]

Although the first part of *The Arbor* is more about Andrea and the second part is more about Lorraine, the lives of mother and daughter are interwoven across the whole. Aesthetically and theoretically, of course, this structure is essential to the film's rejection of chronological time. But it also opens up a space, located only in and through the film itself, for the two to communicate. One scene, for instance, brings the two together through a montage across time and space: as Lorraine in *The Arbor* reads on stage the final words spoken by Lorraine in *A State Affair*, Barnard cuts away to archive footage of Andrea, smoking and listening, as it were, in the audience. In this opening up to a possible reconfiguration of memory and its narratives *The Arbor* evokes Freud's concept of *Nachträglichkeit,* translated into English as 'deferred action' or 'afterwardness'. Jean Laplanche and Jean-Bertrand Pontalis give this definition of Freud's term:

> experiences, impressions and memory traces may be revised at a later date to fit in with fresh experiences or with the attainment of a new stage of development. They may in that event be endowed not only with a new meaning but also with psychical effectiveness.[8]

They go on to point out that the possibility of revision specifically counters the concept of psychoanalysis that reduces 'the subject's history to a linear determinism envisaging nothing but the action of the past upon the present'. They also quote Freud's letter to Wilhelm Fliess of 1896:

> I am working on the assumption that our psychical mechanism has come into being by a process of stratification: the material present in the form of memory traces being subjected from time to time to a *rearrangement* in accordance with fresh circumstances – to a *re-transcription*.[9]

Laplanche and Pontalis add that it is not lived experience that undergoes revision but memory traces that are a residue of trauma, the legacy of material that surpassed the subject's understanding at the time of the original event. *The Arbor* enacts the process of *re-transcribing* traumatic memory. Through its temporal organization, the film precisely inscribes a rejection of linear determinism appropriate for the story of a young woman whose experience resists incorporation into a meaningful context.

Laplanche later expanded his thoughts on *Nachträglichkeit* with a new translation of the word as 'afterwardsness'. He argues that hidden in these kinds of memory traces is 'a message from the other':

> Even if we concentrate all our attention on the retroactive temporal direction, in the sense that someone reinterprets their past, this past cannot be a purely factual one, an unprocessed or raw given. It is impossible therefore to put forward a purely hermeneutic position on this – that is to say, that everyone interprets their past according to their present – because the past already has something deposited within it that demands to be deciphered, which is the message of the other person.[10]

Andrea's gradual breakdown and her disappearance from Lorraine's life represents 'something deposited within it that demands to be deciphered'. *The Arbor* returns at the end to the footage of Andrea and one-year-old Lorraine boarding the train to London. As Andrea cuddles her child affectionately and talks proudly about Lorraine's good qualities, the material nature of film seems to merge with the psychoanalytic message. The film records a 'real event' that is preserved across time to be returned to its history reconfigured and re-transcribed. But the process stops short of a coherent narrative, and reaches out, by analogy, to a feminist concept of history and psychoanalysis, as though these two disciplines might enable the political task of decipherment demanded by the 'message'. In the last resort, *The Arbor* insists on moving beyond the immediate personal relation, to insist that the audience hear the ghostly voices from post-industrial ruins that are struggling to address the future. The film ends, immediately after the shot of Andrea and Lorraine in the 1980s, with a long tracking shot along Brafferton Arbor. In the distance, a group of boys are playing football. Clio Barnard says:

> There is a need to engage emotionally with the fallout of depravation, marginalisation and neglect in the UK today . . . The recent return to right wing politics is scary. We live in a time when the gap between wealth and poverty has increased. This inequality leads to social dysfunction, the neglect of communities and the neglect of individuals. This is an important time to reflect on the complexity of circumstances that lead to neglect and abuse and our collective responsibility towards the most vulnerable in our society.[11]

Andrea and Lorraine: before the future.

PART THREE:
BETWEEN PAST AND PRESENT

INTRODUCTION: ART AND MOVING IMAGES — TRANSITIONAL SPACES OF SPECTATORSHIP

At first glance the selection of artists discussed in this section might seem arbitrary. And I did, indeed, write about each in disparate circumstances and for different reasons. However, as I brought the essays together, I noticed that certain themes link some artists and then further themes suggest other links and create varying patterns of interconnection across the section. Two initial points caught my interest. First of all, going back in time, all four artists share a common grounding in the radical aesthetics that developed particularly around both conceptualism and film theory in the 1970s. But over the intervening years, as digital technology transformed exhibition conditions, as galleries and museums opened up to moving-image art, the relevance of film and film theory seems, on the face of it, to have fallen by the wayside. So second, I would like to use this particular conjuncture of artists to speculate about different ways in which old questions about radical aesthetics might have persisted into this new environment. It is, of course, a given that memories of my own intellectual and aesthetic origins and allegiances, rooted as they are in the 1970s, have inflected my interest.

Although a juxtaposition between Mary Kelly and Morgan Fisher would not necessarily have occurred to me outside the context of this book, thinking about their early work in conjunction suggested unexpected crossovers. First of all, within their historical context, both were influenced by 1960s conceptualism; second, both took on, as radical art projects, two ideological institutions whose power crucially depended on the very invisibility of their workings: for Kelly, the place of the mother under patriarchy; for Fisher, the place of cinema within Hollywood. I was struck by the way that these two very diverse projects both address their objects (maternity, cinema) through rigorously devised aesthetic strategies out of which a dialogue between an idea and its mode of signification emerges.

Kelly has acknowledged the influence of conceptualism, especially as a radical presence in the UK when she first arrived in 1968. Feminists working out of the Women's Liberation Movement had their own political rationale for rejecting all traditional forms of art and associated ideas and Kelly always describes herself as an artist whose work is informed by feminism. She has, however, mentioned that: 'It seems significant to me now that I used a strategy similar to theirs [conceptualists] but tried to turn it around so that it didn't refer specifically to the institution of art but to elsewhere.'[1] The 'elsewhere', for Kelly, was the institution of patriarchy. She has summed up the project of *Post-Partum Document* (1973–9) as describing 'the subjective moment of the mother–child relationship. An analysis of this relationship is crucial to an understanding of the way in which ideology functions in/by their material practices of childbirth and child care.'[2] While the work drew on her own experience of motherhood, its analytic structure and theoretical frame of reference reduces the autobiographical to a minimum, also subsuming the presence of the artist into the rigorous application of process and procedure.

Sabine Folie has described the relation of Fisher's films to the Hollywood system:

to reveal how profane and yet complex the things really are on which our perceptions are based, and which manipulations are required to produce such a thing as a Hollywood movie:

a gigantic apparatus, endless amounts of footage that need
to be cut and montaged in order to create the illusionism
of a linear story that is nonetheless an artefact through
and through, the product of a deception that, as Morgan
Fisher admits, we all like to submit to.[3]

There is a sense in which the body of Fisher's 16mm films could be
understood as, if not sections of a single work, a project unified by
an analysis of those aspects of the Hollywood production process that
remain invisible. As Christophe Gallois puts it: '[The films] address
cinema from the angle of its devices, technicians, conventions and
standards – all the elements surrounding film yet excluded from our
usual viewing experience.'[4]

Although for counter-cinema of the 1960s–1970s, strategies for
making visible the invisible were aesthetically and conceptually central,
and Bertolt Brecht was a significant rediscovered influence, there was
something different about Fisher's films. His habitual Hollywood
cinephilia, his location in Los Angeles and his occasional work in the
film industry gave him a kind of closeness to and engagement with the
object of his critique. But even so, pre-figured procedures minimalized
the artist's personal involvement with the work, in spite of his occasional
presence on film and on the soundtrack, most particularly in *Standard
Gauge* (1984).

As both movements, feminist and conceptual, rejected the traditional
concept of artistic creative autonomy and as the parameters and
possibility of the artwork were stripped to zero, there is an interesting
parallel between Kelly and Fisher's methodological practice. Both artists
were gleaners, gathering into their work, in the first instance, found
objects taken from their relevant emotional and intellectual frames
of reference. Kelly's psychoanalytic investigation of the mother–child
relationship was built out of actual objects, indexical residues left by
the everyday process of maternal care. For his material investigation of
the cinema, Fisher frequently re-used found film footage, the discarded

residues of Hollywood productions on which he might, or might not, have been working.

Mark Lewis and Isaac Julien would both have been at art school in the late 1970s and early 1980s and thus the first generation to absorb as students the mix of feminist, Marxist and post-colonial theory with the radical, political aesthetic of the contemporary avant-garde. Although both artists now work in gallery spaces, traces of the cinematic past persist in their work: 'cinema' continues to be a point of reference and framework for thought right into the 'post-cinematic' recent present. Francesco Casetti has argued, in his fascinating book *The Lumière Galaxy* (2015), that a mix of past and present characterizes this particular technological moment in time at which the cinema stands 'suspended between no-longer-being and trying-to-be-something-else'.

> The cinematic dispositive no longer appears to be a predetermined, closed, and binding structure, but rather an open and flexible set of elements; it is no longer an *apparatus*, but rather an *assemblage*. And it is not the 'machine' that determines the cinematic experience; rather, it is the cinematic experience that finds – or even configures – the 'machine.'[5]

As the cinematic experience bridges the pre- and post-digital, Casetti sees the present as intermediate and threshold-like: the cinema, even in its transformed environment, is remembered and still embedded in cultural consciousness. He points out that this moment is unlikely to last, as younger and younger generations grow up with fainter memories and a more tenuous experience of cinema as it was. Both Julien and Lewis's moving-image work can be imagined within a framework in which the cinephilia of archaic cinema still impacts within digital work and the modes of aesthetic thought digital technology produces.

In my essay on *Ten Thousand Waves,* I discuss the importance of citation and quotation of film for Julien, which stretches back into his earlier work. But his elegant use of *mise en scène* and the drama of his landscapes constantly evoke the cinema as spectacle, the power of its compositions, its use of colour, lighting, framing and so on. Lewis has often used formal, pre-determined filmic procedures that expose and celebrate the limits and possibilities of the cinematic apparatus. While the mechanics of the production of the film image (that had also been important to Fisher) are exposed, Lewis brings a kind of elegiac celebration to the spirit of Brecht. Although he has made many, and different, kinds of films, these experiments pre-figure his later work with rear projection, once again an exploration of the cinema and its apparatus.

But there are two sides to the 'reminiscences' of cinema. Film memories may be incorporated visually and pictorially into the work itself. But there are also questions about exhibition and mode of address, which replay and reference theories of spectatorship. To go back to the 1970s: there was a sense then in which cinema came to be understood to be more than itself in the pages of *Screen* and in debates around independent cinema in the UK. In arguments that were first formulated in France but rapidly translated into English, the conventions surrounding film's fusion of vision and narration combined to subordinate the spectator to dominant ideology, complicit in assuring the identity of the bourgeois male subject. The position has been succinctly summed up by Jacques Aumont:

> the dominant form of cinema is driven by a wish for continuity and centering; both these characteristics are seen as constitutive of the subject; and the ideological function of the cinema con-sists mainly of constituting the individual as subject by placing him or her imaginarily in a central position. The apparatus plays an essential role in all this. It is that which, although invisible, enables us to see.[6]

Political cinema would, in response, aspire to disrupt the continuum of narrative point-of-view and decentre its accompanying gaze, and thus generate an alternative, active, deciphering spectator. Aumont notes in passing and laments that, by the time of writing in the late 1980s, these theoretical debates were being left behind and losing their currency.

The original theoretical discourse might seem creaky and archaic today, somewhat similar perhaps to the cinema machine itself, but the issues raised by the theoretical avant-garde of the past resonate with today's moving-image exhibition in the gallery. Casetti points out that the new, open, concept of 'cinema' has brought back to contemporary memory the medium's actual, historic disunity and heterogeneity, its multiple genealogies and variable structures. And he pauses on the experiments on the 1960s that challenged the coherence of film, breaking out into multiple film forms and formats. In keeping with my argument here, he makes a forceful contrast between the avant-garde and the more playful approach of today's bricoleurs: 'They [the avant-garde] functioned in a strongly critical dimension and were well aware that the subject was inscribed into the dispositive.'[7]

To recapitulate: 1970s theory and its political avant-garde focused critique most particularly on a centred point of view and the narrative continuum of conventional cinema. Although both Lewis and Julien have moved beyond the visual austerity and minimalism that character-ized the 1970s, the structural strategies of their installations find ways of disrupting and disturbing easy spectatorship. As Julien's work has spread across multiple screens, he has explicitly commented that his intention is to put traditional viewing habits into question:

What I call parallel montage relates to the choreography of the gaze. There's a question of performance in the work but it doesn't end there, it's also the way the screens are articulated architecturally and how people are relating to them in the space. Some people come in and just sit down – maybe they're tired. But let's say that when we're looking at moving images we fall into certain habits and I'm trying to break those habits in a gallery context.[8]

Echoing the 1970s rejection of linear narrative patterns, the spectator has to decipher the work and accept both the lack of a commanding point-of-view and the necessity of observing the screens in different configurations and successions. And just as Casetti refers back to experimental film beyond the single screen in the 1960s, so Julien remembers the 'expanded cinema' of the 1980s that flowed into the later post-digital gallery installations: 'both kinds of work questioned the whole traditional idea of viewing cinema.'[9] The spectator's thought must reconfigure and rethink time in a process further complicated by the different temporal layers within the piece itself as Julien's work constantly refers back to the past: stories of migrations across history interweave with stories of exemplary black travellers.

From quite early on Mark Lewis's films have featured complex camera movements, very often as cinematic portraits of a particular place or space, in which the camera's trajectory traces a topographical or architectural relation with the site. But from about 2011, about the time of *Black Mirror*, *National Gallery* and *Beirut*, his camera took on a greater autonomy. Lewis's camera had always been detached from point of view. But in these later works its presence begins to overwhelm the buildings, architecture and city sites filmed, as in his city films shot in Toronto and São Paulo in 2014, veering off into complex and uncompromising visual figurations. For Lewis, this camera is descended from Dziga Vertov's *Man with a Movie Camera* (1929), in which the camera eye is essentially embodied and mechanical, intrinsically differing from and superior to the human eye. Freed from a spectator's narrative point of view and perspectival orientated space, in Lewis's later city films the camera emerges as a visual force that is less and less subordinated to what is filmed, more and more detached from gravity and architectural proportion. In terms of the theoretical debates of the 1970s, in which Vertov, of course, had a privileged place, this cinema replaces address to the human subject with an uncanny and defamiliarized spectator experience. Elie During has pointed out:

However, in this case, what announces the mute presence of a world before or after mankind is perhaps above all a new model of the cinematographic subject itself: a subject without a point of view, casting upon the world a floating gaze, literally without perspective . . . unless rather it unfolds all perspectives at once to lay them out before our eyes, transparently stacked upon each other as in an isometric drawing. A vision without a point of view, a survey without distance.[10]

Lewis's constant return to the idea of a 'promise of modernity that never happened' materializes in the urban projects of the 1950s and '60s that he films and in the camera's mechanical way of experiencing the world.

I have argued that there is a theoretical dimension to Julien and Lewis's installation pieces, which disrupts habits of spectatorship and undermines expectations of point of view. Very relevant here are Viktor Shklovsky's influential thoughts on habit, with which I ended my essay on Lewis's rear projection work. Habit might, perhaps, be imagined as the glue that holds convention and normal ways of seeing in place; art, Shklovsky suggests, should work as a 'defamiliarising' or 'estrangement' process: 'The technique of art is to make objects "unfamiliar", to make forms difficult, to increase the difficulty and length of perception because the process of perception is an aesthetic end in itself and must be prolonged.'[11]

A final note on developments within Mary Kelly and Morgan Fisher's work. Fisher stopped making films in 1986, with *Standard Gauge*, and has since only made the film *()* (2003). In the 1990s he turned to painting and sculpture and his work is now widely exhibited in galleries and museums. In the new gallery context, his 16mm films remain intact and are projected in suitably designed spaces. Theoretical and material reflections on the history of cinema continue to preoccupy his work, not through moving images but through art installations. For instance, he has used a set of nine mirrors to 'mirror' the range of aspect ratios used across the history of cinema. Even in the context of a double painting, he continues to make spectatorship 'difficult'. Sabine Folie points out:

> The Pendant Pair Paintings are mounted not side by side but facing each other, so that they can be experienced only in sequence – diachronically, with a temporal gap intervening. The beholders, in other words, are not seated in a movie theater, watching the moving picture; they must move through the room in order to perceive the pictures in sequence – even more, they must perform a rotation.[12]

At first glance, there is a paradoxical sense in which the very juxtaposition of projected film to paintings and other works draws attention to its archaic status: dignity is lost with the loss of the specificity of cinema. However, on second thoughts, the projector and film exemplify Walter Benjamin's concept of the 'outmoded' and a return of the archaic to a new kind of cultural context and value. The projector, once either invisible or intrusive, has found new presence beyond its original use value, now even an object of curiosity for those who have grown up since the death of cinema. Not all Fisher's current work is related to film. Yet here, too, there is a bridge between the past of celluloid and its displacement, not onto the digital, but into a variety of different framed forms and sculptural structures, still in dialogue with material and conceptual aspects of cinema.

In her installation *Love Songs* (2006), Mary Kelly too takes up the question of dislocation and continuum between past and present. For Kelly, her intellectual and political origins in feminism had always been inseparable from the continuum of her life and work. But during the 1990s, seeing through the eyes of a younger generation, she realized that feminism as represented by the Women's Liberation Movement of the 1970s now belonged to history, to the past of an older generation. *Love Songs* configures these imaginary and symbolic concepts of time using the immaterial material of light as its key medium. Rosalyn Deutsche evokes the exhibition as a whole as 'a theater of not-forgetting' and, specifically about the installation *WLM Demo Remix*, she continues:

> *WLM Demo Remix* portrays a trans-generational haunting.
> A legacy of an earlier generation of feminists appears to a new
> generation. Likewise, the women in the later image inhabit
> those in the earlier one. Using a slow dissolve to combine past
> and present images, a technique that imitates the scene of the
> unconscious mind, the loop begins with the later image – the
> photo of the restaging – which gradually fades and disappears
> as the earlier image emerges and grows clearer.[13]

I began by pointing out that the four artists discussed here in Part Three all have roots in the ideas and aesthetic debates around radical film and art in the 1970s. In their late works the question of time recurs, albeit in very different ways, revisiting various formative cultural or political conjunctures, as though looking back at a primal scene. Morgan Fisher's recent exhibitions have incorporated 16mm film, the medium through which he originally reflected on the cinema more generally. Mark Lewis's city films and installations conjure up modernity's promise to reconfigure society, now only a memory metaphorically represented in modernist architecture and city planning. Isaac Julien has returned repeatedly to stories of migration, from Franz Fanon to Morecombe Bay, with his own family's journey always in the background. In *Love Songs*, Mary Kelly reconfigures her own formative moment in the Women's Liberation Movement into a dialogue with feminists today. Addressing the passing of time and raising the issue of artists' responsibility towards history's closures, these works all reanimate something from the past, very nearly under erasure, that has made a crucial contribution to the legacy of modernity.

MORGAN FISHER: FILMS ON PROJECTION AND THE PROJECTOR

The act of making a film, of physically assembling the film strip, feels somewhat like making an object: that film artists have seized on the materiality of film is of inestimable importance, and film certainly invites examination at this level. But at the instant the film is completed, the 'object' vanishes. The film strip is an elegant device for modulating standard beams of energy. The phantom work itself transpires on the screen as its notation is expended by a mechanical virtuoso performer, the projector.[1]

Between 1968 and 1974 Morgan Fisher made eight films that reflect in different ways on the production of the film image. The films, all 16mm, belong to the conceptual or minimalist avant-garde of the time but, as a Los Angeles-based film-maker, Fisher also worked on the edge of Hollywood, editing for Roger Corman's New World Pictures and filming stock footage for Haskell Wexler. His industry experience occasionally found its way into his experimental films as, for instance, the incorporation of discarded 35mm rushes into his 16mm work *Standard Gauge* (1984). Furthermore, unusually for an American avant-garde artist, he avidly consumed Hollywood movies; as evoked by Stuart Comer: '[Fisher delighted] in downtown Los Angeles[,] devouring triple bills of Budd Boetticher, Robert Aldrich and Sam Fuller films for 50 cents a pop.'[2] If Hollywood offers a proto-cinematic framework for Fisher's films, their post-cinematic framework came to be the art gallery and the museum. From the early 1990s, Fisher turned to painting, object construction, and a final (at least at the current time of writing) film, *()*, made in 2003; he has had retrospectives at the Whitney Museum of American Art (in 2005) and the Museum of Contemporary Art, Los Angeles (2006, both curated by Chrissie Iles, and many other significant solo shows such as 'Morgan Fisher: The Frame and Beyond' (curated by Sabine Folie and Ilse Lafer) at the Generali Foundation, Vienna, in 2012 and 'Morgan Fisher: Films and Painting and In Between and Nearby', curated by Alex Sainsbury, at Raven Row, London, in 2011.

When I was invited by Christa Blümlinger and Jean-Philippe Antoine to participate in the symposium 'Morgan Fisher: un cinéma hors-champ?' at the Université Paris 8 Vincennes Saint-Denis in April 2012 I decided to concentrate on the place of projection and the projector in Fisher's work. Not only has the projector always been the most repressed of industrial cinema's machines, but it was also neglected by the avant-garde discourse of self-reflexivity. Now, in the digital era, invisibility has been overtaken by disappearance and the projector gains poignancy as its use fades into history.

The projector, seen up close, is a clunky, awkward and noisy piece of machinery, diametrically unlike the 'phantom' screen image, the immaterial and glamorous illusion that its beam of light creates. But the projection mechanism is the true source of the cinema's magic: it turns the reels of film and throws their images onto the screen, tricking the human eye into creating the illusion of movement as the series of individual frames are transformed into a stable and continuous flow. These two distinct effects have always been the source of the cinema's primal mystery so that all subsequent sources of fascination, from stars to suspense, have depended on the correct functioning of the projector. It is here that the paradox of projection lies: the cinema's most repressed mechanism is also the site of the manipulation of human perception that makes those marvellous effects come into being. The Maltese cross is the device that pauses the filmstrip in the gate. Turning continuous movement into intermittent movement, it ensures that the spectator's eye fails to see the individual frames as they move and halt at the correct speed, whether 16 or 24 frames per second. The phi phenomenon describes the basic perceptual mechanism of the illusion of movement, enabling the still frames of the filmstrip to appear as moving images on the screen.

To capture the illusion of movement, the cinema's pioneers drew on the long history of the various 'philosophical toys' that had emerged over the course of the eighteenth and nineteenth centuries. In this sense, if the screen and the viewing space of the cinema lead back to the camera obscura, the projector's manipulation of perception is derived from those biological and fantastical experiments. I have referred to these processes as 'mysterious' and 'magical' not only because the actual biological processes involved are complicated and not consciously considered by most film spectators, but because the history of film theory has been haunted by varied explanations for the perception of the illusion movement such as the persistence of vision (an afterimage retained by the eye after the object has disappeared from sight), once a quite generally accepted theory but now apparently discredited.

Although there are, of course, mechanical similarities between the camera and the projector (the Lumière brothers' invention could function as both), the temporalities involved in making a film and its projection are obviously very different. Film as recorded material is, in the first instance, singular: the camera records its images once (however many takes a shot might demand), and, out of the editing process, an 'object' (as Hollis Frampton puts it), a final and defined 'film', emerges. Reproduced from a unique negative into many positives, film exhibition then becomes multiple and repeatable, ranging from the massively popular hit to the exclusively elite, but inevitably depending on the standardization of both mechanism and practice of projection.

Morgan Fisher made three films around projection: *The Screening Room* (1968), *Phi Phenomenon* (1968) and *Projection Instructions* (1976). *Projection Instructions* carves out the possibility of the 'once-off', both in the performance of projection and the variability of the image shown, insisting that, unlike most other objects that are mechanically reproduced, the film image projected is contingent, not given, and that the projector as 'virtuoso performer' can modulate its sounds and images. While the performance goes against the grain of the standardization on which cinema depends, it brings the projection mechanism into visibility, along the lines that avant-garde and radical film practices have given to other aspects of the apparatus.

It was in an interview with Scott MacDonald, film critic and chronicler of the avant-garde, that Fisher pointed out the projector's neglect within the avant-garde tradition of self-reflexivity. When questioned about *Projection Instructions*, he replied:

> the projector has remained enshrined as an objective, almost scientific, instrument. Normal projection is a hidden assumption even in the few examples of avant-garde work that have taken projection as a subject, where, for example, the projector serves as a device that extrudes light or inflects the space through which the beam passes before it strikes the screen. Even then, the projector's autonomy as a mechanism that functions of itself remains inviolable. There's obviously nothing wrong with conventional projection, but I still find it strange that work of every kind, including advanced work, relies on correct projection. I wanted to see what could be done by bringing that standard into question: there is no correct way to show *Projection Instructions*. It is, so to speak, an objective film, one that gives the projectionist a chance to be an interpretive artist.[3]

In contrast to the normal exercises needed to establish that the projector is working correctly, Fisher gives his 'instructions' as a score that the projectionist can play as he or she chooses, allowing a personal interpretation and adjustment of focus or sound level and so on,

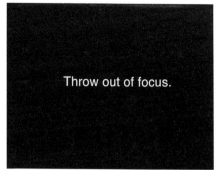

Projection Instructions (1976).

countering the way that the projectionist is 'tyrannized by the film's ...
demands'.[4] Projection can thus be reconfigured as a performance with a
potential for deviance from the norm. As Scott MacDonald points out,
a film, whether fictional, factual or experimental, absorbs its spectators
into the world of the screen, so that any abnormality in projection is
automatically perceived as a breakdown, as a disturbance: the illusion
begins to falter, the narrative time and the credible space that the film
has carefully created is jolted into the here and now of the theatre.

While *Projection Instructions* draws attention to the work of the
projectionist, Fisher's earlier *Screening Room* draws attention to its site:
the cinema. In a deviation that (once again) defies the normal practices
of film exhibition, Fisher created *Screening Room* as a piece that could
only work at a specific cinema and that would need to be remade for
subsequent screenings. He describes his film as a 'site-specific work'.
In its first stage, the camera has filmed, with a tracking, point-of-view
shot, its own entrance into the interior of a cinema; once inside, it halts
and, with a zoom on the screen, finds the flickering light of the projector's beam. This 'one-off' encounter between camera, cinema space,
screen and projector later becomes a film, projected for an audience
in the very location of its filming. Although *Screening Room* may, of
course, be shown repeatedly, it is only 'here' that it can fulfil its aesthetic
and theoretical purpose. This 'one-off' or 'here' conjures up, in reverse,

the fact that cinema was born to travel and that, transcending the (site-) specifics of culture or geography, it could aspire to address the world precisely due to the standardization of projection. Furthermore, *Screening Room* tells a story in its own right as it recounts the process of 'handing over' from one piece of cinematic apparatus to another. At a certain point, the camera's part in the film process is over, its recording function relegated to its own private, now past, moment. The process of projection gives film an infinite future and public presence, repeatedly and collectively. (In an interesting cinematic gesture, *Screening Room*'s key 'baton exchange' from camera to projector is done via a zoom: out from the camera and into the screen.) Morgan Fisher has said:

> The film brings you to where you are sitting watching it . . . A good narrative film – and I love good narrative films – makes you forget the world outside that of the film, it makes you forget about the space you are sitting in, that you even have a body. Although the film is not reflexive about production, as many of my other films are, by making you aware of these things it is reflexive about the circumstances in which you view it. The film uses illusion to bring you to the space where you are sitting, a situation about which you can have no illusions.[5]

A film's performance is, obviously and essentially, repeatable; it usually takes place at the regular times given by a cinema's advertisements, or the times announced in newspapers, for example. In this way, the repetition of film projection is integrated into the temporal rhythms of everyday life with their various resonances of, say, a squandered afternoon or a romantic night out. Ultimately, due to repeated screenings and poorly maintained machines down the exhibition hierarchy, the once pristine celluloid receives a further layer of inscription in the form of scratches and dirt that bear witness to the damage caused by projection over the life of a film print. The 'magic' and the 'illusion' of cinema are overlaid by the film's own ageing. Fisher's film installation

Passing Time (1979) is a loop that displays the words 'passing time'. Not only does the spectator experience time passing during the screening, but each projection also leaves various marks on the celluloid, as the print itself is subjected to passing time. Projection gives film material its own historical dimension: the indexical images recorded photographically on celluloid are overlaid by equally indexical marks, dust or scratching that have no representational significance except as traces of the physical movement of the film's images through the machine and, thus, its ageing.

Standard Gauge consists of the discarded bits of 35mm film gleaned by Fisher from Hollywood rubbish bins, and re-filmed in 16mm; the film thus refers in particular, in terms of the production of film images, to laboratory processes.[6] But some of the bits are taken from the heads and tails of the film reel that address only the projectionist and the process of preparing the film for screening. As the bits of film are shot as strips, with their still-frames visible, there is a vivid sense of the contrast between the inert material handled, examined and threaded by the projectionist, and the illusion as it comes to life on the screen. This insistent inertness of *Standard Gauge* leads directly back to Fisher's earlier experiments that specifically explore the process of projection: *240x* (also known as *Maltese Cross*) and *Phi Phenomenon*.

Fisher's film *Phi Phenomenon* consists of a ten-minute (the length of a 16mm roll of film) static shot of an ordinary wall clock with its second hand removed. That is it. In his comments on the film, Scott MacDonald notes:

> Our minute by minute recognition that the hands of the clock have moved is like a slow-motion version of the phi phenomenon mechanism itself. And the fact that the phi phenomenon mechanism remains invisible, even though we know what it is and when we should be able to see it, reminds us that at the heart of the process of film beats a mystery that no one as yet fully understands.[7]

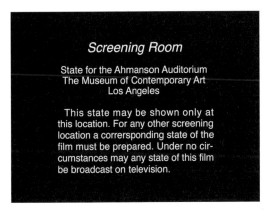

Phi Phenomenon (1968).
Screening Room (1968).

This observation is reminiscent of Jean Epstein's 1946 essay 'The Intelligence of a Machine', in which the author points out that the cinema's fusion of the static and the mobile, the discontinuous and the continuous, seems to fly in the face of nature, 'a transformation as amazing as the generation of life from inanimate things'.[8] This process of transformation is achieved by the projector, its Maltese cross mechanism and its manipulation of the phi phenomenon.

Phi Phenomenon raises a key question for avant-garde film aesthetics: to what extent is a film's self-reflexivity dependent on an actual representation of its process of production in the final work? Most self-reflexive films reference a specific cinematic mechanism and this is indeed the case in those of Fisher's films that 'foreground' the workings of the projector. But *Phi Phenomenon* does not show, or even suggest, the mechanism of projection explicitly (apart, of course, from its title), but rather conjures it up implicitly in the emptiness of space and time as the clock's minute hand completes its given ten-minute journey. The projector comes to figure, not through explicit reference to either its physical presence or its functioning, but implicitly, in and out of the waiting spectator's reverie and reasoning. Scott MacDonald makes the further point that 'Fisher is primarily a conceptual film-maker: the simple straightforward elegance of his films is not an end in itself;

it is a means of generating new forms of film thought'.[9] MacDonald's emphasis on 'film thought' is not only relevant for Fisher's films, but usefully places his work in the historical context of conceptualism and minimalism in the late 1960s and through the 1970s. Once again, however, *Phi Phenomenon* seems to break out of the restrictive boundaries of medium reflexivity and contemporary film artists' concerns with materiality. The passing of time as charted by the clock's face and the duration of time experienced while watching it bring to the surface of the spectator's consciousness questions about time itself. This is, in the first instance, a 'new form of film thought' (that is, how cinema represents time), but it also creates another framework for reflecting on time, beyond and outside film and its apparatus.

There is, in *Phi Phenomenon*'s relation to 'film thought', the intermittent movement of the clock's minute hand that evokes the cinema's fusion of stillness and movement, that is, the frame's staccato halt for 16 or 24 times per second in front of the camera's or projector's gates. For avant-garde film-makers such as Tony Conrad, Paul Sharits and Peter Kubelka, the filmstrip's frames have served as a primary point of aesthetic reference. Their flicker films consist of patterns made by frames of different densities (black-and-white or colour) in a potentially infinite sequence of variations and repetitions. In this context, the smallest units of film (the single frame) appear, unusually, in their own right and form sequential patterns, extendable to the given length of the roll of film or even into infinity. In *Phi Phenomenon*, the intermittent movement of the clock's hand evokes the movement of the filmstrip and its frames, creating a repetitive pattern, varied only by the numbers that mark its progression. But these small intervals of time are part of the film's larger, integral duration, the ten minutes of the 16mm roll of film that Fisher has used as an unbroken 'chunk' of time in so many of his films. Out of awareness of the roll's given and limited time the film gains a necessarily finite nature, enclosed between a beginning and an end, countering the sense of infinite repetition associated with the frames. Simultaneously, this 'chunk' of uninterrupted time is charted precisely on the clock's face, so that the original ten minutes of recording (the moments at which the camera captured the clock's image on celluloid at some point in 1968) is exactly reproduced by the screening time. The spectator's thoughts easily shift back and forth across cinema's double temporality: a return to the 'then' time of the clock and its recording, its past in the presence of the camera, and the 'now' of that same clock in any particular screening, in the presence of the projector. The experience of time as duration, the passing of *that* 'twenty minutes to two to ten minutes to two' in 1968, exaggerates the spectator's sense of time passing for *this* ten minutes, enjoyed or endured as the case may be. *This* particular ten minutes becomes heavy with 'time consciousness'. As Fisher removed the clock's second hand, the passing of the clock's time is (to all intents and purposes) barely visible. As Scott MacDonald points out, the actual movement of the minute hand eludes the spectator: you know it moves, it progresses across the clock face, but the moment of movement seems to be impossible to catch. Thus the minute hand moves imperceptibly in an illusion of movement of its own, fusing with the one, derived from the phi phenomenon, that brings mobility to the sequential still images of the filmstrip.

Within the cultural tradition of the avant-garde, 16mm screenings have often taken place with the projector in the room, so its *brr-brr-brr* noise accompanies the image on the screen like a self-reflexive soundtrack. Thus, in addition to the title *Phi Phenomenon*, the mechanism of projection would, in its original screenings, intrude into the spectator's consciousness alongside questions of perception: that is, how does the film spectator perceive the film image on the screen or observe the mysterious process by which projection enables each biological eye to translate the inert or distorted celluloid material into a correct approximation of human vision (without slippage of frames or an intrusive flicker) and achieve the magical illusion of movement? While *Phi Phenomenon* does, from this perspective, conjure up forms of 'film thought' (to use MacDonald's term), its self-reflexivity is generated not by representations of the cinematic apparatus (as in other films by Fisher and, indeed, by avant-garde film-makers more generally), but via the immediacy of the screening room, the projection and the experience of the film.

Phi Phenomenon also plays on the human mind's propensity to think analogously. For instance, the relation between the clock's face and its concealed clockwork suggests an analogous relation between the screen and the projector. The meaningful image that the spectator looks at is, in both cases, generated by a mechanism hidden at the back, that is, behind the clock's face or in the projection box at the rear of the theatre. If the clock's face on the screen mimics the flatness and meaningfulness of the screen itself, the projector, too, depends on cogs and wheels to turn the film reels, just as clockwork turns a clock's hands. Furthermore, the analogy between the displayed and the concealed also leads on to other questions of value. As Fisher points out so clearly in *Projection Instructions*, the projection process involves a human worker who must, like his or her machine, remain invisible, behind the scenes. In this sense, Fisher's attention to the projectionist resembles his other tributes to the cinema's concealed labour force, most particularly in its industrial, mass-produced form. In *Standard Gauge* he draws attention to the work of the laboratory technicians and those bits of film that address them, such as 'The China Girl', that are associated with these behind-the-scenes processes.

The uninterrupted image of the clock face opens up time and space for other levels of reverie that ultimately drift off beyond 'film thought'. The comparative emptiness of the screen space and the lack of distraction during the film's ten minutes leave the spectator free to wander into his or her own stream of consciousness. As *Phi Phenomenon* foregrounds the contrast between a hidden mechanism and the apparently self-sufficient image generated (the time on the clock face, film images on the screen) it is easy to slip into a more general reverie about the social and political significance of this spatial division: that is, any facade that conceals its own mechanics might come to mind. Fisher has said that 'any single bit of machinery can be made to stand for the entire system of machines and what they are capable of doing.'[10] From this perspective, the mind can move from the clock and projector to further analogies, for instance, to the relation between the industrial machine and the labour force, on the one hand, and the commodity and the consumer on the other. In Marx's theory of commodity fetishism, the commodity proclaims the self-sufficiency of its value and represses the workers' labour that has produced it. Analogously, conventional film projection focuses the spectator's attention on the allure of the screen, repressing the labour of the projectionist and the projector. To counter such an alluring, perfect surface, the avant-garde tradition of self-reflexivity, to which Fisher belongs, makes visible a film's means of production, in a gesture against its pseudo-autonomy. As this argument is both drawn from and extends Marx's concept of commodity fetishism, the spectator's stream of consciousness while watching *Phi Phenomenon* can wander back to the image of the clock itself and wander away to its social and political resonances and connotations. Many historians have drawn attention to the place of clock time in capitalist society, for instance, the regulation of labour time within established hours of work and the equivalent regulation of leisure time. Watching *Phi Phenomenon*, I remembered the image of the clock in King Vidor's *The Crowd* (1928), its hands almost seeming to stop as the clerical workers wait for the precise second of their release at the end of the working day. In a very different line of association, I remembered that the organization of time represented by the clock face, sixty minutes to an hour, is a legacy of Babylonian culture. The implications of this key contribution to world civilization from ancient Iraq would not have had much relevance in 1968, but are unavoidable today.

The division between an alluring surface and the mechanism it conceals, as I have suggested, can be found in certain kinds of structures: projector/screen, clockwork/clock face, labour/commodity. But the division can lead further to mythic stories of the beautiful automaton, such as Olimpia in E.T.A. Hoffmann's 'The Sandman'. Here, too, the unsightly mechanism that creates her lifelike movements is concealed by her beautiful facade. She is emblematic of the human mind's pleasure in artifice as such, or, as Marina Warner puts it, 'the enchanted enigma of appearances'. Out of these, in Laurent Mannoni's term, 'arts of deception', cinema emerges with its mechanism of projection and the phi phenomenon on which it depends.

However wide-ranging the reveries induced by *Phi Phenomenon* might be, the image of the clock, as Thom Andersen points out, ultimately returns the spectator to questions of time:

> In a clock, the salient features of a face are present in mechanical form: a series of intense micro-movements on a receptive immobile surface. It has been 'envisaged' or 'facified' and so it stares at us. *Phi Phenomenon* had a privileged position in early writing on Fisher's films despite its anomalous position because there is so much that can be written on clocks and time, and it opens a space and time in which ideas can arise. By inviting us to watch a mechanical representation of time, time translated into space, it allows us to speculate about time and our experience of it.[11]

As a film that 'projects the projector', it foregrounds to an unusual extent this particular dimension of cinematic time. By and large, cinematic time, like that of the photograph, is located in the past, at the moment its images were captured and then integrated into an overarching discourse (whether fiction or documentary) possessed of its own temporal structure. Film projection, on the other hand, always take place in the present tense of any individual screening experience but, most importantly, it also 'projects' the film into its own future, to those screenings that have always prolonged the life of any film (while taking their toll on its actual material).

Morgan Fisher has pointed out that, in the chronology of the cinematic apparatus, the projector is its final machine, taking a finished film to the public. In 'For a Metahistory of Film', Hollis Frampton refers to film as the 'last machine'. As the mechanical projector is replaced by the digital, this doubled sense of finality has now literally been overtaken by technological change. The projector has no future, along with so many of the machines that stand for the industrial age. The projector, the clumsy and all-too-material machine that produced the phantom image on the screen, is now itself a phantom.

MARK LEWIS: FILMS ON TIME, SPACE AND REAR PROJECTION

Rear projection was a cost-cutting special effect used by Hollywood studios to save on star and location time, later replaced by more reliable video and digital effects. This device, always a bit tawdry, mocked for its clumsy visibility, has been given by the passing of time a kind of archaic, aesthetic preciousness and a retrospective theoretical interest. Mark Lewis has used rear projection in three gallery installations and one film, partly as a homage to an outmoded technology, but more significantly to reflect on its intricate dislocations of screen time and space, that is, on its cinematic attributes. The first was *Rear Projection: Molly Parker* (2004); then *Nathan Phillips Square, A Winter's Night, Skating* (2009, shown in the Canadian Pavilion at the Venice Biennale); and then *The Fight* (2008). Lewis then made the documentary film *Backstory: Hansard Rear Projection,* a tribute to the Hansard family and their rear projection studio, one of the best in Hollywood since the 1930s that was, in 2009, about to close down.

Lewis's interest in an archaic industrial object is in keeping with an accentuated sense of passing time that I mention in the introduction to Part Two of this book. From time to time, acute and perceptible cultural, political or economic change interrupts a smooth sense of historical continuum, separating out one 'era' from another. Recent developments in visual media technology bear witness to this phenomenon as the digital relegates celluloid to an ever more distant past. Nothing divides the history of the cinema into pre- and post-digital so clearly as the world of special effects, as instanced by the total disappearance of rear projection. When the device appears today in an old movie, it conjures up that bygone technological age, pointing to the changing nature of cinema, its roots in the machine age, the twentieth century and the cultures of modernism and modernity.

It was the temporal and spatial discordances inherent to rear projection that first caught Lewis's attention. He wrote, in 2003, 'the two elements march to different beats':

> Back projection, certainly early back projection, brings together so inefficiently two completely different types of film experience that we can hardly not notice their montage effect: we experience the two visual regimes as separate and unwoven, literally as collage. Therefore, that which is designed to make the transition scenes relatively seamless . . . in fact makes transition truly palpable. On the face of it, this is a paradoxical condition, achieved against the putative intentions of the scene itself.[1]

Whether or not the process was 'truly palpable' in its heyday, rear projection was an essential part of the production processes of the Hollywood studio system. The technology had existed for some time, but it was adopted widely in response to problems posed by the arrival of synchronized sound: how to record audible dialogue, on location, while preserving star impact? The process made it possible to split a scene or sequence into two parts, separating location from performers. The narrative setting, shot during pre-production, would be taken to a specialized studio and the 'plate' (as the pre-existing moving footage was known, as opposed to the immobile 'transparency') would then be projected on to a translucent screen. Placed in front of it, the stars, carefully arranged and with limited mobility, could then be conveniently filmed in the studio and their dialogue easily recorded. Thus stars could be shot in close-up, their words clearly audible and their emotions clearly visible, while the appropriate dramatic setting, landscape scenery or urban streets, rolled behind them. In the early days of the talkies, location recording was difficult to nearly impossible and rear projection technology quickly improved with increased demand. Although sound technology improved over the years, as rear projection enabled productions to stay in the studio, its use was irresistibly attractive to the schedule- and budget-conscious front office and also, occasionally, had a certain aesthetic appeal to some directors.

Dominique Païni refers to the introduction of location into the studio as an 'aggregation' of spaces; quite often, however, the aggregation was overtaken by a sense of dislocation. In a further paradox inherent to the rear projection process, as Lewis has pointed out, the location footage sometimes seemed incompatibly 'realistic', as though documentary footage had intruded into wholly staged narrative dramas.

> The juxtaposition can produce a unique and strangely beautiful montage effect. Highly artificial looking, these scenes of studio and location, of fiction and documentary, quickly became the orthodox means by which actors and audiences were both 'taken' into a simulated real while also being distanced from it. An early example of rear projection illustrates this point: *Her Man* (Tay Garnett 1931) shows stars Helen Twelvetrees (Frankie) and Philip Holmes (Danny) in conversation as they are 'driven' in a little carriage through the streets of a Caribbean port such as Havana. Perhaps partly due to its date, the studio and the background are particularly poignantly dislocated: the background has a distinctly documentary feel as the street scenes include an unusual amount of detail.[2]

Many Hollywood directors despised rear projection and film critics and historians have, by and large, followed their lead. But, perhaps once again due to passing time, rear projection's clumsy visibility has recently received some interesting critical attention. In her essay on Edgar G. Ulmer's *Detour* (1945), Vivian Sobchack convincingly demonstrates not only that rear projection made an essential aesthetic contribution to the film but that these processed shorts were characteristic of film noir more generally. She says:

> Not merely a tacky effect of low-budget production, back projection is an aesthetic element that well serves noir's philosophical worldview, transforming it not only into something literal and materially realized but also producing a subtle, yet significant, effect on the viewer's sensual comprehension of cinematic meaning.[3]

It is better known that Alfred Hitchcock returned persistently to plates and transparencies, not only in the railway carriage, a favourite site of drama for Hitchcock from the 1930s (*The Lady Vanishes*, 1938) to the 1950s (*North by Northwest*, 1959), but in many other settings. In fact, Hitchcock's near obsession with this special effect went beyond convenience, and he continued to use the method long after it seemed antiquated to his technicians, not to mention critics and audiences. For instance, when *Marnie* came out in 1964, critics condemned its 'processed shots', most particularly the one in which Marnie is first shown riding her horse. For Hitchcock it was essential to combine close-up with action. In a pre-production meeting he said: 'Now we show her riding . . . and then we go to Closeups which will mean plates and things for her Closeups showing her enjoying it and her hair blowing and it's very important that we establish here one big Closeup of the hair blowing as she's riding.'[4]

The intensity and reality of the previous location scene in which Marnie rides away from the camera mutate into repetitive gesture in the studio as an artificial landscape unwinds behind her. Marnie's screen space has become strange and disorienting, foregrounding emotion over credible action. As Hitchcock no doubt intended, the character's loss of any sense of time and place, transported as she is by the pleasure of riding, is further realized by the discordance of time and place characteristic of rear projection. This dreamlike shot dissolves into the stylized overhead shot of a street in Baltimore, Marnie's childhood home.

In his essay for the exhibition catalogue *Hitchcock and Art: Fatal Coincidences*, Dominique Païni argues that Hitchcock used rear projection for its dreamlike qualities, the uncertainty that double filming brought to the cinema, and ultimately for its modernity. He says the effect 'creates a semblance of reality without erasing the illusory device that goes with it'.[5] In a comment on the dance sequence in Hitchcock's *Saboteur* (1942), a sequence that has had particular influence on Lewis, Païni points out that the different aspects of Hitchcock's use of rear projection come together in the interests of an overarching emotional effect as he

> isolates his dancing couple from the surrounding action and spirits them away from the other characters. This cinematic sleight-of-hand lends the situation an air of enchantment. The scene is a perfect example of the dramatic, poetic and visual power of Hitchcock's transparencies at this point in the 1940s.[6]

This paradoxical, impossible space, detached from either an approximation to reality or the verisimilitude of fiction, allows the audience to see the dream space of the cinema. But rear projection renders the dream uncertain: the image of a cinematic sublime depends on a mechanism that is fascinating because of, not in spite of, its clumsy visibility. Païni describes rear projection's characteristic montage of time and space in terms of strata of scenery, in which nature may become 'portable', and the ultimate space results from an aggregate in which film studio and the actual location sequence, filmed in the 'real world', remain uneasily separate. Elisabeth Bronfen takes the question of uncertainty, unease and instability further, with the extremely interesting suggestion that Hitchcock used rear projection to signify trauma just beyond the reach of film language:

Hitchcock's use of rear projection consistently controls our response to the world on screen by appealing to our willingness not so much to suspend our disbelief as to indulge in an attitude of disavowal: 'I know that this is only a cinematic fiction but all the same I am viscerally involved.' The transparent artificiality produces a mood of instability that draws our attention to something beyond the fictional world fabricated on screen, to a real that remains un-representable yet haunts the film image – be it the personal trauma of the characters or the political trauma of global warfare.[7]

Lewis has argued more generally that this accumulation of dislocations between the studio and the plate points directly to a contradiction at the heart of Hollywood cinema. In principle, rear projection folds one level of time invisibly into another and the figures in the studio foreground fuse with the projected space behind them. But, because of its inherent imperfections, the usually invisible mechanics and processes of film production can disrupt the seamless coherence of the spectacle and even intrude into the spectator's consciousness. As this kind of Brechtian reference to production processes was, with some exceptions, taboo within the strict conventions of Hollywood, for Lewis, rear projection introduced a touch of modernism into this bastion of mass culture. In its very clumsiness, the device embodied this complex contradiction: through rear projection, even if accidentally and unconsciously, the materiality of modernism found a way into the ultimate mass-entertainment industry of modernity.

These kinds of considerations were important as background for Lewis's interest in rear projection, but his actual work with the device, the 'recycling' of the now-archaic rear projection technology, produces another layer of time. His installations are based on citation, a shift in context that resurrects its original, industrial, use while drawing attention to its aesthetic, intrinsically paradoxical qualities. From an initial cinephile interest in rear projection, a mixture of curiosity and

pleasure, Lewis began to search for any still-functioning studios. He found the Hansard Studio in Hollywood that the Hansard family had operated successfully over three generations. It was there (for the sake, in the first instance, of precision and accuracy) that he made the portrait of Molly Parker, *Rear Projection: Molly Parker*. But in 2006 the studio was rapidly going out of business. Lewis, his imagination caught by the family anecdotes and the poignancy of this story of technological decline, returned to Hollywood in 2008 to make a documentary: *Backstory: Hansard Rear Projection*. He was given access to the archive at Paramount Studios, where he selected some plates from

Backstory (2009).

their stock-footage collection and some that had been made for specific productions (the studio not only allowed him to use their plates, but had new prints made for him). He and his cinematographer, Brian Pearson, filmed some more material relevant to the Hansards' story. The surviving father-and-son team, located in front of backdrops typical of the device, tell of the success of their family business until it was overtaken and displaced by electronic (green- and blue-screen) effects and finally computer-generated imagery. Here, in a compressed and poignant form, is a first-hand account of the modern object's trajectory to the 'outmoded' that so fascinated Walter Benjamin. A mechanism, once incorporated into the everyday of its own historical moment, falls into disuse and finally becomes archaic: but recycled obliquely back into history, it can acquire new unexpected interest and aesthetic significance.

The sense of dislocated time produced by a revitalization of the archaic, furthermore, conjures up the dislocation built into the rear projection mechanism itself. The two come together in the opening shot of *Backstory*. Mr Hansard Senior is placed in the studio, the 'star', as it were, of Lewis's film; he performs his usual role of technical expert, aligning the positioning of the plate with the camera and carefully going through the motions of co-ordinating the lighting balance between the screened image (a swimming pool with swimmers and divers) and the studio. He demonstrates the precise technological skill for which the Hansard studio had always been known, but his words and gestures are performative rather than professional, enacted for an artist's documentary rather than for the industry. The present is all-too-vividly superimposed on a lost past. In this sequence, onto the temporal and spatial dislocation of rear projection, the 'now' of the studio superimposed on the 'then' of the plate, the 'then' of the outmoded technology is recorded in the 'now' of the documentary. As these layers fuse into an uneasy but fascinating mismatch within the single screen image, in a projected future, a spectator will impose a final layer of time and space onto those already on the screen, realizing the odd relationship between this outmoded technology and the contemporary artist's work.

In his work on the Molly Parker portrait, Lewis drew on rear projection's 'sanctification' of the star image, but also on a certain kind of Renaissance painting that places its sacred figures, as it were, in close-up, superimposed on a faraway landscape that stretches into the distance. Lewis drew particular attention to this topography in the catalogue for his 2006 exhibition at the FACT Centre, Liverpool, where the *Molly Parker* work was first exhibited. He included particular images in which the foreground, occupied by the central figure, is detached from its background in an arrangement that recalls the aggregated spaces of rear projection: Jan van Eyck's oil painting *The Virgin of Chancellor Rolin* (1435–6), for example, and various portraits by Memling, Velázquez and others. The paintings in which the figure is located in an interior use windows and arches to separate the foreground from the background and suggest rear projection's frames within frames, as in rear projection's motor-car or railway-carriage effect. The paintings in which the figure is in an exterior space have more difficulty with the transition between foreground and background so that the effect is more pronounced and often even more beautiful. In *Rear Projection: Molly Parker* Lewis was referring particularly to the stratification of exterior space, the opposition between the flattened foreground, occupied by the figure in the Renaissance portrait, situated in close-up, and the distant landscape background.

The Hollywood film industry was axiomatically built around stars. The studio space could highlight their beauty, literally enhanced by controlled lighting effects, and their most highly dramatic moments and characteristic poses were exaggerated by the stasis enforced by the technical device. Here again, there is a link to the spatial and conceptual organization of the Renaissance portraits that superimpose highly emblematic figures against natural worlds. Whereas the holy figures (the Virgin, Christ, saints or donors) had to be raised out of ordinary surroundings, brought close to the spectator for reverence, contemplation or supplication, they were also embellished with extraordinary beauty and dramatized by characteristic gestures or poses. Through rear projection, the stars were similarly located in a foreground, flattened plane that enhanced their emblematic qualities against the background. Defined by characteristic attributes, these iconic figures are given a privileged position for the spectator's eroticized gaze, possible edification and even adoration.

Lewis's two main rear projection installations, however, shift the balance between foreground and background, plate and star. In both

Rear Projection: Molly Parker and *Nathan Phillips Square, A Winter's Night, Skating* the plate has an aesthetic importance of its own, accentuating the already given dislocations of time and space. Both the sites have a special and personal significance for Lewis and his memories of his Canadian childhood. In *Molly Parker* the plate had been shot in the Ontario countryside, near Algonquin Park, where Lewis had already shot several films, across two seasons. The scene begins in autumn, with

Rear Projection: Molly Parker (2004).

characteristically lush red and golden colours, then suddenly mutates to the deep snow of a Canadian midwinter. Here, the duality of rear projection, its folding of doubled time and space within a single image, is exaggerated by the background transformation. Molly's dress seems reasonably compatible with the autumn setting but adds to the discordance between studio and plate when the scene turns to winter. In keeping with Lewis's frequent return in earlier (and later) films to abandoned buildings, a disused roadside gas station and café stands in the background, with its sign 'Howlin' Wolf' still prominently displayed. The abandoned buildings carry the idea of the disused and the obsolete across from the technology to the image itself (and vice versa).

Furthermore, Molly is filmed with a complex camera movement that combines a track with a zoom (a 'trombone' effect), further flattening and making strange her figure's relation to the background screen; at the moment when Molly is almost in close-up, the plate shifts

Rear Projection: Molly Parker.

from autumn to winter and the camera repeats the effect in reverse and moves back to its original position. The camera movement adds a further layer to the fusion of temporal and spatial impossibility in the work. As Elie During has pointed out:

> The combined use of an optical tracking shot (zoom in) and a kinetic tracking shot (track out) leads to a variation of the focal length while keeping the framing unchanged. As a result, the

Nathan Phillips Square, A Winter's Night, Skating (2009).

entire space is affected by a strange distortion. The cinematic subject is eclipsed for a moment, since no 'natural' point of view can correspond to an event of this kind. It is as if the form of the shot presented itself in its truth: a pure movement of the mind. The power of fascination of the dolly zoom lies precisely in the fact that it superimposes – in a single gesture – two a priori contradictory movements (advancing and withdrawing, moving closer and moving further away), at the cost of squashing all depth of field.

He continues: 'In all cases, the issue is indeed folding one time onto another, or refolding one time into another, in other words, inscribing simultaneously, within the same image, disjointed temporal perspectives, or distinct temporal orders and timescales.'[8] In its combination of the two effects (rear projection and trombone camera movement) the *Molly Parker* installation disrupts the traditional securities of cinematic visual convention, creating on various levels a modernist sense of distanciation. Rear projection already confounds point of view, denying either protagonist or spectator a coherent relation to the screen space, and concurrently folds 'one time into another'.

While in *Molly* the camera movement is executed in the studio, in *Nathan Phillips Square, A Winter's Night, Skating* the significance of the plate is accentuated by an extremely mobile camera and its relation to the architecture and the setting of the skating rink. In the studio space a young couple skate around each other, apparently intent on flirtation, in a quite residual gesture to the rear projection scene in Hitchcock's *Saboteur* where Robert Cummings and Priscilla Lane fall in love while dancing in front of a rear projection of a formal party. Toronto's Nathan Phillips Square skating rink has a double significance for Lewis, both personal and historical. First of all, he had skated there as a child; but the plaza (opened in 1965) stands for a period of modern architecture to which he frequently returns. In a Canadian context, the architecture represents a moment in the 1950s to '60s in which the country detached itself from a somewhat kitsch Britishness and discovered a national and international modernity. For instance, in addition to other modernist buildings, Lewis has returned in several films to celebrate Mies van der Rohe's 1969 Toronto-Dominion Banking Centre. He refers to the period, perhaps nostalgically, as 'a promise of modernity that never happened'. In this spirit, the camera breaks with gravity and perspective and the great metallic arches spanning the space seem to be invested with their own mobility. This style of filming city and building space is, for Lewis, the essence of the moving image: it was not so much the speed and movement of the early modern city that inspired the invention of cinema, but rather the cinema itself that animated the city and mobilized modernity.

Between *Rear Projection: Molly Parker* and *Nathan Phillips Square, A Winter's Night, Skating*, Lewis filmed his third rear projection installation: *The Fight*. This work is the reverse of the other two, as the focus of its movement and its drama is located in front of the screen, without foregrounding the camera's presence. The scene recreates a fight between a group of French nationals and a group of Roma that Lewis had witnessed in the south of France. He had been struck by the way that the violence and the insults exchanged between the two groups produced a kind of rhythm: physical contact was restricted to certain, quite formal, movements and the bodies of the two sides moved in synchronization, forwards into confrontation and then back to regroup. The scene is filmed in front of a transparency, a static camera projection, and its theatricality is augmented by a street stall, like a backdrop, that stands behind the group, hung with T-shirts, scarves and other typical tourist objects. It took Lewis three days of rehearsals to perfect the participants' strangely balletic movements: of the individuals within the groups, of the two distinct groups and of the rhythmic explosion and containment of violence. The scene's emblematic and non-naturalistic performativity is enhanced by the indifference of the passers-by as they wander through the transparency in the background. The length of the piece, at just over five minutes, is long enough both to establish the rhythmic nature of the performance and, as certain movements and gestures recur, to imply that the fight will go on for ever, without narrative structure and without conclusion.

At the end of *Backstory*, the Hansard father and son discuss the end of the rear projection era. Billy is now employed by Sony simply as a projectionist, showing films, rushes and so on to industry people who were once his clients. Both vividly evoke the present uselessness of their once productive equipment. Mr Hansard senior says: 'I don't see a couple of years in the future, it will be a couple of months before I take this stuff down to Catalina and use them as sea anchors.' And Billy adds, 'They'll make a nice diving reef for the fishes.'

There is a sense in which Lewis is attracted to things, buildings or objects that are marked by a history of human use. This is obviously the case with the disused and abandoned buildings and places that recur across his work, but his celebration of modernity is acutely of a moment of historical optimism, coincident with cinema, that never managed to fulfil its promise. But Lewis's use of rear projection revolves around the injection of new life into an archaic device and resonates directly with Walter Benjamin's idea that a return to seemingly outdated objects might invest them with new value and meaning. As Benjamin puts it in his essay on Surrealism:

> [Breton] was the first to perceive the revolutionary energies that appear in the 'outmoded', in the first iron constructions, the first factory buildings, the earliest photos, the objects that have begun to be extinct, grand pianos, the dresses of five years ago, fashionable restaurants when the vogue had begun to ebb from them.[9]

In his vast *Arcades* project, Benjamin looked back at nineteenth-century Paris and suggested that obsolescence brings with it a kind of utopian detachment from use which releases an outmoded building or technology for an altered aesthetic. Lewis's rear projection installations reproduce the shift from use value to cultural value: recycled within a new context, the original object becomes a point of reference back across time but loses its original significance. To resurrect the paradoxes

The Fight (2008).

of a forgotten, widely despised technology is to project a parallel, non-teleological approach to history that zigzags and can leap-frog across time to make unexpected links between a 'then', in the case of the film industry, and a 'now' that quotes it. The act of quotation pays tribute to the hidden, overlooked complexities of the original device but also confuses the linear relation between past and present.

I have argued that rear projection brought with it an estrangement effect, which Viktor Shklovsky, in his original use of the term, understood as enforcing a disruptive pause in the continuum of human habit. In the case of cinema, the 'habit' might be understood in terms of the spectator's absorption into the coherence and homogeneity of a fiction and its credibility. The artificiality and the temporal and spatial uncertainty of rear projection always hovered uneasily within the temporal and spatial norms imposed by Hollywood convention. All too often, the absurdity inherent in the device risked exposing the mechanism's fragility, bringing with it that uncanny sense of a modernism displaced that had wandered into the inappropriate setting of mass entertainment. However slight the estrangement effect might be, it has allowed Mark Lewis to celebrate a device widespread within the film industry of modernity as an unwitting parallel to its contemporary modernisms.

ISAAC JULIEN: DISPLACING THE SPECTATOR, *TEN THOUSAND WAVES*

First, a kaleidoscope: Isaac Julien's *Ten Thousand Waves* installation (2010) is made up of an arrangement of nine large double-sided screens, with the footage of the original film travelling from screen to screen.[1] The images move in a constantly shifting and seemingly arbitrary succession around the space, enhancing the movement of film itself. The spectator looks around bewildered, uncertain which way to turn or how to follow the fleeting patterns of images. The sensation is reminiscent of an aurally enhanced kaleidoscope: colours, textures, perspectives and sounds interact with each other. In time, recurring figures and scenes begin to form into more coherent patterns, and the installation's meanings and emotions begin to take shape. But in quite another way, the kaleidoscopic effect continues. It gradually extends beyond aural and visual profusion to the heterogeneity of the installation's content: fusions of fact and fiction, story and images, quotation and reference, archive and reenactment. The variety of material and narrative is characteristic of the essay form, partly objective, partly subjective, dealing with thought and ideas outside a linear, logical structure. The essay film can enhance the form with a variety of media material and, through montage, it can create specifically cinematic juxtapositions and relations.

While Julien's films have always been essayistic, in *Ten Thousand Waves* the structure of the installation precipitates the essay film into new aesthetic and theoretical dimensions. This is due, in the first instance, to the complementary relation between its multiple thematic strands and its multiscreen form; the film's themes literally travel around the nine screens, linking the heterogeneous materials together visually and theoretically. Rather than the single-screen essay film's sequential images, the montage of ideas can spread simultaneously around the topography of the installation. Perhaps because there is no single vantage point at which all the nine screens of *Ten Thousand Waves* can be viewed at once, the feeling of kaleidoscopic immersion persists, advanced by both the work's strands (ideas, stories, voices and so on) and the scale of the installation, the patterns formed by the arrangement of screens, their sculptural effects and the highly cinematic nature of the images themselves.

There is a resonance between the kaleidoscope effect, a reminder of pre-cinematic optical culture, and the post-cinematic digital culture to which a multiplicity of screens and variety of devices have returned. While the cinema of the single screen and the static spectator exists in-between these two, film images are still omnipresent and unavoidable, if becoming, perhaps, more and more ghostly. This is very much the case in *Ten Thousand Waves* and references to cinema's past recur throughout. Gradually, the spectator's immediate encounter with the external space of the installation screens gives way to awareness of its internal structuring around various strata of history. As the temporal dimension comes more to the fore, it merges with the movements of people across time and space that lie at the heart of the work.

Second, a paradox and a palimpsest: at first sight, *Ten Thousand Waves* (which is primarily set in China, was filmed in Chinese locations, and draws on moments of China's history and legend) seems to be quite distant from the concerns that have characterized Julien's previous films and installations, culturally and geographically. However, from another perspective, *Ten Thousand Waves* paradoxically reworks, reconfigures and re-contextualizes material (both form and content) that has pre-occupied him since the very beginning of his career. Mobility and flow have always been of central significance for Julien's 'travelling cinema'. Going back, for instance, to early film works, *Looking for Langston* (1989) took him to the Harlem Renaissance and the great African

American poet Langston Hughes; *Frantz Fanon: Black Skin, White Mask* (1996) took him to Fanon's Caribbean origins, to France and then to Algeria; and recent works have come to be increasingly about migration and the relation between cultures, for instance *True North* (2004) and *Fantôme Afrique* (2005) leading to *Western Union: Small Boats* (2007) all revolve around themes of travel and migration. And as *Ten Thousand Waves* now also travels across nine screens, its stories of migration mix with images of globalized capital and the paradox begins to resolve into a palimpsest. The installation forges a dialogue with selected and relevant aspects of Chinese culture and history that echo and respond to Julien's long-standing themes, his political ideas, visualizations and experiences. His own personal, intellectual, political and aesthetic histories animate *Ten Thousand Waves* as though words or images had been overlaid by a later superimposition but are still inscribed into its texture. This sense of layering also relates to Julien's use of reference and citation, as he inscribes his themes and ideas into the unfamiliar politics and economics of twenty-first-century capitalism in China. Furthermore, just as the theme of migration in *Ten Thousand Waves* reaches back to his earlier work, so the theme of capital reaches forward to his next project, *Kapital* (2013).

The installation, whose film lasts 49 minutes, opens with all nine screens engulfed by extraordinary CGI-enhanced ocean waves. On an immediate level, this vividly evokes the fearful nature of the sea; on another level, it establishes visually the highly metaphoric significance of 'waves'. Both levels of significance lead to two contrasting kinds of 'movement' that lie at the heart of *Ten Thousand Waves*, connecting its intertwined layers: the migration of impoverished peoples under globalized capitalism, and the circulation of capital itself, through both manufacturing and finance, and particularly, in this context, as it flows into contemporary China. Julien's point of departure was the 2004 tragedy of Morecambe Bay, in northwest England: on 25 February of that year, 23 Chinese migrant workers and asylum seekers, employed as cockle-pickers, were caught at night by a fast high tide and drowned.

These waves were actual and deadly, and are conjured up repeatedly on the soundtrack of *Ten Thousand Waves* in Wang Ping's poems on 'the cold North Wales sea'.[2]

As the child of St Lucian parents who immigrated to London in the 1950s, Julien has a persistent interest in movements of people, cultures and ideas, phenomena with roots in his own story. In *Western Union: Small Boats* he turned to stories of contemporary migrations, those of Africans struggling, in overcrowded boats, to cross the Mediterranean to southern Europe. While it was real waves that engulfed the 'small boats' of those searching for a 'better life', the word has yet another metaphoric significance, in the racist concept of migrant 'waves' threatening fragile indigenous economies and identities.

Early in *Ten Thousand Waves*, grainy black-and-white archive footage taken from a police helicopter on that night in 2004 shows the rescue of one survivor from a sandbank in the rising tide; then the camera moves across the empty, bleak surface of the sea. Almost more poignant are the voices: the woman responsible for the cockle-pickers pleads for help, and the rescue workers report on the hopelessness of their task. These sounds and images of Morecambe Bay, and Julien's own black-and-white video of the mudflats, haunt the installation's screens and form the core of its historical and emotional thought. *Ten Thousand Waves* brings the fate of the Chinese cockle-pickers into a structural relation with its second key theme, which leads the film into mainland China. While the migrant workers represent the movement of people in global capitalism, the new Shanghai represents the movement of global capital itself. In the early 1990s, the Chinese state developed the Pudong area of the city as a financial centre, and its flamboyant buildings represent the sudden arrival and rapid growth of Chinese capitalism. Julien uses the Pudong Hyatt Hotel to underscore the internationalism of the new China, filming the city from one of its bedrooms so that the exotic high-rise buildings seem to hover like a backdrop in a futuristic movie. The buildings of Pudong and the migrants in Morecambe Bay stand at opposite ends of the social and economic spectrum, emblematic of the conditions of contemporary Chinese capitalism that brought both into being. These resonant images, as they emerge out of the confusion and inscrutability of the world today, form a kind of Benjaminian 'constellation' within the intellectual structure of the installation. Walter Benjamin says, 'To thinking belongs movement as well as the arrest of thoughts. Where thinking comes to a standstill in a constellation saturated with tensions, there the dialectical image appears. It is the caesura in the movement of thought.'[3]

Out of the emblematic 'dialectic' of Pudong and the Morecambe Bay migrants, two other strands emerge, bringing the reality of history and geography, politics and economics into an encounter with fiction, legend and myth reaching back into China's past. Morecambe Bay leads to the legend of 'The Tale of Yishan Island' and Pudong to Shanghai in the 1930s. In interviews, Julien has often explained that he re-created the figure of Mazu (played by Maggie Cheung), the goddess of seafarers and the legendary rescuer of endangered fisherman, as a poignant counterpoint to the Morecambe Bay disaster. Threaded into the later parts of the installation is an enactment of the legend: a group of fishermen journey through the exquisitely beautiful landscape of Guangxi province, watched over by Mazu. Filmed against a green screen, Mazu flies, goddess-like, across the landscape and moves easily between continents and epochs. Julien creates a cinematic passage between eras and incidents, cutting between the police-helicopter footage of Morecambe Bay and Mazu's gaze as she hovers protectively over the fishermen's journey.

To bring a legendary past into contemporary Pudong, Julien cites and quotes from the emblematic film *The Goddess* (1934), directed by Wu Yonggang and starring Ruan Lingyi as a mother who becomes a prostitute to support her son. Shanghai had become the capital of a flourishing Chinese film industry by the early 1930s, coinciding with the rise of urban life, the idea of the 'new woman' and the various cultures of modernity. Ruan was the superstar of the period, but also

a brilliant actress who could portray both melodramatic suffering and
the aspirations of new womanhood; her performance was perfectly in
tune with the very end of silent cinema, revolving particularly around
gesture and very subtle, emotional facial expression. In spite of her
extensive fan base, Ruan was hounded by the press for her unconventional private life and her love affairs; she committed suicide in 1935
(on International Women's Day) at the age of 24. Julien uses extracts
from the original film and also filmed reconstructed scenes in the
same Shanghai studio where *The Goddess* had been shot in 1934.
Zhao Tao, an important star of Chinese cinema today, walks through
the vast spaces of the Shanghai studio, travelling on a 1930s tram
and reenacting scenes from *The Goddess*. Here the continuum of place,
the studio, emphasizes the gap in
historical time: the footage of Ruan
takes on a documentary aura, the
indexicality of the medium over-
whelming the fictional nature of her
performance. As Zhao also appears
in the Pudong Hyatt scenes, she
takes the film from 1930s Shanghai,
when the city was at its apex of
modernity and sophistication, into
the present day of global capital-

ism. Time is layered into the installation, with the figure of the later
actress relating to the earlier one, once again, as in a palimpsest. And
the layering is further complicated as Maggie Cheung had played
Ruan Lingyi in Stanley Kwan's film of her life, *Centre Stage* (1991).
Bringing the references fleetingly together, Cheung flies past the
window as Zhao stands in the contemporary Pudong hotel.

Ten Thousand Waves links the story of *The Goddess* to the stories
of the cockle-pickers in Morecambe Bay. The bits of black-and-white
archive film are weighed down by the past and by the tragedies they
represent. The helicopter footage carries the memory of the 23 deaths

and the circumstances of casual cruelty that caused them, while the footage of *The Goddess* is overshadowed retrospectively by Ruan's impending suicide. Furthermore, Julien himself has noted the parallels between the roads taken by the 1930s prostitute and the contemporary migrant workers, both driven from the expectations of normal everyday life by the need to survive. 'My film juxtaposes [the image of the prostitute] with the words of a contemporary male cockle picker, "I have no time to watch my son grow," making an explicit connection between the two generations of Chinese workers and [finding] similarities in their plight.'[4] Zhao's persona links back to Ruan but also suggests a young woman forced into prostitution today. As Julien has put it:

Isaac Julien, *Green Screen Goddess, Triptych,*
(Ten Thousand Waves), 2010, Endura Ultra photograph.

Zhao Tao's character is moving as it were in time from the 1930s
to the present as she passes from the historical Shanghai Film
Studio to the high-tech Pudong area, and she could also be a
relative of someone involved in the Morecambe Bay tragedy.[5]

The 'The Tale of Yishan Island' and *The Goddess* sequences have a crucial aesthetic and theoretical significance for *Ten Thousand Waves*. Both bring the present into a relation with the past, and vice versa, folding two levels of time into each other, one across decades, the other across centuries. Through the process of folding, as different temporalities are juxtaposed and interwoven, time is taken out of its tendency to slip into the horizontal. Julien describes his method as one of montage, or even bricolage. Patterns takes over from a linear temporal structure, as themes and stories, facts and fictions mesh with each other not only conceptually but actually and physically across the nine screens. The palimpsest-like structure of time layered into strata spreads out into a network of interconnected points, reminiscent, once again, of Benjamin's concept of constellation. These aesthetic and theoretical strategies, realized by the succession of linking, travelling images, are layered further by Julien's use of quotation and reference. As Peter Wollen puts it in his discussion of quotation in Jean-Luc Godard's *Vent d'Est* (Wind from the East, 1970):

> One of the main characteristics of modernism . . . was the play of allusion within and between texts . . . The effect is to break up the homogeneity of the work, to open up spaces between

Isaac Julien, *Blue Goddess (Ten Thousand Waves)*, 2010, Endura Ultra photograph.

different texts and types of discourses ... The space between the texts is not only semantic but historical too, the different textual strata being residues of different epochs and different cultures.[6]

In addition to the networks of associations created by its interwoven strands and themes, the figures that inhabit the screens of *Ten Thousand Waves* bring their own allusions into play, setting in motion paths of association, as though in a textual stream of consciousness. Maggie Cheung is, of course, an iconic figure of recent Hong Kong cinema. In addition to her role as Ruan in *Centre Stage*, she is particularly associated with the films of Wong Kar-wai, while the special effects with which she flies over landscapes (and fleetingly in the film studio and Pudong) evoke her presence in spectaculars such as Ang Lee's *Crouching Tiger, Hidden Dragon* (2000). Zhao also conjures up allusions to Chinese cinema, most particularly to Jia Zhangke's film *The World* (2004), a complex story of internal and external migrations set in a theme park in which the world's most famous monuments are reproduced in reduced size and in an allegorical evocation of global-

ization. Through the presence of video artist Yang Fudong, these references to Chinese cinema are extended into contemporary Chinese art. In the intricate scenes that move from the 1930s film studio to contemporary, lush Shanghai interiors evocative of the 1930s, Zhao and Yang meet in the personas of prostitute and client, as though the artist had wandered into fiction and the actress into art.

These performers are living quotations. They evoke Julien's

relationship to Chinese culture, initially mediated, as he has recounted, through his long-standing love of its cinema and then his recent engagement, both as an artist and an intellectual, with China as a key site of contemporary art as well as of aesthetic and political debate. But the 'living quotations' also address the spectator, triggering associations that transcend the specific textual context and allow an extratextual reverie of its own. The beautiful sequence in which technicians appear with Cheung in a green-screen studio, for instance, reminded me first of avant-garde aesthetics, with their revelation of the mechanics of illusion. But I was then reminded of the scene in Stanley Donen's *Singin' in the Rain* (1952), when Don (Gene Kelly) turns on the studio effects, particularly the wind-machine, to create an atmosphere for his love song. Archival footage included in *Ten Thousand Waves* can also activate associations, as, for instance, with film of the Cultural Revolution in which posters of Mao conjure up both an icon of Pop art and the dictator himself. From a British perspective, the Morecambe Bay tragedy brings to mind not only the conditions to which asylum-seekers and migrants were reduced, as the Labour government bowed to the strident xenophobic voices of the country's popular press, but the persistence and proliferation of these tendencies now, culminating in the disastrous referendum on Europe of 2016.

Julien's expanded, multiscreen works, most particularly *Ten Thousand Waves*, have allowed him to develop his long-standing reflections on the relation between time and space as 'in between-ness'. He has described one of the aspirations behind his work as 'creolizing vision'. Out of this idea, homogenous spaces of geography and linear narratives of history mutate as time is slowed down until it spreads into space, evoking the metaphor of the threshold, or of a halted journey. (Perhaps this confusion, or fusion, of temporal and spatial dimensions is realized emblematically in his use of the bullet shot in *Baltimore* (2003).) Very often over the course of his career, in works such as *The Attendant* (1993), *The Darker Side of Black* (1994) and *Paradise Omeros* (2002), Julien has referred to the beyond-traumatic journey of African

Isaac Julien, *Yishan Island, Voyage (Ten Thousand Waves)*, 2010, Endura Ultra photograph.

slaves across the Atlantic. It would seem as though his form of political poetics aspires to deconstruct precisely the trajectory of that journey, and to offer its victims a saviour in a legendary figuration, such as the one offered by Mazu. In a discussion of the death of the Morecambe Bay cockle-pickers, Julien has said, 'What resonated for me was that they drowned, they drowned in the sea, and that connects with the slaves' passage across the Atlantic, in which so many were lost in the ocean.'[7] In *Ten Thousand Waves* he continues to engage with the difficult relation between art and politics, that is, how art finds images for the growing gap between the power of capital and 'the wretched of the earth'.

The uncertain vision (its kaleidoscopic design) built into *Ten Thousand Waves* has an important theoretical grounding in Julien's intellectual background and the influence of 1970s film theory on his aesthetic formation. Although those debates might seem faraway from his complex multi-screen installations of recent years, there are threads that make connections between the two. Both Julien and his collaborator Mark Nash refer occasionally to this theoretical context and implicitly to *Screen* (of which Nash was editor from 1977 to 1981), with its critique of mainstream cinema and its support for politically radical, avant-garde alternatives. A key critique, derived from Louis Althusser, argued that the camera itself aligned the spectator with dominant ideology: the gaze, centred and privileged, reproduced the imagined sense of wholeness and coherence characteristic of the bourgeois subject. While the traditions of the avant-garde consistently, and for a variety of aesthetic reasons, decentred the spectator's eye and challenged this ideological gaze, the development of multiple-screen installations finally achieves a form of spectatorship in which the subject's position is essentially fragmented and displaced. As Mark Nash points out: 'Starting with *Fantome Créole*, Julien has explored the possibilities of a presentation that does not allow the viewer to see the whole work from one vantage point.' He discusses the various formations, for example: 'one has to move around to see the "whole thing" and there were always one or two screens that one was not able to see.'[8] Julien himself makes the point that his fragmentation of cinematic continuity through his method of 'parallel montage' also finds a formal realization in the structure of the installation:

> What I call parallel montage relates to the choreography of the gaze. There's a question of performance in the work but it doesn't end there, it's also the way the screens are articulated architecturally and how people are relating to them in the space. Some people come in and just sit down – maybe they're tired. But let's say that when we're looking at moving images we fall into certain habits and I'm trying to break those habits in a gallery context.[9]

Due to the necessary restriction of the installation in the differing museum and gallery topographies, there is no original to these works, once again reflecting a traditional avant-garde distrust of the value invested in the precious art object. Nash underlines this when he points out that, furthermore, the installations have single screen and photographic versions, 'which undercut the sense of there being an original or definitive version'.[10]

While these considerations may be traced to film theory debates of the 1970s, the moving image installation is transforming spectatorship so radically that the residues of a past intellectual context fade as new aesthetics come to the fore. The spectators' mobility varies their vantage points when watching the changing conjunction of images on the screens. On one level this involves actual, physical movement, a walking from place to place within the installation, but the arrangement of the screens also produces movement of eye and of attention. Cinema has traditionally absorbed its spectator into the images and narratives played out on a single screen. *Ten Thousand Waves* creates a mobile attention that plays into the new forms of multiple viewing on the multiple screens of everyday life today. The spectator's gaze has mutated into a series of glances, always prepared to be caught, to pause, and then restlessly move on. Attention is not so much distracted as divided, and simultaneity coexists with sequence. Furthermore, the key theme of movement in *Ten Thousand Waves* (that of peoples and that of capital) interacts with this complex spectatorial experience.

In *Ten Thousand Waves*, Julien has woven together an intricate series of themes layered as in a palimpsest and threaded across citations and living quotations. Not only do these patterns defy linearity and sequence, but the installation's conceptual structure cannot be separated from its material structure as the images and ideas flow from screen to screen. Emotion is built into the formal aspects of *Ten Thousand Waves*. In its elegiac memorial to the cockle-pickers, it also remembers the dead of generations past and the work seems to be haunted by ghostly presences. The figure of Mazu represents a legendary goddess but she also hovers over the whole work with a phantom-like insubstantiality, bringing the past into the present just as the ghost represents the refusal to be laid to rest.

MARY KELLY: SPEAKING MATERNAL SILENCE, *POST-PARTUM DOCUMENT* AND *THE BALLAD OF KASTRIOT REXHEPI*

This, the last essay in the *Afterimages* collection, serves several different purposes here. Mary Kelly's work fits in with that of the other artists collected in Part Three (although her work is not derived primarily from the moving image). As I am focusing on two of Kelly's installations that are specifically about motherhood, this chapter also relates closely to Part Two of the book, and I will return to some of the arguments made in the introduction to that section. Writing once again about *Post-Partum Document* (1973–9) has allowed me to go back, across four decades, to think about the weaving together of psychoanalysis and feminism in both that work and *Riddles of the Sphinx* (dir. Laura Mulvey and Peter Wollen, 1977).

Griselda Pollock's essay 'Still Working on Subjectivity' emphasizes that *Post-Partum Document* and *Riddles of the Sphinx* were the products of the specific context of the 1970s: how the dialogue between feminism and psychoanalytic theory affected representation and women's relation to language and to art. Pollock begins the essay with *Riddles of the Sphinx*, pointing out that the Sphinx, in the film, signifies the 'fate of the feminine': 'The Sphinx, like the feminine, is cast outside the gates of culture, silenced by phallocentric language, rendered archaic and monstrous, and denied the means to think of rethink her negative positioning in a phallocentric society.'[1] Across the essay, she argues that the first step towards 'thinking or rethinking' this negative positioning would be the feminist 'thinking and rethinking' of the Oedipus Complex through both theory and poetics. Pollock emphasizes the importance of Mary Kelly's appearance in *Riddles of the Sphinx*, in which she reads from *Post-Partum Document* (still at the time a work in progress). Our shared intellectual and political backgrounds led both works back to the Oedipus Complex, to the 'primal scene', as it were, of the fate of the feminine. But they tell the story rather differently. In *Riddles of the Sphinx*, we showed the mother resisting the father's place in the final stage of Oedipal separation; she searches for alternatives, retreating into a female world. For some feminists at the time this implied an essentialist position on women's relation to the Oedipus Complex, as though the Symbolic Order could simply be bypassed. But the film shifts away from the character and her narrative. In the last three tableaux of Louise's story the focus is on language itself, not in its conventional association with the paternal law, but as a hinterland in which words and images hover on the edge of meaning and muteness gestures towards the maternal as a potential and valuable source of symbolization. Although Kelly radically reconfigures the Oedipal trajectory, she follows it through to its end, to the child's socialization at school. For both the film and the installation the problem of the mother is central to a feminist representation of the Oedipal experience; both revolve around (the problem of) signifying the maternal and also opening up signification for the maternal. Pollock invokes Julia Kristeva's work on poetics, also dating from the mid-1970s, to suggest

that there was a critical conjunction between the poetics of an independent cinema and the poetics of conceptualism that opened up a fluid, intertextual aesthetic and theoretical space for a distinctive moment of feminist avant-garde practice; an avant-garde moment 'in, of and from the feminine' as defined by a feminist critical consciousness of the unconscious. This avant-garde would create knowledge about the feminine that existing discourses or theories could not and did not provide

... [These works] had to imagine a new kind of spectator: an active reader of signs.[2]

For Peter and me, the film form (within an avant-garde framework) offered an immediate possible conjuncture between the problem of language and patterns of space and time. In the first instance, 'language' meant lack of it. We drew on Kristeva's concept of the semiotic and the chora: 'the unnameable, improbable, hybrid, anterior to meaning to the One, to the father and consequently to the maternally connoted to such an extent that it merits [in Plato's term] "not even the rank of syllable."'[3] Although Kristeva is locating the maternal as a source for a radical and anti-patriarchal poetics, a child and future poet's language, we turned the concept of the 'anterior' back to the mother as subject of the pre-Oedipal, to find (in Kristeva's term) an 'indefinite *fuzziness*' of language.[4] In the traditional psychoanalytic view, the sharp shock of castration closes the 'middle of the journey', leaving the mother abandoned and the child ready to move into the paternal social and cultural sphere. Peter and I wanted to imagine an in-between space, a pause that spatializes time, in which to reflect on an intertwining of the verbal and the visual, 'reaching out towards' or 'on the verge of' expressing the muteness of the semiotic. Once again, the politics of representation can only be formulated out of the politics of feminism in confrontation with the woman's negative position in the patriarchy. As Kelly has put it:

Because of the coincidence of language with patriarchy, the feminine is, metaphorically, set on the side of heterogeneous, the unnameable, the unsaid. But the radical potential of women's art practice lies precisely in this coincidence, since, in so far as the feminine is said, it is profoundly subversive.[5]

Mary Kelly has sometimes referred to film as an influence as she developed *Post-Partum Document*'s aesthetic strategies. Although she had worked with film early in her career, for instance on the Berwick Street Collective's *Nightcleaners* (1972–5), it was the extended shot, unfolding in durational time, that particularly influenced her. She has commented specifically on the five-minute opening shot of Straub–Huillet's *Othon* (1970):

> HANS ULRICH OBRIST: What was it about Straub and Huillet that struck you?
>
> MARY KELLY: It was real time. It was running the whole reel of film for one shot, driving into Rome, in *Othon* . . . That just took my breath away. I thought that's what I wanted to do in the exhibition. Working on *Nightcleaners* it hadn't really occurred to me how I could use something like diegesis in the context of the exhibition.
>
> When Peter Wollen saw the first showing of *Post-Partum Document* at the ICA he said 'Well, it's a diegetic space' . . . It wasn't just literally the narrative but, as I tended to call it, the narrativization of space that was interesting to me, the way you pulled people in and through that story.[6]

In conversation with me, in 1983 at the Institute of Contemporary Art in London, she commented on film as an influence from another perspective. She had been struck by the way that *Penthesilea: Queen of the Amazons* (the first film I made with Peter Wollen in 1974) was divided into sections: 'I thought: why can't an art work be like a film? Why can't it be drawn out and you be drawn into the work and read it through like a film? The way you organized *Penthesilea* into sequences was very appealing.'[7]

There is a sense in which any reconfiguration of the Oedipus Complex has to engage with its structure as narrative, as a transition from one state to another. One of the most striking aspects of *Post-Partum Document* is its organization in duration and in sequence, both of which, as formal strategies, negotiate with the temporality of narrative. In this case the conceptual framework of the Oedipal trajectory opens out a rich and compelling space for the maternal voice. Kelly has built sequences and duration into the structure of her installations, although in varying ways across the development of her work. In the crucial first instance of *Post-Partum Document*, the 'narrativization of space' echoes the exploration and analysis of the Oedipal narrative that the work is about. At the same time, the various sections, each of the six Documentations that chart the mother's journey and the child's development, break up the continuum of the narrative, holding in suspense at each stage the inevitable journey towards the mother's ultimate loss of the child. Although Kelly works in detail with the beginning and the end of the Oedipal trajectory, *Post-Partum Document* extends the 'middle of the journey', as she explores the minutiae of transition. It is here that words and objects, the stained liners, the first scribbles, the mother's memorabilia, the child's gifts, ultimately his actual writing, create an intimate but recognizable discourse. Across the space, the child moves forward and the mother holds on to precious moments, holding back time, with the objects of signification that ultimately become the artwork itself.

Post-Partum Document, while establishing Kelly's working practice in duration and sequence, also constitutes another founding instance for her art: the practice of collection as a key methodology that continues throughout her work. Time is inscribed into *Post-Partum Document* through the trace, the object and the document, each one carrying forward a present moment, an instant, into the future in which it becomes both a sign of and physical residue of the past. The processes of collection and presentation of objects play a key part in this staging and imagining of event and its affect. The objects emerge to fill the gap left by the mother's separation from that of her child and share, like a photograph, the indexical sign's temporal ambivalence. This methodology is reminiscent of the gleaning process (as discussed in Part Two, 'Alina Marazzi'). The gleaner follows the harvest to collect discarded items and, outside the formal process of harvesting for a commercial market, invests what would otherwise be waste or rubbish with a new value. Furthermore, a double temporality lies at the heart of gleaning, as the objects once discarded gain a new life and a new value. Kelly has commented on the further contradictions and ambivalence at stake in the tension between temporalities:

> What I've emphasised in the relation is a moment of transgression where separation threatens a woman's representation of

Mary Kelly, detail of *Post-Partum Document*: Documentation VI: Pre-writing alphabet, exergue and diary, 1978, Perspex unit, white card, resin and slate.

herself as essentially and naturally maternal and creates a kind of chasm that resounds with questions. The woman questions the socially given meanings for the feminine. So I guess the kind of language I'm aspiring to is one that will prolong that rupture.[8]

In the process of the mother's encounter with the space of rupture (separation, chasm), a possibility of questions, meaning and language emerge. The questions and the objects occupy and extend the Oedipal process, fragmenting linearity and extending figuratively into the more transformative temporality of a threshold. The metaphor of a threshold represents an attempt to shift the figuration of time away from an imaginary pattern derived primarily from a foreclosing of the past (a hastening towards the end of an era), into an imaginary pattern derived from space, of holding past and future suspended in an uncertain present.

During the 1970s and '80s, Kelly had, by and large, drawn on her own experience for the source material of her 'collections': first motherhood and then, in *Interim* (1984–9), recorded conversations with her friends and comrades from the Women's Movement. This close relationship between her experience and the material collected was disrupted in the early 1990s by the eruption of war, civil wars and their atrocities. In response, Kelly produced three installations: *Gloria Patri* (1992), on the First Gulf War, was a meditation on the nature of masculinity and the military; *Mea Culpa* (1999) on the legacy of brutalities inflicted on civilians by oppressive regimes; and then *The Ballad of Kastriot Rexhepi* (2001). In the process of moving from a known into an unknown world, Kelly continued her earlier methodology of collection and became a 'gleaner' of emblematic stories. Newspapers and the news media in general became her primary source material, which she accumulated into a private archive from which she could select documentation, anecdotes and statements. The process of collecting raw material, sifting through its mass not necessarily with a pre-fixed purpose, finally selecting one item, involves an elongated engagement with the meanings and significances of the stuff itself. Thus Kelly has to read through and study her archive, but also has to read conceptually to select and present the chosen item. This takes time and involves reflecting on the relevant historical period, setting in motion the layering of time that will emerge in the final installation. She has remarked that this process sometimes takes her years. Ultimately, not only does the presence of the primary sources mark the evolution of the work itself, but the time involved in the sifting and selection process creates a relationship between document and work. It is as though Kelly acts as mediator, an aesthetic filter, between the original event and its appearance in the gallery.

Kelly used sequence and series as well as anecdote and stories for *Interim* and *Gloria Patri* but with very different forms of spatial organization from *Post-Partum Document*. Her work on women caught up in the atrocities of war demanded a new formal approach to the material, as though in recognition of its actual difficult and traumatic nature; also, due to the structural importance of narrative sequence, she returned to her early use of narrativization of space. For *Mea Culpa*, Kelly selected five incidents of contemporary atrocity; in each case a mother witnesses a violent, brutal attack on her child (for instance, *Phnom Penh, 1975*) or her home (as in *Sarajevo, 1992*). *The Ballad of Kastriot Rexhepi* evolved around the story of a lost child and thus inevitably recalls the first (Oedipal) maternal loss. Kastriot, an infant of eighteen months, had been left for dead by his Albanian parents as they fled from Serbian invaders, who, noticing that he was still alive, adopted and renamed the child Zoran. Having been reclaimed and renamed by Albanians, eventually, at the age of 22 months, Kastriot was reunited with his parents and photographed for the press; it was recorded that his first word had been 'Bab', Albanian for 'Dad'. Kelly found an account of this unlikely happy end to a story of the horrors of war in a local Los Angeles newspaper and she became particularly interested in its generic, mythic connotations, taking it out of its literal setting. As she has noted, the mythic story paralleled the child's acquisition of language and the story's happy end is marked by a recognition of the father, as though emerging from a long Oedipal journey. Griselda Pollock has pointed out:

> The artist who made *Post-Partum Document (1973–79)* as a study of the mutual subjectivization/socialization of the maternal and infant pair could not but notice the psycho-symbolic significance of this time-scale which raises the child's story from within events of the Kosovo war and the scourge of ethnic cleansing to a mythic status without losing its historically specific clothing.[9]

These works with maternal trauma affected the aesthetic form of Kelly's work in three specific ways. First of all, the stories moved beyond the anecdotal: no longer incorporated, as in some earlier works, into an encompassing framework, the events were translated into words that became the visual core of the installations. At first glance, the use of language seems to have displaced all Kelly's other formal materials, found or constructed objects rigorously arranged into category and pattern. Language in *Mea Culpa* and *The Ballad of Kastriot Rexhepi* is not resonant of the Symbolic Order but much closer to the kind of poetics of the semiotic analysed by Kristeva as specifically outside patriarchal culture. The story is told in rhythmic metre, and the flow of the narrative is punctuated by the imagined or actual words of the participants, designed to maximize, in Kelly's words, 'the emotional or affective residue of the event'.[10] In order to find an appropriate print medium for these small narratives, Kelly began to experiment with compressed lint, extracted in units from the filter of her washing machine. For *Mea Culpa*, the units were combined into panels, one for each story and one on each wall of the gallery space. For *The Ballad of Kastriot Rexhepi*, in collaboration with the composer Michael Nyman, Kelly turned Kastriot's story into a ballad in four stanzas. The units form a continuous narrative, divided into a series of 49 panels wrapping around four walls of the gallery at eye level. Thus these installations return to the structure of narrativized space. Kelly has described the visual effect of the *Kastriot* installation as similar to a 360-degree pan or an anamorphic lens. She says: 'The composition of the lint panels is based on the a-b-a structure of a transverse sound wave with the text running through the middle as a rest line.'[11] The wave physically frames the story itself, in a counterpoint to its own rhythm, in which words conjure up images in series, almost like an invisible sequence of pictures

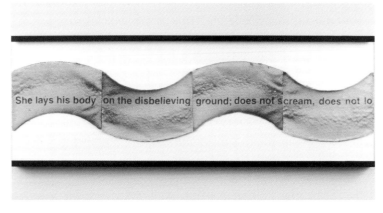

The Ballad of Kastriot Rexhepi, 2001, close-up detail of compressed lint.

The Ballad of Kastriot Rexhepi, detail.

The Ballad of Kastriot Rexhepi, installation view, Santa Monica Museum of Art.

or frames cut from the celluloid strip of a film. As Kelly herself has pointed out, the wave comes into its own at the moment in which *The Ballad of Kastriot Rexhepi* is performed by a singer and a string quartet: the music and the words animate the ballad itself, running along the line of the text, inserting it, now very precisely, into the present tense of performance. The wave contributes to this moment of animation, while also reaching back to the poignancy of the past to which the installation ultimately refers.

Mary Kelly's collected material and gleaned objects mediate between indiscriminate traces of the past and the social, cultural and historical significance they acquire once incorporated or inscribed into an artwork. The process is reminiscent of Lacan's use of metaphoric objects to mediate between those indiscriminate traces of the unconscious and their significance once reconfigured by the conscious mind. In his 1953 essay 'The Function and Field of Speech and Language in Psychoanalysis', Lacan draws on figures and images from the 'memorialisation' of history to evoke ways in which the individual psyche 'memorialises' its own past experiences. These are metaphors of storage and preservation: for instance, hysterical symptoms as monuments, childhood memories as archival documents, 'my history' as legend, and 'lastly, in the traces that are inevitably preserved by the distortions necessitated by the linking of the adulterated chapter to the chapters surrounding it, and whose meaning will be re-established by my exegesis.'[12] Lacan's figures and images, furthermore, lead towards the more elusive psychic structures of collective social experience; history as a metaphor for the individual's past broadens out, extending to 'history' as the account of shared social and cultural formations. Mary Kelly's work similarly materializes the stuff of a socially constructed unconscious, for instance, by translating the Oedipus Complex into monuments, documents and legends, ultimately to construct a new feminist exegesis. In her recent work, arising out of violence and trauma, the new exegesis emerges stark and unadorned by any mediating object; language itself demonstrates both its failure and its aspiration to speak the unspeakable.

Mary Kelly's great work, *Post-Partum Document*, took on the conventional psychoanalytic understanding of the Oedipus Complex to reconfigure its structure and the narrative, turning the patriarchal order upside down. This is, in the first instance, due to its feminist politics: as the installation traces the child's Oedipal development through the mother's experience, maternal muteness acquires a double voice (of Kelly as artist, Kelly as mother) and a narratorial point of view. But *Post-Partum Document* also challenged the patriarchal order historically and socially, giving a voice to silence in a further sense: most radically, it is a work of feminist art. Emerging out of maternal marginalization, out of the private and personal sphere, the installation claimed a public discourse for something that its surrounding culture and ideology found confusing and unrecognizable. The impact of the first (at the Institute of Contemporary Art, London, in 1976) and subsequent exhibitions have gathered momentum across time to become an essential part of art history, affecting and expanding art and art-historical language. Furthermore, the words and ideas of feminist critics as they wrote about *Post-Partum Document*, their commentaries and analyses, have established a terrain and a frame of reference for today's feminist engagement with aesthetics, theory, art practice and beyond.

APPENDIX: TEN FREQUENTLY ASKED QUESTIONS ON 'VISUAL PLEASURE AND NARRATIVE CINEMA'

WHAT WAS THE CONTEXT FOR 'VISUAL PLEASURE AND NARRATIVE CINEMA', AND WHY DID YOU CHOOSE TO WRITE ABOUT HOLLYWOOD FILMS?

Although I have written about the context for the essay before, for instance, in the Introduction to the second edition of *Visual and Other Pleasures* (2009), I'll recapitulate some key points. The two sections of the question do, in fact, go together. A lot of things were changing around the end of the 1960s, post-1968, and at the beginning of the 1970s, but there were three changes that deeply affected me and my relation to the cinema: the rise of the Women's Liberation Movement, the arrival in the UK of new kinds of cinema, and a new awareness of the history of women's film-making. I had spent most of the 1960s going to Hollywood movies of the '50s (these were the great films of the end of the studio system) with Peter Wollen and other friends, all of us left intellectuals, all followers of the *Cahiers du cinéma*. This was not casual film-going but a passionate attachment to a popular cinema and definitely an experience of 'visual pleasure'. Then the Women's Movement turned me into a critic and analyst of films I had loved . . . films that had once moved me to tears now seemed irritating in their persistent insistence on woman as spectacle. The essay could not have been written before the impact of feminism on what had been my very intense relationship with Hollywood cinema. Nor could it have been written in the context of film studies. Quite soon after 1975, by the time film studies came into existence, it would hardly have been acceptable, in the academic context, to think and write in terms of such sweeping statements and manifesto-like style.

The old cinema of the Hollywood studio system had, anyway, gone into decline. A wide range of avant-garde and experimental films had begun to arrive in the UK, opening my eyes to a completely different kind of film-making. It was very exciting to see films by Chantal Akerman, Joyce Wieland and Yvonne Rainer, for instance, when they were shown at the National Film Theatre in London in 1973. Avant-garde and experimental traditions and the new possibilities of 16mm made it possible to envisage the new women's cinema that I mention in 'Visual Pleasure'. Also crucial for the context were ideas and debates in journals such as *Afterimage* or *Screen* as well as publications such as *Women and Film* and special issues of other journals on women's film-making. For me, the Women's Event at the Edinburgh Film Festival in 1972 was a turning point: with Claire Johnston and Lynda Myles I researched and programmed one of the first ever women's film festivals. This archaeological excavation of women's cinema history underlined how difficult it had been for women to establish themselves in any sector within the industry: their work tended to be found in early cinema and in experimental films. This experience also made me realize that only a women's cinema could and would radically challenge the dominant codes and conventions that exploited the image of women.

I should also mention that during the late 1960s and early '70s, the work of contemporary French theorists began to be translated into English. For me, even before I encountered Freud in my Women's Liberation reading group, the *New Left Review*'s publication of Louis Althusser's essay 'Freud and Lacan' (issue 55, May–June 1969) introduced me to the idea that psychoanalytic theory and the concept of the unconscious would be significant for feminist thought. Perhaps, in addition to the three contexts I mentioned above, this 'theoretical consciousness' was also transforming cultural horizons in Britain at the time.

FREUD IS WELL KNOWN TO HAVE BEEN A MISOGYNIST. WHY DID YOU USE PSYCHOANALYSIS FOR A FEMINIST ARGUMENT?

I have often reminisced about the feminist reading group the Family Studies Group, which I joined in 1971. Our discussions reached a new stage when we encountered Freud. This was one of the most exciting intellectual moments of my life and particularly so due to the context of collective, feminist reading and discussion. Freud's concepts and vocabulary addressed some of our key interests. How is the unequal distribution of power between male and female structured? What role does sexuality play in this structuring? And what is the relevance of the mother's position within the patriarchal order? When it was the group's turn to edit the London Women's Liberation Movement's publication *Shrew*, we featured a short essay by Juliet Mitchell: 'Why Freud?' Mitchell begins by summarizing numerous reasons for feminists' (and women's generally) long-standing distrust of Freud and then sketches out some initial counter-reasons that she would develop at greater length in various publications over coming years, most influentially *Psychoanalysis and Feminism* (1974).

There are two sides to Freud's thought that are of interest to feminism. The first, and the simplest, is that his analysis of the male psyche under patriarchy was also an analysis of women's oppression, an account of a society which entrenched male power in the gendered unconscious. For instance, women may well object to Freud's emphasis on the power of the phallus and, with it, the idea of the female body as castrated, but as Juliet Mitchell has succinctly pointed out, 'To Freud, if psychoanalysis is phallocentric, it is because the human social order that it perceives refracted through the individual human subject is patrocentric.'[1] This was the social reality of his time and was still ours. The second side to Freud's theory of femininity is more complex, certainly for Freud himself who, as has been often pointed out, opened his lecture 'On Femininity' with the image of woman as riddle, addressing the women in his audience with the words: 'You are yourselves the problem.' And here, again, the question divides into two. First of all, how do babies become girls and how do girls become women? And then: what is the place of the mother in the Oedipus Complex? In traditional psychoanalytic theory these questions revolve around the castration of the female figure. While misogynistically visualizing women as 'lacking', the concept also leads to the very interesting question, for a feminist critique of patriarchal imagery, of male fetishism.

In my thoughts about motherhood, as a site in/from which a feminist poetics could materialize, I have gone back to the Freudian Oedipus Complex. But, by and large, rather than the ins and outs of gender construction, I have tried to use psychoanalysis to decipher the kind of symptomatic imagery that the male unconscious conjures up. I found it was not difficult to identify certain images, often of surface enchantment and secret disgust, a kind of 'vernacular fetishism' that revealed (not very hidden) symptoms of the 'patriarchal unconscious'. A surface enchantment disavows the actual female body, the source of anxiety. It was for this kind of analysis that I first used psychoanalytic theory in my essay 'Fears, Fantasies and the Male Unconscious', and I still remember a sense of exhilaration upon discovering that the psychoanalytic tools actually worked![2]

This led to the 'Visual Pleasure and Narrative Cinema' essay; here I was interested in deciphering and exposing the unequal balance of power intrinsic to Hollywood's dominant scopic codes in three cumulative steps. First, the gender-indifferent human pleasure of looking that then led, second, to the visual-component instincts of sexuality: exhibitionism and voyeurism. While Freud argued that the passive and the active drives were present in both masculine and feminine sexuality, it was, third, convenient to name exhibitionism as passive and voyeurism as active. To my mind, overriding Freud's careful lack of determinism, visual codes of many Hollywood films addressed the spectator as active and voyeuristic, inscribing this dominant position into the language of film itself. Freud revealed how patriarchy was inscribed into the social unconscious. To change the world as it is, you have to understand what it is.

WHY DID YOU REFER TO THE SPECTATOR AS 'HE' THROUGHOUT 'VISUAL PLEASURE AND NARRATIVE CINEMA'? ISN'T THIS A SEXIST REPRESSION OF THE FEMALE SPECTATOR? WHAT ABOUT THE WOMEN IN THE AUDIENCE?

When I wrote the essay, I wanted it to be 100 per cent polemical. Mandy Merck has referred to it as 'Mulvey's Manifesto',[3] and it was indeed designed to be uncompromising and un-nuanced. But I also hoped that by conjuring up the male universal, homogenizing subject 'he' (that we all knew), especially in the context of an overtly feminist argument, there might be a further element of shock. I now think it might have been sensible to draw attention to this as a device, but the essay was not intended to be 'sensible'. The idea was to dramatize Hollywood's masculine mode of address as an in-built sexist repression of the female spectator. From quite another perspective, I was drawing on my own experience. When I began to 'look at' films with feminist detachment, I realized how easily I had, in the past, adopted the masculine spectator's position, enjoying a sense of gender shift unavailable to a heterosexual man. A similar narrative 'masculinization' of occasional Hollywood heroines led to my follow-up essay 'Afterthoughts on "Visual Pleasure and Narrative Cinema" inspired by King Vidor's *Duel in the Sun* (1946)': '[The heroine's] oscillation, her inability to achieve stable sexual identity, is echoed by the woman spectator's "masculine" point of view. Both create a sense of the difficulty of sexual difference in the cinema that is missing in the undifferentiated spectator of "Visual Pleasure."'

I used Freud again but, this time, to argue for a more androgynous female spectator, a more masculinized heroine that I ultimately discarded as 'uneasy in her transvestite clothes'. Perhaps this was a too-easy throw away. But once again, I found that Hollywood's neurotic concern with gender identity could provide interesting source material. The male/female binary oppositions of 'voyeurism' and 'exhibitionism' or 'passive' and 'active' were infinitely more schematic on the screen than they ever were in Freud and, equally, infinitely less complex than in life.

Later I began to write about the Hollywood movies made for and about women, attuned to a feminine sensibility, that came to be known as melodramas. While these films showed that Hollywood could, within very limited constraints, consciously address a female audience, the exception, however, proved the rule. The melodrama confirmed the extent to which spectatorship was gendered: usually organized around a dominant male point of view and, in this case, deviating for a minor genre, derogatorily known as 'women's weepies'.

WHY DID YOU NOT MENTION RACE IN 'VISUAL PLEASURE AND NARRATIVE CINEMA'?

The essay was primarily intended as a critique of images of woman in patriarchal society, using Hollywood cinema, which I knew well, as a striking and obvious case in point. Looking back, it seems strange to me that I did not then think of studio-system Hollywood as an apartheid cinema, as I do now. Although I was reasonably aware of American history and culture and had a definite interest in African American literature and music, it was some time before I began to realize that the whiteness of the Hollywood screen was due to a conscious implementation of racist policies in the film industry. The structure of the gaze around gender, however, was obvious to me and could be conceptualized psychoanalytically. To address the question of racism would have demanded a much more historically informed and serious argument.

I did wonder why the coming of sync sound in the U.S. had not been a tide-turning moment, bringing the great black performers of the 1920s (who had, through their presence on records, on the radio and on Broadway, had a transformative impact on U.S. popular culture) to the screen. Some obvious questions were: why, when Hollywood adopted sync sound, was the emblematic first figuration of the new musical genre a white performer in black face? Why were the first attempts at introducing black music and dance to the screen (always in movies with an all-black cast) doomed to fail, with only a few (albeit very interesting) follow ups across the decades? The answers lie, of course, in the deep-rooted nature of American racism. Any hopes the black performing community might have invested in the coming of sync sound were quickly dashed. While Hollywood song and dance stars were to be uniquely white, many of the routines that then appeared in musicals were, of course, taken from black music and dance culture.

The cinema was particularly subject to racist taboo and the depiction of interracial romance was formally prohibited by the Hays Code of 1930. Furthermore, the threat of interracial desire had to be erased from spectatorship, creating yet another rationale for black performers' exclusion from the screen. When, very rarely, black musicals were produced, the powerful presence of both male and female performers transcended the often-demeaning frame story: that is, they were playing themselves and their extraordinary song and dance numbers today gain a sense of documentary reality. These films are a vivid reminder of what has been lost to the history of Hollywood cinema and its musical culture due to racism.

WHY DID YOU NOT MENTION A QUEER GAZE OR GAY AND LESBIAN SPECTATORS IN 'VISUAL PLEASURE AND NARRATIVE CINEMA'?

Looking back on the essay, I seem to have missed a lot of possible nuances in the argument, especially where a potential female or lesbian spectator is concerned. The section on voyeurism and the 'male gaze' in 'Visual Pleasure and Narrative Cinema' has achieved some kind of cliché status over the years, but the section on fetishism, and the absence of the male gaze, is less clearly argued and usually overlooked. So far as I remember (rather indistinctly), I hoped that the section on fetishism would 'save' some of Hollywood for a 'visual pleasure' that was not totally subordinated to male voyeurism and sadism. I now see that this argument could have found a complicity between the woman as spectacle and a female spectator that would be pleasurable but not dominating. Unlike male-dominated genres, my idea of fetishism flattened the screen, diffused space and fused the fascinating image of the female star with the fascination of film and the screen itself. I said:

> The beauty of the woman as object and the screen space coalesce: she is no longer the bearer of guilt but a perfect product whose body, stylised and fragmented by close-ups, is the content of the film and the direct recipient of the spectator's look ... The most important absence is that of the controlling male gaze within the screen scene.

The woman as spectacle is perhaps even more central to the argument (object, product and so on), but she dominates the language of film, has become an icon of *photogénie* and thus the visual pleasure of cinema itself. Rather than arguing that the very perfection of the female body, the exquisite fetish, acts as a defence against male castration anxiety, I could have argued that women spectators, untroubled by castration anxiety, could find visual pleasure in a female, and so too a lesbian gaze when the performance of femininity is 'the content of the film and the direct recipient of the spectator's look'.

Once again, the essay was very much a single-issue manifesto, but the argument takes in the 'problem' posed by the male figure as spectacle of visual pleasure. Hollywood cinema's anxious emphasis on gender roles, the split between male voyeurism and female exhibitionism, the active male gaze directed at a passive female figure complemented by the active role of the male protagonist in the story, all protected a male star from two intense dangers: the active female gaze and the homosexual gaze. When I wrote the 1975 essay, I did not know about the male panic sparked by Rudolf Valentino in the 1920s. According to Miriam Hansen, as Valentino attracted an active female gaze, his screen image, in the eyes of dominant ideological discourse, was necessarily effeminate, passive and anathema to true masculinity. Paradoxically, the heterosexual female gaze in the cinema rendered him queer on the screen.

Throughout film history, queer spectators have, of course, read against Hollywood's conformist grain, finding their own visual pleasures and queering the gaze, playing with and against the way in which the gender rules and roles were inscribed into the language of the cinema itself. It is now well known that gay movie-goers either could recognize, or heard through the grape vine, which straight screen figures were gay in real life (Rock Hudson, for instance) and created their own ironic fan commentaries. But the real strides made since 1975 in gender and sexual politics have changed the meanings of male and female, masculinity and femininity, that were inscribed into the essay. So too, of course, has film spectatorship changed.

YOU SEEMED TO THINK THAT A NEW, FEMINIST LANGUAGE OF CINEMA WAS ABOUT TO EMERGE WHEN YOU WROTE 'VISUAL PLEASURE AND NARRATIVE CINEMA'. HAS THAT HAPPENED? DO YOU THINK FILMS MADE BY WOMEN CAN CHANGE THE WAY WOMEN ARE PORTRAYED ON SCREEN?

There is rather a disconnect in the 'Visual Pleasure and Narrative Cinema' essay between the confident assertion that a new cinema had already been born and a rather cautious assessment of its actual potential: 'a politically and aesthetically avant-garde cinema is now possible, but it can still only exist as a counter-cinema.'[4] I did have a lot of confidence in the potential of 16mm, cheaper and lighter to enable women to make films (see my answer to the first FAQ) and even to bring about an avant-garde revolution. The emphasis on a counter-cinema came from two directions. The conceptualism and feminism conjuncture had reacted against any idea of the artist as a self-sufficient, inspired individual. And I was also influenced by Peter Wollen's theoretical elaboration of counter-cinema from his analyses of late Godard in 'Godard and Counter-Cinema: *Vent d'Est*' (1972) and Claire Johnston's pamphlet 'Women's Cinema as Counter Cinema' (Society for Education in Film and Television, 1973). Peter and I had made our first film, *Penthesilea: Queen of the Amazons*, in 1974 (shortly before the publication of the 'Visual Pleasure' essay in 1975), which we thought of as a 'scorched earth' film or film-making returned to zero. Our ideas had advanced by the time we made *Riddles of the Sphinx* in 1977, but by this time we were working in the very lively independent film movement that had grown up in the UK during the 1970s, and also many more films made by women had come into distribution. The feminist avant-garde of this period definitely became a point of reference in the future but 16mm was a short-lived gauge and a sense of a coherent 'avant-garde' was lost in the political reversals of the 1980s.

I do not believe that, even then, there was a 'feminist language of cinema' as such. But women, by and large, want to visualize and narrate material that is close to their lives and their immediate concerns, which very often involve imaginative and unusual forms of visualization and narration. Furthermore, women's critical writing plays a crucial role as, all too often, when women do get to make films they fail to get the equivalent attention and publicity that goes to men. This is especially important for innovative, experimental and generally 'off the radar' films. Laura Marks, in her book *The Skin of the Film: Intercultural Cinema, Embodiment and the Senses* (1999), brings small and easily overlooked films into critical visibility.

But it was also important, alongside films made to be 'shock troops of change', that women could get work in the film industry. The first women cinematographers had just graduated from the National Film School (Diane Tammes, for instance, who worked with Peter and me on *Riddles of the Sphinx* and all our subsequent films).

Although it is still a struggle for women to work in film, whether technically or creatively, over the years the number of films made by women has grown, not necessarily penetrating the mainstream industry, not necessarily enough, but expanding into independent sectors (especially when supported by state funding). Recently campaigns and public debate (at Cannes or the Academy Awards, for instance) have drawn much-needed attention to discrimination in the film industry in general.

Certainly, by now, there are more films made by women than can be contained in an idea of 'women's cinema'. I would end by saying that only the production and circulation of films made by women, in large numbers, can transform the image of women on the screen, but women also bring to cinema issues, ideas and perspectives that benefit everyone, across society and regardless of gender.

DO YOU THINK HOLLYWOOD HAS CHANGED DURING THE PAST DECADES? WHAT DO YOU THINK OF *WONDER WOMAN*?

I have not been particularly drawn to Hollywood cinema recently. I do believe strongly in the various feminist campaigns to improve women's participation behind the camera, as writers and directors, as well as to improve images of women on the screen: Melissa Silverstein's always lively commentary 'Women and Hollywood', for instance. And I think that, even though it might seem superficial, the Bechdel test can throw up interesting results. Patriarchal strategies will be hard to shift until women have a much greater share in the power of image-making and while the statistics of inequality remain shocking. When we organized the Women's Film Event at the Edinburgh Film Festival in 1972, I actually believed that equality would be achieved by the turn of the century. At least there is some discussion now of a 50 per cent quota. Independent films in the U.S. are becoming much more significant and bringing women directors into the public eye. We are seeing a new generation of women directors emerge, such as Ava DuVernay, who as an African American further shifts the eternally entrenched ideologies of Hollywood.

I thoroughly enjoyed *Wonder Woman*, which comes out of the mainstream, blockbuster industry and thus, in principle, is special effects and violence orientated. It was interesting and inspiring to see how Patty Jenkins, as a woman director, could affect the brand and its conventions. Peter Wollen and I had used bits of the original comic in our first film, *Penthesilea: Queen of the Amazons* (1974), which were wittily ironic and, I thought, feminist in tone, so I was rather anxious about the 2017 movie. But the wit survived, playing on surprise and role reversals. I was moved, too, by the anti-war spirit of the film, its setting in the First World War, its use of centenary consciousness and the awareness today that it should have been 'the war to end all wars'. So Diana as superhero is actually a pacifist. I almost always agree with the *New York Times* film reviewer Manohla Dargis, who summed up her best ten films of 2017 with these words:

> I love all the movies on my list, but more than any other this year, *Wonder Woman* reminded me that we bring our entire histories when we watch a movie – our childhood reveries, our adolescent yearnings and adult reservations. I've always loved *Wonder Woman* in all her imperfection, including in the old TV show, and I loved her here because all my adult reservations were no match for this movie.[5]

WHY IS 'VISUAL PLEASURE AND NARRATIVE CINEMA' STILL READ TODAY? DO YOU THINK IT'S STILL RELEVANT?

This question has puzzled me for some time. Soon after the essay came out in 1975 it began to be taken up and republished in edited collections, probably because film studies and women's studies were beginning to be established. I felt a bit ambivalent about an essay that had been written completely outside an academic context and without any academic purpose in mind becoming, as it were, 'a standard text'. Even using psychoanalytic theory as a 'weapon' without much rationalization or explanation of terms or concepts was meant to be a provocation. At some point I stopped giving permission for its republication but requests kept coming in and I thought: why be precious about it? And, in spite of its manifesto style, it was carefully written and very carefully structured so that all the sections of the argument fitted into a symmetrical pattern. My contradictory attitude to Hollywood cinema as well as the undercurrent of excitement about the emerging, avant-garde 16mm cinema both reflected changing critical perspectives.

Furthermore, it was written at a time when films were watched in cinemas, in the specific conditions of the darkened theatre and the illuminated screen. When new technologies radically changed conditions of spectatorship I thought that 'Visual Pleasure and Narrative Cinema' would lose currency. During the 1990s, first on video and then on DVD, I experimented with new ways of watching movies; I discovered that, just as feminism had transformed my relationship with Hollywood, so the new ability to alter the flow of films opened up completely new and unexpected relationships with cinema. Out of this, I wrote *Death 24x a Second: Stillness and the Moving Image*, in which I specifically discuss new kinds of spectatorship that render the gender-based arguments of 'Visual Pleasure' completely archaic. In spite of all this, the essay lives on and on. And I am, of course, surprised but pleased when people, very often women but also men, come up to me or write to me, even to this day, to say that the essay influenced their ways of watching and thinking about films. In 2015, the fortieth anniversary of 'Visual Pleasure and Narrative Cinema', events organized around the essay not only demonstrated that it could still generate good discussion and ideas, but traced the intellectual history of the essay in very interesting and unexpected ways. Also, in 2015, the journal *Afterall* published a small, elegant book in which a visual essay by the artist Rachel Rose accompanied the original text. The book seemed to me to solve the problem of the essay: it could shake off any remnant of use value and, following the path of Walter Benjamin's obsolescent object, it could take on a new life, new use value and a new future.

However, writing in December 2018, I have noticed that the idea of the male gaze has recently more or less entered (if not ordinary, at least cultural) language. Quite often the term is related back to the 'Visual Pleasure' essay, but obviously as it gains in currency it takes on more of a life of its own. There is a sense in which 'the male gaze' has become part of the widespread critique of mainstream film, for its day-to-day sexism, for the lack of women directors, for the lack of good female parts and so on. This is, to my mind, a long overdue development and I am extremely gratified that the phrase, alongside 'the female gaze', has now moved into current feminist debate and with relevance (and use value!). But it seems to me that my personal thoughts about 'Visual Pleasure and Narrative Cinema' are not really that relevant today, as the essay no longer belongs to me but to continuing and contemporary discussions on the topic. After all, spectacle has proliferated massively since 1975, and its politics are more urgent than ever.

HOW HAVE NEW TECHNOLOGIES AFFECTED FILM SPECTATORSHIP? HOW HAVE THEY AFFECTED WOMEN'S SPECTATORSHIP IN PARTICULAR? IN YOUR BOOK *DEATH 24X A SECOND: STILLNESS AND THE MOVING IMAGE,* YOU PROPOSE THAT NO LONGER ARE AUDIENCE MEMBERS FORCED TO WATCH A FILM IN ITS ENTIRETY IN A LINEAR FASHION. DOES THIS MEAN THAT THE AGE OF FILM VOYEURISM IS OVER?

When I was writing *Death 24x a Second: Stillness and the Moving Image* in the years leading up to its publication in 2006, I used my own experiments with spectatorship (pausing, repeating, slowing down sequences in films that I knew well) to evolve my ideas for the book. At that time, I thought that this kind of spectatorship, with its special relation to cinephilia and curiosity about film form, would spread rapidly: a 'democratization of textual analysis', as I envisaged it. But over the years I have questioned people, in seminars, lectures, among friends and so on, about any ways in which their modes of spectatorship have changed, whether or not they have adopted the forms of viewing discussed in *Death 24x*. I have been surprised by how many people still watch films with the correct narrative flow and at the standard pace. I realize that this kind of experimentation does presuppose a cinephilia, a curiosity about the forms, language and style of film that is still comparatively restricted. However, the vastly increased availability of films through streaming, DVD publication and so on has enormously, if paradoxically, increased interest and knowledge of cinema and its history. This is another form of democratization: knowledge about the cinema is no longer restricted to an elite but is part of the popular.

Although none of these points relate specifically to women and feminist spectatorship, it is now possible (the democratization of textual analysis!) for anyone, any curious young woman, for instance, to analyse exactly how the male gaze was and is constructed, to speculate about a feminist alternative and develop a knowledge of the language of film that is essential for any alternative way of seeing to come into being. I can imagine a counter culture in which women share their experiences, their insights and the kind of theoretical speculations that could emerge out of thoughtful film spectatorship. And of course, the Internet would be the most suitable site for this kind of exchange.

Clearly, the possibility of playing with imagery and performing gender can be achieved more simply in this technological age, just as fluidity of gender is now more socially accepted. There is an important balance to be maintained, I think, between the explosion of media imagery that bombards young people today and young women's readiness to create alternatives and to experiment with images, always building on their awareness of how commodity culture functions, and most particularly through a refinement of their theoretical skills. To work theoretically on images today is not necessarily an academic or difficult exercise; it should be part of the everyday life experience of everyone exposed to the rapidly advancing commodification of the digital. I welcome the new possibilities of recording images and creating stories, commentaries, documentaries, essay films and so on out of found footage or recycled material. Already it is possible to see on YouTube remixes and mash-ups (of course of varying degrees of interest), but this nonetheless shows that creative resources can be developed as alternatives to the vast, present-day proliferation of ready-made media. However, it is also important to remember that YouTube is infinitely more powerful than any of the Hollywood studios ever were. In this sense, these new forms of empowerment are simultaneously supping with the Devil.

HOW HAS THE APPEARANCE OF NEW VIEWING PLATFORMS, PARTICULARLY SMALL SCREENS SUCH AS PHONES, AFFECTED FILM SPECTATORSHIP?

I have never watched a film or a television programme or any moving image work on my phone. This seems to me to be an intractable difference between generations, although I do quite often see 'older people' apparently absorbed in something unfolding on their phones. At the risk of seeming luddite, I doubt that the visual language and cinematic nuances of great films can transcend the limitations of the small screen and I tend to think that it becomes, in miniature, a primarily narrative medium. That is, people watch features or television series on their phones as they might read a book, absorbed in story, character and suspense. But the phone is, furthermore, a multimedia platform: the beep of an arriving text or email message, or rival narratives, news stories from the outside world, for instance, make their own demands. The solitary nature of phone spectatorship offers no protection from the intrusions of everyday life: the journey ends or an irritated companion wants to chat. Thus the question of 'phone spectatorship' is not simply to do with smallness of the screen but to do with a porous, permeable space. On the other hand, people can evolve and customize their own viewing conditions in their own domestic surroundings, out of extremely high-quality equipment, the availability of films and the quality of distribution through an online film club such as MUBI.

In a brilliant juggling act, Francesco Casetti takes up these kinds of arguments in *The Lumière Galaxy: 7 Key Words for the Cinema Today* (2015). He emphasizes that the present state of the cinema is contradictory: films recognizably persist across the explosion of change brought about by the digital, but they are consumed within completely new technological environments, transformed by new conditions of access and experience (thus: films are watched on your phone). Furthermore, Casetti points out that this kind of relocation of cinema affects the configuration of film history in which, rather than the past leading simply to the present, the past can be illuminated by the present: 'we create a constellatory temporality, far from a progressive and causal logic, but, on the contrary, a kind of back and forth that moves us in many different directions and opens for us many different paths.'[6] There is an optimism in his argument, both about the cinema's survival and also about the theoretical implications of the past/present dialectic. At the same time, Casetti cannot avoid the inherent uncertainty built into this period of transition, the fragility of the threshold space, in which the familiar cinema seems to grow faint. In a poignant phrase, he notes that 'darkness', once the absolute condition for film spectatorship, 'has disappeared': 'vision occurs ever more frequently in broad daylight, on modes of transportation, in city squares and even at home.'[7]

Although, of course, collective film-viewing in the darkened cinema, with the film seen in continuum, is still very much available today, there is an unavoidable sense of generational shift. My generation (I was born in 1941) is the last to have had a childhood of films seen only in the cinema, and I find it hard not to feel, in some sense, sorry for recent generations who have grown up in a polymorphous viewing world. Even while watching a movie, they find it hard not to reach for their phones; even when surrounded by the complexities and confusions of everyday life, they seem to be fixated on the small screen. However, as Casetti points out, the cinema has moved from a technological straightjacket into a lived flexibility. Certainly, the spectator of 'Visual Pleasure and Narrative Cinema' has given way to infinitely more complex, and ultimately playful, ways of relating to the screen. And on the screen gender images are now, in some kind of synchronicity, also more complex, more flexible and more playful than the spectatorial straightjacket I wrote about in 'Visual Pleasure and Narrative Cinema'.

REFERENCES

PREFACE

1 Sheila Rowbotham, *Woman's Consciousness, Man's World* (Harmondsworth, 1973), p. 29.
2 Alina Marazzi, *Un'ora sola ti vorrei* (Milan, 2006), p. 53. Translation author's own.
3 Julia Kristeva, 'Women's Time', *Signs*, VII/1 (Autumn 1981), p. 18.

PART ONE: A LAST CHAPTER

INTRODUCTION: FINAL THOUGHTS ON WOMAN AS SPECTACLE

1 bell hooks, *Black Looks* (Boston, MA, 1992), p. 120.
2 James Snead, *White Screens Black Images: Hollywood from the Dark Side* (London, 1994), p. 8.
3 Once a decade, *Sight and Sound* asks critics to name the best ten films of all time.
4 See Jacqueline Rose, 'A Rumbling of Things Unknown', *London Review of Books*, XXXVIII/8 (26 April 2012), pp. 29–34. In this portrait essay, Rose gives a vivid account of Marilyn Monroe's political awareness, especially of her identification with black America and its struggles.
5 It is said that audiences coming out of the first release of *Lola Montès* advised the waiting queue not to bother.
6 Jacques Rancière, *Intervals of Cinema*, trans. John Howe (London, 2014), p. 39.

MAX OPHÜLS, *LOLA MONTÈS*

1 Following numerous adventures across Europe, dancer and courtesan Lola Montez (1821–61, born Eliza Rosanna Gilbert) reached the summit of her notoriety in the 1840s due to her affair with King Ludwig I of Bavaria (he bestowed on her the title Countess of Landsfeld). Driven from Bavaria by the 1848 Revolution (and the king's abdication), she ultimately left Europe and moved to the U.S. in the early 1850s. There, her fleeting relationships and public performances continued until her health rapidly deteriorated in the late 1850s.

2 See Claude Beylie, *Max Ophüls* (Paris, 1963), p. 158.

3 Georges Annenkov, *Max Ophüls* (Paris, 1962), p. 93.

4 Gilles Deleuze, *Cinema 2: The Time Image* [1985], trans. Hugh Tomlinson and Robert Galeta (London, 2005), p. 81.

5 Ibid., pp. 81–2.

6 Georges Annenkov, *Max Ophüls* (Paris, 1962), p. 85.

7 Mary Ann Doane, 'Remembering Women: Psychical and Historical Constructions in Film Theory', in *Psychoanalysis and Cinema*, ed. E. Ann Kaplan (London and New York, 1990), p. 46.

8 Gilles Deleuze, *Cinema 2: The Time Image*, trans. Hugh Tomlinson and Robert Caleta (Minneapolis, MN, 1989), p. 78.

9 The Ringmaster's relation to Lola is reminiscent of the ambivalence so often encountered in a director's relation to his favourite star, in which personal fascination is sublimated into the inexorable exploitation of an actual woman as spectacle for mass consumption.

10 François Truffaut, *Les films de ma vie* [1975] (Paris, 2007), p. 250.

ALFRED HITCHCOCK, *VERTIGO*

1 Edward Said, *On Late Style: Music and Literature Against the Grain* (New York, 2006), p. 14.

2 Walter Benjamin, *The Arcades Project*, ed. Rolf Tiedemann, trans. Howard Eiland and Kevin McLaughlin (Cambridge, MA, 1999), p. 8.

3 See Part Three, 'Mark Lewis: Films on Time, Space and *Rear Projection*' for further discussion of Hitchcock and the rear-projection process.

4 Dan Aulier, *Vertigo: The Making of a Hitchcock Classic* (New York, 1998), p. 67.

5 Ibid., pp. 67–8.

6 Philip Wylie, *A Generation of Vipers* [1943] (New York, 1955), p. xii. By 1955 the book had been through twenty printings and selected in the same year by the American Library Association as one of the most

important non-fiction works of the first half of the twentieth century. A representative quotation:

> Let us look at mom. She is a middle-aged puffin with an eye like a hawk that has just seen a rabbit twitch far below. She is about twenty-five pounds overweight . . . In a thousand of her there is not sex appeal enough to budge a hermit ten paces off a rock ledge. She none the less spends several hundred dollars a year on permanents and transformations, pomades, cleansers, rouges, lipsticks, and the like – and fools nobody except herself. (Wylie, *A Generation of Vipers*, pp. 201–3.)

7 Ibid., p. 216.
8 Annette Michelson, 'On the Eve of the Future: The Reasonable Facsimile and the Philosophical Toy', in *On The Eve of the Future: Selected Writings on Film* (Cambridge, MA, and London, 2017), pp. 23–4.
9 Ibid., p. 24.
10 Raymond Bellour, 'The Ideal Hadaly', *Camera Obscura*, V/3 (1986), p. 131.
11 Ibid.
12 Christian Metz, 'Disavowal, Fetishism', in *Psychoanalysis and Cinema: The Imaginary Signifier* (London, 1982), p. 72.
13 Gilles Deleuze, *Cinema 2: The Time Image*, trans. Hugh Tomlinson and Robert Caleta (Minneapolis, MN, 1989), p. 46.
14 Ibid., p. 81.
15 Said, *On Late Style*, p. 16.
16 Benjamin, *The Arcades Project*, p. 8.

MARILYN MONROE: EMBLEM AND ALLEGORY OF A CHANGING HOLLYWOOD

1 In early interviews, both stars avoided the problem of having a mother in a mental home by saying they were dead. Both, however, set the record straight in later years.
2 Gary Vitacco-Robles, *Icon: The Life, Times, and Films of Marilyn Monroe*, vol. 1: *1926 to 1956* (eBook, 6 March 2014).
3 Donald Spoto, *Marilyn Monroe: The Biography* (London, 1994), pp. 121, 195.
4 Ibid., p. 284.
5 Ibid., p. 290.
6 Ana Salzberg, *Beyond the Looking Glass: Naricissism and Female Stardom in Studio Era Hollywood* (Oxford and New York, 2014), p. 144.

7 Pasi Valiaho, *Mapping the Moving Image: Gesture, Thought and Cinema, c. 1900* (Amsterdam, 2010), p. 17.

8 *Photogénie* was the term used by certain French avant-garde film-makers of the 1920s to describe the way that the camera could use its mechanical properties and its relation with light, shade and the materiality of celluloid to transform ordinary things or, indeed, people into something specifically cinematic.

9 Roland Barthes, *Camera Lucida: Reflections on Photography*, trans. Richard Howard (New York, 1981), p. 96.

10 Lawrence Crown, *Marilyn at Twentieth Century Fox* (London, 1987), p. 210.

THE DECLINE AND FALL OF HOLLYWOOD ACCORDING TO JEAN-LUC GODARD'S *LE MÉPRIS*

1 Jean-Luc Godard, *Godard on Godard*, ed. and trans. Tom Milne (London and New York, 1972), p. 173.

2 Michel Marie, *Le Mepris* (Paris, 1990), p. 14.

3 Thomas Schatz sums up the radically changed conditions in the Hollywood industry that lay behind the disappearance of the films *politique des auteurs* critics loved and re-evaluated: 'Gone was the cartel of movie factories that turned out a feature every week for a hundred million movie-goers. Gone were the studio bosses who answered to the New York office and oversaw hundreds, even thousands of contract personnel working on the lot. Gone was the industrial infrastructure, the "integrated" system whose major studio powers not only produced and distributed movies but also ran their own theatre chains.' Thomas Schatz, *The Genius of the System: Hollywood Filmmaking in the Studio Era* (New York, 1988), p. 4.

4 Godard, *Godard on Godard*, p. 11. Rather strangely, given his later dismissive comments about *Il disprezzo*, Godard says of Mankiewicz, 'I would not hesitate to accord him as important a place as that occupied by Alberto Moravia in European literature.' Ibid., p. 13.

5 Tom Gunning, *Fritz Lang: Allegories of Vision and Modernity* (London, 2000), p. 6.

6 Jacques Aumont, 'Godard's *Le Mépris*', in *French Film: Texts and Contexts*, ed. Susan Hayward and Ginette Vincendeau (London, 2000), p. 176.

7 '"Nowadays", Gene Kelly declared bitterly (*Cahiers du cinéma*, 85), "the cinema is becoming a means of expression for the writer instead of the director." This is the complaint one might make about Mankiewicz:

that he is too perfect a writer to be a perfect director as well. Basically, what is missing from *The Quiet American* is cinema. It has everything – brilliant actors, sparkling dialogue – but no cinema.' Godard, *Godard on Godard*, p. 84.

8 Tom Gunning analyses this anecdote and demonstrates that Lang elaborated it considerably over the years, in Gunning, *Fritz Lang*, pp. 8–9.

9 Ibid., p. 6.

10 Colin MacCabe, *Godard: A Portrait of the Artist at 70* (London, 2003), p. 155.

PART TWO: THE NEXT CHAPTER

INTRODUCTION: TIME REBORN – WOMEN'S STORIES, WOMEN'S FILM

1 Mary Beard, 'The Public Voice of Women', *London Review of Books*, XXXVI/6 (20 March 2014), pp. 11–14.

2 See Part Three, 'Mary Kelly: Speaking Maternal Silence' for an extended discussion of these points.

3 Peter Brooks, *The Melodramatic Imagination* (New Haven, CT, 1984), pp. 72–3.

4 Yvonne Rainer, *Feelings are Facts* (Cambridge, MA, 2006), pp. 393–6.

5 Julia Kristeva, 'Women's Time', trans. Alice Jardine and Harry Blake, in *The Kristeva Reader*, ed. Toril Moi (New York, 1986), pp. 187–213. Originally published as 'Le Temps des femmes', in *34/44: Cahiers de recherche de sciences des textes et documents*, 5 (Winter 1979).

CHANTAL AKERMAN, *JEANNE DIELMAN, 23 QUAI DU COMMERCE, 1080 BRUXELLES*

1 In 1975, Edinburgh also presented retrospectives of Alain Robbe-Grillet, Jacques Tourneur, Shūji Terayama and Martin Scorsese.

2 Lynda Myles, the director of the Edinburgh Film Festival at the time, confirms this impression: 'I remember that there were virtually no walk-outs and that the audiences seemed totally in thrall.' Personal communication, 29 May 2016.

3 Interview with Chantal Akerman, Criterion DVD, 2009.

4 Akerman has explained that the precision invested in preparing and cooking meals, the insistence on cleanliness and order, were characteristic not only of her own mother but of her father's three sisters, all of whom shared this culture of the domestic. Ibid.

5 Ivone Margulies, *Nothing Happens: Chantal Akerman's Hyperrealist Everyday* (Durham, NC, and London, 1996), p. 64. Margulies's book has thrown essential light on *Jeanne Dielman*, placing it in its contemporary cultural context as well as brilliantly analysing its structure, ideas and use of cinema. This pioneering study has greatly influenced my understanding of *Jeanne Dielman*.

6 'Chantal Akerman on *Jeanne Dielman*: Excerpts from an Interview with *Camera Obscura*, November 1976', *Camera Obscura*, 2 (Autumn 1977), p. 120.

JULIE DASH, *DAUGHTERS OF THE DUST*

1 The last lines of *Illusions* (dir. Julie Dash, 1982), spoken by Mignon Dupree (Lonette McKee) as she decides to stay on in Hollywood and fight to get African Americans onto the screen.

2 Julie Dash, 'Dialogue between bell hooks and Julie Dash, April 26, 1992', in *Daughters of the Dust: The Making of an African American Woman's Film* (New York, 1992), p. 32.

3 Ibid., p. 34.

4 Michael Glover Smith, 'Filmmaker Interview: Julie Dash', https://whitecitycinema.com, 18 November 2016.

5 Dash, 'Dialogue between bell hooks and Julie Dash, April 26, 1992', p. 29.

RAKHSHAN BANI-ETEMAD, *UNDER THE SKIN OF THE CITY*

1 Peter Brooks, *The Melodramatic Imagination* (New Haven, CT, and London, 1995), pp. 56–81.

2 The protagonist's name is a homage to the great Iranian poet Forough Farrokhzad (1935–1967).

3 Rakhshan Bani-Etemad interview with Milos Stehlik, www.firouzanfilms.com, May 2012.

ALINA MARAZZI, *UN'ORA SOLA TI VORREI*

1 A description of *La lingua della nutrice* by Elizabetta Rasy, quoted in *Italian Feminist Thought: A Reader*, ed. Paola Bono and Sandra Kemp (London, 1991), p. 63.

2 Christa Blümlinger, *Cinéma de seconde main: Esthetique du remploi dans l'art du film et des nouveaux medias* (Paris, 2013).

3 Alina Marazzi, *Un'ora sola ti vorrei* (Milan, 2006), pp. 49–50. This is Alina Marazzi's account of making the film, published as an accompaniment to the DVD.

4 Jamie Barron, *The Archive Effect: Found Footage and the Audiovisual Experience of History* (London, 2013), p. 18.

5 Ibid., p. 53.

6 Ibid.

7 Ibid., p. 18.

8 Jacques Derrida, *Archive Fever: A Freudian Impression* (Chicago, IL, 1996), p. 36.

CLIO BARNARD, *THE ARBOR*

1 'Fairy tale Film-maker: Cleo Barnard Interview', *Evening Standard* (23 October 2013).

2 Paul Harrison, *Inside the Inner City: Life Under the Cutting Edge* (London, 1983), p. 25.

3 Max Stafford-Clark, 'Introduction' to Andrea Dunbar and Robin Soans, *Rita, Sue and Bob Too / A State Affair* (London, 2004), p. 1.

4 Simon Reynolds, *Retromania: Pop Culture's Addiction to its Own Past* (London, 2011), pp. 312–13.

5 Cecília Mello, 'Art and Reality in *The Arbor* (2010)', in *Film and Media Studies*, XII (2016), pp. 115–28: p. 119.

6 Clio Barnard, 'Director's Statement', in *The Arbor* DVD booklet (2011), n.p.

7 Ibid.

8 Jean Laplanche and Jean-Bertrand Pontalis, *The Language of Psychoanalysis* (London, 1988), p. 111.

9 Ibid., p. 112.

10 Jean Laplanche, *Essays on Otherness* (London and New York, 1999), p. 265.

11 Barnard, 'Director's Statement'.

PART THREE: BETWEEN PAST AND PRESENT

INTRODUCTION: ART AND MOVING IMAGES – TRANSITIONAL SPACES OF SPECTATORSHIP

1 'Mary Kelly in Conversation with Margaret Iverson', in *Mary Kelly*, ed. Mignon Nixon (Cambridge, MA, 2016), p. 115.
2 Mary Kelly, 'Notes on Reading the Post-Partum Document', ibid., pp. 2–3.
3 Sabine Folie, 'The Frame and Beyond: On the Exhibition at the Generali Foundation', in *Morgan Fisher: Off-screen Cinema*, ed. Jean-Philippe Antoine and Christa Blümlinger (Paris, 2016), p. 12.
4 Christophe Gallois, 'Behind the Scenes: Notes on the Films and Paintings of Morgan Fisher', ibid., pp. 165–6.
5 Francesco Casetti, *The Lumière Galaxy: 7 Key Words for the Cinema* (New York, 2015), p. 69.
6 Jacques Aumont, *The Image* (London, 1997), p. 142.
7 Ibid., p. 92.
8 Andrew Maerkle, 'Not Local, Trans-global: An Interview with Isaac Julien', in *Isaac Julien: Ten Thousand Waves* (London, 2010), p. 104.
9 Isaac Julien, 'Screen', in *Isaac Julien: Riot* (New York, 2013), p. 193. Julien specifically reminisces about the expanded work of his days at St Martin's School of Art and the London Filmmakers' Co-op.
10 Elie During, 'Turning Movements: Fragments on Mark Lewis', in *Mark Lewis: Impossible Films*, ed. F. Bovier and H. Taieb (Geneva, 2016), p. 34.
11 Victor Shklovsky, 'Art as Technique', in *Russian Formalist Criticism: Four Essays*, ed. Lee T. Lemon and Marion J. Reis (Lincoln, NE, 1965), p. 12.
12 Folie, 'The Frame and Beyond', p. 27.
13 Rosalyn Deutsche, 'Not-forgetting: Mary Kelly's *Love Songs*', in *Mary Kelly*, ed. Mignon Nixon (Cambridge, MA, 2016), p. 161.

MORGAN FISHER: FILMS ON PROJECTION AND THE PROJECTOR

1 Hollis Frampton, 'For a Metahistory of Film: Commonplace Notes and Hypotheses', in *Circles of Confusion: Film – Photography – Video – Text, 1968–1980* (Rochester, NY, 1983), p. 115.
2 Stuart Comer, 'The Kid Stays in the Picture', in *Morgan Fisher: Films and Painting and In Between and Nearby* (London, 2011), n.p.

3 Scott MacDonald, 'Interview with Morgan Fisher', *Film Quarterly*, XL (Spring 1987), p. 32.
4 Ibid.
5 Melissa Gronlund, 'Morgan Fisher: The Man Who Wasn't There', *Sight and Sound* (2010), accessed www.bfi.org.uk, March 2019.
6 I was interested to discover that Fisher had worked as an editor on Stephanie Rothman's *The Student Nurses* (1970), made for Corman's New World Pictures, and found footage from the film appears in *Standard Gauge*. The *Student Nurses*, and Stephanie Rothman's next film *The Velvet Vampire* (1971), became cult films for early feminist film fans when shown at the Edinburgh Film Festival in 1971.
7 Scott MacDonald, 'Morgan Fisher: Film on Film', *Cinema Journal*, XXVIII/2 (Winter 1989), p. 17.
8 Jean Epstein, 'L'Intelligence d'une machine', in *Ecrits sur le Cinema* (Paris, 1974), p. 259.
9 MacDonald, 'Morgan Fisher: Film on Film', p. 13.
10 MacDonald, 'Interview with Morgan Fisher', p. 27.
11 Thom Andersen, 'Pebbles Left on the Beach', in *Morgan Fisher: Two Exhibitions*, ed. Sabine Folie and Susanne Titz, exh. cat., Verlag der Buchhandlung Walther König (Cologne, 2012), p. 198.

MARK LEWIS: FILMS ON TIME, SPACE AND REAR PROJECTION

1 Mark Lewis, 'Foreword', *Afterall*, VIII (2003), p. 2.
2 Ibid.
3 Vivian Sobchack, '*Detour*: Driving in a Back Projection or Forestalled by Film Noir', in *Kiss the Blood off My Hands*, ed. Robert Miklitsch (Champaign, IL, 2014), p. 117.
4 'Alfred Hitchcock: A Friendly Salute', *Take One*, 50 (1976), p. 36.
5 Dominique Païni, 'The Wandering Gaze: Hitchcock's Use of Transparencies', in *Hitchcock and Art: Fatal Coincidences* (Montreal, Milan and Paris, 2000), p. 58.
6 Ibid., p. 63.
7 Elisabeth Bronfen, 'Screening and Disclosing Fantasy: Rear Projection in Hitchcock', *Screen*, LVII/1 (2015), p. 34.
8 Elie During, *Turning Movements: Fragments on Mark Lewis* (Geneva, 2016), p. 45.
9 Walter Benjamin, 'On Surrealism', in *One-way Street, and Other Writings*, trans. Edmund Jephcott and Kingsley Shorter (London, 1969), p. 12.

ISAAC JULIEN: DISPLACING THE SPECTATOR, *TEN THOUSAND WAVES*

1 I saw the version shown at the EYE Filmmuseum, Amsterdam, in 2012. Each exhibition has its own configuration of screens and the number vary according to the size of the gallery space. The installation *Ten Thousand Waves* also exists as a single-screen film *Better Life*.

2 At one point, Julien intended *Ten Thousand Waves* and *Western Union: Small Boats* to be part of a single project, and commissioned Wang Ping's poems for both works, but eventually decided to include them only on the soundtrack of *Ten Thousand Waves*.

3 Walter Benjamin, *The Arcades Project*, ed. Rolf Tiedemann, trans. Howard Eiland and Kevin McLaughlin (Cambridge, MA, 1999), p. 475.

4 Isaac Julien, Introduction to a screening of *The Goddess* (1930), EYE Filmmuseum, Amsterdam, 27 September 2012.

5 Andrew Maerkle: 'Not Global, Trans-local: Interview with Isaac Julien', in *Isaac Julien: Ten Thousand Waves*, ed. Isaac Julien, exh. cat., Victoria Miro Gallery (London, 2010), pp. 97–105: p. 102.

6 Peter Wollen, 'The Two Avant-gardes', in *Readings and Writings* (London, 1982), p. 102.

7 Julien in conversation with Cynthia Rose, 2013.

8 Mark Nash, 'Electric Shadows (Dian Ying)', in *Isaac Julien: Ten Thousand Waves*, ed. Isaac Julien, exh. cat., Victoria Miro Gallery (London, 2010), pp. 37–44: pp. 38–9.

9 Maerkle, 'Not Global, Trans-local', p. 104.

10 Nash, 'Electric Shadows (Dian Ying)', p. 41.

MARY KELLY: SPEAKING MATERNAL SILENCE, *POST-PARTUM DOCUMENT* AND *THE BALLAD OF KASTRIOT REXHEPI*

1 Griselda Pollock, 'Still Working on the Subject', in *Rereading Post-Partum Document: Mary Kelly*, ed. S. Breitwieser (Vienna, 1998), p. 238.

2 Ibid., p. 243.

3 Julia Kristeva, 'From One Identity to Another', in *Desire in Language: A Semiotic Approach to Art and Language*, ed. Leon S. Roudiez (Oxford, 1980), p. 133.

4 Ibid., p. 135.

5 Mary Kelly: 'Notes on Reading the Post-Partum Document (1977)', in *Mary Kelly*, ed. Mignon Nixon (Cambridge, MA, 2016), p. 3.

6 'Mary Kelly in Conversation with Hans Ulrich Obrist', in *Mary Kelly: The Voice Remains: Works in Compressed Lint, 1999–2017* (New York, 2017), pp. 12–13.

7 'Mary Kelly and Laura Mulvey, in Conversation: Discussion of Mary Kelly's *Post-Partum Document*', ICA Talks, 1982. Tape recording accessed courtesy of the British Library.

8 'Mary Kelly in Conversation with Paul Smith', in *October Files*, vol. XX: *Mary Kelly*, ed. Mignon Nixon (Cambridge, MA, 2016), p. 21.

9 Griselda Pollock, 'Mary Kelly's *The Ballad of Kastriot Rexhepi*: Virtual Trauma and Indexical Witness in the Age of Mediatic Spectacle', in *October Files*, vol. XX: *Mary Kelly*, p. 137.

10 Mary Kelly, '*The Ballad of Kastriot Rexhep*: Notes on Gesture, Medium and Mediation', in *La Balada de Kastriot Rexhepi*, exh. cat., Comunidad Autónoma de la Región de Murcia (Murcia, 2008), p. 101.

11 Ibid., p. 103.

12 Jacques Lacan, 'The Function and Field of Speech and Language in Psychoanalysis' [1953], in *Ecrits* (London, 1977), p. 50.

APPENDIX: TEN FREQUENTLY ASKED QUESTIONS ON 'VISUAL PLEASURE AND NARRATIVE CINEMA'

1 Juliet Mitchell, 'Introduction' to *Feminine Sexuality: Jacques Lacan and the école freudienne*, ed. J. Mitchell and J. Rose (London, 1982), p. 23.

2 Laura Mulvey, 'Fears, Fantasies and the Male Unconscious', in *Visual and Other Pleasures* (London, 1989), pp. 6–13.

3 Mandy Merck, 'Mulvey's Manifesto', in *Camera Obscura: Feminism, Culture and Media Studies*, XXII/3 (2007), pp. 1–23.

4 Laura Mulvey, *Visual and Other Pleasures* (London, 1989), p. 16.

5 Manohla Dargis, 'Best Movies of 2017', *New York Times*, 6 December 2017.

6 Francesco Casetti, *The Lumière Galaxy: 7 Key Words for the Cinema Today* (New York, 2015), p. 213.

7 Ibid., p. 205.

BIBLIOGRAPHY

Annenkov, Georges, *Max Ophüls* (Paris, 1962)

Aulier, Dan, *Vertigo: The Making of a Hitchcock Classic* (New York, 1998)

Aumont, Jacques, 'Godard's *Le Mépris*', in *French Film: Texts and Contexts*, ed. Susan Hayward and Ginette Vincendeau (London, 2000)

Barron, Jamie, *The Archive Effect: Found Footage and the Audiovisual Experience of History* (London, 2013)

Benjamin, Walter, *The Arcades Project*, ed. Rolf Tiedemann, trans. Howard Eiland and Kevin McLaughlin (Cambridge, MA, 1999)

Berardi, Franco, *After the Future* (Edinburgh, Oakland, CA, and Baltimore, MD, 2011)

Beylie, Claude, *Max Ophüls* (Paris, 1963)

Blümlinger, Christa, *Cinéma de seconde main: Esthetique du remploi dans l'art du film and des nouveaux medias* (Paris, 2013)

Brooks, Peter, *The Melodramatic Imagination* (New Haven, CT, and London, 1995)

Dash, Julie, 'Dialogue between bell hooks and Julie Dash, April 26, 1992', in *The Making of an African American Woman's Film* (New York, 1992)

Deleuze, Gilles, *Cinema 2: The Time Image*, trans. Hugh Tomlinson and Robert Galeta (London, 2005)

Derrida, Jacques, *Archive Fever: A Freudian Impression*, trans. Eric Prenowitz (Chicago, IL, 1996)

Doane, Mary Ann, 'Remembering Women: Psychical and Historical Constructions in Film Theory', in *Psychoanalysis and Cinema*, ed. E. Ann Kaplan (London and New York, 1990)

Gunning, Tom, *Fritz Lang* (London, 2000)

Harrison Paul, *Inside the Inner City: Life Under the Cutting Edge* (London, 1983)

Laplanche, Jean, and Jean-Bertrand Pontalis, *The Language of Psychoanalysis*, trans. Donald Nicholson-Smith (London, 1988)

Leyda, Jay, *Films Beget Films* (London, 1964)

MacCabe, Colin, *Godard: A Portrait of the Artist at 70* (London, 2003)

Marazzi, Alina, *Un'ora sola ti vorrei* (Milan, 2006). Alina Marazzi's account
of making the film accompanies the DVD.

Margulies, Ivone, *Nothing Happens: Chantal Akerman's Hyperrealist
Everyday* (Durham and London, 1996)

Marie, Michel, *Le Mepris* (Paris, 1990)

Mello, Cecília: 'Art and Reality in *The Arbor* (2010)', *Film and Media
Studies*, XII (2016)

Metz, Christian, 'Disavowal, Fetishism', in *Psychoanalysis and Cinema:
The Imaginary Signifier* (London, 1982)

Michelson, Annette, 'On the Eve of the Future: The Reasonable Facsimile
and the Philosophical Toy', in *On the Eve of the Future: Selected
Writings on Film* (Cambridge, MA, and London, 2017)

Rasy, Elizabetta, *La lingua della nutrice*, in *Italian Feminist Thought:
A Reader*, ed. Paola Bono and Sandra Kemp (London, 1991)

Reynolds, Simon, *Retromania: Pop Culture's Addiction to its Own Past*
(London, 2011)

Said, Edward, *On Late Style: Music and Literature Against the Grain*
(New York, 2006)

Salzberg, Ana, *Beyond the Looking Glass: Narcissism and Female Stardom
in Studio-era Hollywood* (New York and Oxford, 2014)

Spoto, Donald, *Marilyn Monroe: The Biography* (London, 1994)

Stafford-Clark, Max, 'Introduction' to Andrea Dunbar and Robin Soans,
Rita, Sue and Bob Too/A State Affair (London, 2004)

Truffaut, François, 'Max Ophuls est mort', in *Les Films de ma vie* [1974]
(Paris, 2007)

Wylie, Philip, *A Generation of Vipers* (Champaign, IL, 1996)

ACKNOWLEDGEMENTS

I would like to credit the following publications in which versions of some of these essays were first published: 'La compulsion à répéter. *Lola Montès* de Max Ophuls', *Trafic*, 98 (June 2016) and 'A Compulsion to Repeat: Max Ophuls' *Lola Montès*', *Afterall: A Journal of Art, Context and Enquiry*, 35 (Spring 2014); 'Cinematic Gesture: The Ghost in the Machine', *Journal of Cultural Research*, XIX/1 (2015); 'Thoughts on Marilyn Monroe: Emblem and Allegory', *Screen*, LVIII/8 (Summer 2017); '*Le Mépris* (Jean-Luc Godard 1963) and its Story of Cinema: A "Fabric of Quotations"', *Critical Quarterly*, LIII/51 (July 2011); 'A Neon Sign, A Soup Tureen: The *Jeanne Dielman* Universe', *Film Quarterly*, LXX/1 (Autumn 2016); 'Social Realism, Melodrama and the Mute Text: Rakhshan Bani-Etemad's *The May Lady* and *Under the Skin of the City*', in *On Women's Films Across Worlds and Generations*, ed. Ivone Margulies and Jeremi Szaniawski (London, 2019); 'Women Making History: Gleaning and the Compilation Film', in *Where is History Today? New Ways of Representing University the Past*, ed. Marcel Arbeit and Ian Christie (Olomouc, 2015); 'Projecting the Projector: Morgan Fisher's Reflections on a "Cinematic Repressed"', in *Morgan Fisher Off-screen Cinema*, ed. Jean-Philippe Antoine and Christa Blüminger (Dijon, 2017); 'Rear-projection and the Paradoxes of Hollywood Realism', in *Theorizing World Cinema*, ed. Lucia Nagib, Chris Perriman, Rajinder Dudrah (London, 2011); 'Ten Thousand Waves', *Isaac Julien: Riot*, exh. cat., Museum of Modern Art (New York, 2013); 'Mary Kelly: An Aesthetic of Temporality', in *Mary Kelly: Projects, 1973–2010*, ed. Dominique Heyes-Moore (Manchester, 2011).

I am extremely grateful to those friends and colleagues who invited me to give conference papers from which some of these essays emerged or to contribute to the books, journals or exhibition catalogues in which others were first published: Raymond Bellour, Martine Beugnet, Christa

Blüminger, Nicholas Chare and Liz Watkins, Ian Christie, Isaac Julien, Mary Kelly, Mark Lewis, Colin MacCabe, Ivone Margulies and Jeremi Szaniawski, Lucia Nagib, Ruby Rich and Rob White.

I would also like to thank Vivian Constantinopoulos for being an exemplary editor, who has helped me evolve the shape of the book in discussion over the last two years; Phoebe Colley for her attentive reading of the manuscript; and Vladimir Seput, who has given me invaluable help with the images and the bibliography.

The author and publishers would like to thank the following for their permission to reproduce the images on the following pages: © Morgan Fisher: pp. 184, 187; © Mark Lewis Studio: pp. 200–201, 204, 205, 206, 209; © Isaac Julien: pp. 216, 217, 218–19, 221; © Mary Kelly: pp. 230, 234, 235.

INDEX